IN SUCH
GOOD
COMPANY

ALSO BY CAROL BURNETT

One More Time
This Time Together
Carrie and Me

IN SUCH GOOD COMPANY

ELEVEN YEARS *of* LAUGHTER,

MAYHEM, *and* FUN

in the SANDBOX

CAROL BURNETT

THREE RIVERS PRESS
NEW YORK

FOR THE CAST AND CREW OF OUR SHOW,
WITH MY EVERLASTING LOVE AND GRATITUDE.

CONTENTS

IN SUCH
GOOD
COMPANY

INTRODUCTION

I recently had the extreme pleasure of receiving the Screen Actors Guild Life Achievement Award, and in accepting the honor I talked about how much I loved going to the movies with my grandmother, Nanny, as a kid. My favorites were the comedies and the musicals. I think that's when I fell in love with the idea of, someday, being a musical comedy performer. Since there wasn't television "back in the covered wagon days," when I was growing up, I never imagined that my dream would be realized by having my own weekly musical comedy variety show on the small screen. But that's exactly what happened.

I've been thinking about that time a lot, and since my memory is pretty good, I decided to put my thoughts down on paper for anybody who might be interested in what we did and how we did it.

In doing the research for this book, I watched all 276 shows, even though at times I felt like Norma Desmond watching herself on the screen in *Sunset Boulevard*!

When I was watching the first few episodes, the first thing I noticed was how I looked. I laughed out loud at my various hairdos, with different shades of red, remembering that I (amateurishly) dyed my hair myself every week using Miss Clairol, because I hated to waste my time sitting in a beauty parlor.

What really stand out are the changes that evolved. Of course the hairstyles, makeup, and costumes were constantly changing. Remember, this was the late sixties into the seventies . . . bell-bottoms, miniskirts, etc. The makeup was exaggerated—heavy eyeliner and large Minnie Mouse false eyelashes . . . upper *and* lower! Even Bob Mackie, our brilliant costume designer, who surprised us every week with his creations, both beautiful and comedic, would admit that he missed the mark on some occasions. But they were rare.

One of the things I noticed was how *I* evolved over those eleven years. I went from the "zany, kooky, man-hungry, big-mouthed goofball," which was who I had fashioned myself into during my early years, including my time as a regular on the Garry Moore television show, into a somewhat more "mature kook."

I always loved doing the physical comedy—falling down, jumping out of windows, getting pies in the face—however, around thirty-seven, thirty-eight years old, three or four years into the show, I found myself enjoying tackling more sophisticated and complex satires and some of the sketches that had a tinge of pathos. "The Family" scenes with Eunice, Mama, and Ed always touched me deeply, because as crazy as they could get, there was always an element of reality—these were people suffering disappointment and regret, raging against fate, doing the best they could.

Naturally, there were a lot of sketches and musical numbers I had completely forgotten. Some of them made me laugh, and some, I admit, made me cringe! But overall, I was transported back to the most wonderful and pleasurable phase of my career.

What follows are many outstanding memories of what occurred during a "regular show week." I'll share anecdotes about our cast members, many of our guests, recurring characters, favorite movie parodies, some of the funny and off-the-cuff questions from our audience and my responses—basically how we all played together in the sandbox—hilariously—from 1967 to 1978.

Some of these stories may be familiar to those of you who know me best, but they needed to be retold in order to give you the whole picture of those eleven wonderful years!

But I'm getting ahead of myself. Let me start over at the very beginning . . .

IN THE SANDBOX

When I was growing up, theater and music were my first loves, so my original show business goals revolved around being in musical comedies on Broadway, like Ethel Merman and Mary Martin. My stage break came in the spring of 1959, when I was cast as Winnifred the Woebegone in the musical comedy *Once Upon a Mattress*, a takeoff on Hans Christian Andersen's fairy tale "The Princess and the Pea." It was an Off-Broadway production at the Phoenix Theatre, directed by none other than the iconic George Abbott, "Mr. Broadway" himself!

The show was originally scheduled for a limited run of six weeks, but it was so popular that it was moved to Broadway and ran for over a year. I got my wish; *I was on Broadway!* Because no one had expected the production to be so successful, there were numerous booking issues that caused our little show to be bounced from theater to theater —from the Phoenix to the Alvin to the Winter Garden to the Cort and, finally, to the St. James. There were a couple of jokes going around the business about the production during this period. I remember Neil Simon quipped, "It's the most moving musical on Broadway! If you haven't seen *Once Upon a Mattress* yet, don't worry, it'll soon be at your neighborhood theater."

My second big break came in the fall of 1959 when I was asked to be a regular performer on *The Garry Moore Show*, a terrifically popular TV comedy-variety series. For almost a year, until the summer of 1960, I doubled up and did both shows. I would perform in *Mattress* on Tuesdays through Fridays at 8:30 p.m. and then do two shows a day on Saturdays and Sundays.

I would rehearse for Garry's show eight to nine hours a day Monday through Friday, and then we would tape his show on Friday, in the early evening, which gave me just enough time to hop the subway and head downtown to arrive at *Mattress* in time for the 8:30 curtain!

I had no days off. Hey, I was young, I told myself—but evidently not *that* young, because one Sunday, during a matinee, I fell asleep . . . in front of the audience!

Normally, the scene involved Princess Winnifred trying her best to get a good night's sleep on top of twenty mattresses, but she couldn't. The mattresses were highly uncomfortable and lumpy, resulting in a very active pantomime in which I jumped up and down, pounding on the offending lumps, and finally wound up sitting on the edge of the bed wide awake, desperately counting sheep as the scene ended. Not this Sunday. As I lay there on top of twenty mattresses, I simply drifted off to dreamland. Our stage manager, who was in the wings, called, "Carol?" And then louder, "Carol!" I woke up with a start and nearly fell off the very tall bed. The audience howled, but the producers changed the schedule after that and moved the Sunday performance to Monday, so I could have Sundays off.

By that time *The Garry Moore Show* had switched to tape, like everyone else, but we still performed in front of a live audience as if it were a live show—no retakes, no stops. We wanted the excitement and spontaneity that went with the feeling of live theater—which was exactly what made the show so good, every Tuesday night on CBS.

The musical numbers and the writing were certainly worthy of being on the Great White Way; in fact, our junior writer was Neil Simon, whom we called "Doc." He had worked for Sid Caesar on *Your Show of Shows*. It's a little-known fact that Neil wrote *Come Blow Your Horn*, his first play, while he was working for Garry, who was one of his first investors!

Garry's show was a great learning experience for me. I remember sitting around the table reading the script the week that the famous vaudeville performer Ed Wynn was the guest. Then in his seventies, he had begun his career in vaudeville in 1903 and had starred in the Ziegfeld Follies beginning in 1914. He told great stories about those days. He got on the subject of "comics vs. comedic actors."

Garry asked him what the difference was.

"Well," Ed said, "a comic says 'funny things,' like Bob Hope, and a comedic actor says things funny, like Jack Benny."

That's what I wanted to be . . . someone who "says things *funny*."

I left *Mattress* in June of 1960, while I was still a regular on Garry's show, but I really never dreamed television was going to be my "thing," even though I found myself falling in love more and more with the small screen. Garry's show allowed me to be different characters every week, as opposed to doing one role over and over again in the theater. In essence we mounted a distinct musical comedy revue every week—week in and week out—in front of a live studio audience, just like in summer stock.

However, I still harbored my dream of starring again on BROAD-WAY and being the next Ethel Merman.

CBS asked me to sign a contract with them after I had been on Garry's show for a few seasons. The deal I was offered was for ten years, from 1962 to 1972, paying me a decent amount to do a one-hour TV special each year, as well as two guest appearances on any of their regular series. However, if I wanted to do an hour-long variety show of my own during the first five years of the contract, *they would guarantee me thirty one-hour shows!*

In other words, it would be *my* option! CBS would have to say yes, whether they wanted to or not!

They called this "pay or play" because they would have to pay me for thirty shows, even if they didn't put them on the air. "Just push the button!" was the phrase the programming executives used. This was an unheard-of deal, but I didn't pay much attention to it, because I had no plans to host my own show—never dreamed I'd ever want to. I was going to focus all of my energy on Broadway.

A MAN'S GAME

By 1966 I had married Joe Hamilton, who had produced Garry's show, and we had our adorable daughter, Carrie, and another baby on the way. My Broadway career had not panned out, which was why we were in Hollywood to begin with, and I was as in demand as a carton of sour milk. We were sitting on orange crates and packing boxes in the living room of a Beverly Hills home we had somehow managed to scrape together the down payment to buy.

We had to do something to earn some money. It was the week between Christmas and New Year's; 1967 was a few days away and our five-year deadline on the pay-or-play clause was about to expire. Joe and I looked at each other, looked around the furniture-less living room, and picked up the phone.

Mike Dann, one of the top executives at CBS in New York City, took the call and sounded happy to hear from me. He asked about our holidays, and I said they had been lovely but I was calling to "push the button" on the thirty one-hour comedy-variety shows they had promised me in my contract five years ago.

Mike honestly didn't remember any of this. He was completely in the dark. Joe took the phone and reminded him in great detail. My guess is that more than a few lawyers were called away from their holiday parties that night to review my contract.

When Mike called the next day, he said, "Well, yes, I can see why you called, but I don't think the hour is the best way to go. Comedy-variety shows are traditionally hosted by men: Gleason, Caesar, Benny, Berle, and now Dean . . . it's really not for a gal. Dinah Shore's show was mostly music."

"But comedy-variety is what I do best! It's what I learned doing Garry's show—comedy sketches. We can have a rep company like Garry's, and like *Caesar's Hour*. We can have guest stars! Music!"

"Honey, we've got a great half-hour sitcom script that would fit you like a glove. It's called *Here's Agnes!* It's a sure thing!"

Here's Agnes? No thanks . . . we pushed the button.

PLAY!

CBS scheduled our show's premiere for Monday, September 11, 1967, opposite *I Spy* and *The Big Valley*, both of which were among the top-watched shows on TV. It was pretty obvious the network didn't think we'd last the whole season; otherwise they would have given us a more forgiving slot where we'd have had more of a chance to get some traction. In truth, we weren't sure we'd last, either. We sighed and decided we'd at least get our thirty shows. We could start unpacking, because, for a year, the bills would get paid.

It was all a gamble, but despite everything, many of the original staff members from Garry's show, like head writer Arnie Rosen, director Clark Jones, choreographer Ernie Flatt, lead dancer Don Crichton, and many more, took the plunge and followed us to California.

Lyle Waggoner came on board to be my handsome foil—I winced in embarrassment while rewatching the shows when I saw myself going gaga and swooning over him, which was a running gag for the first few seasons. Eventually, much to my relief, we deep-sixed the "swooning over Lyle" bit and he morphed from just being the show's good-looking announcer to getting laughs as different nuanced characters. He turned into a very good sketch performer.

Vicki Lawrence had no professional experience when we brought her on. It was fascinating to watch her grow out of her awkward, young teenage stage and into a very clever and confident comedienne and singer/dancer.

Harvey Korman was a consummate comedic actor from the get-go, but I also saw him evolve over the years in ways that were astonishing. He never fancied himself a singer or a dancer. If our choreographer, Ernie Flatt, tried to give him a dance step to execute, he would freeze in his tracks, but if you gave Harvey the *role* of a dancer, he would improvise dance steps that made him look like Gene Kelly . . . well, I won't go that far, but you'd swear the guy was born to move. It worked the same way with singing; he could sing up a storm if he was playing the part of someone who could sing!

We did a lot of movie takeoffs on the show, and I swear he seemed to channel those famous actors—Ronald Colman in our version of *Random Harvest*, Zachary Scott in *Mildred Pierce*, and who could ever forget his Clark Gable in our *Gone With the Wind* parody?

Tim Conway was a frequent guest in the early years and joined us every week in the ninth season! Much more about him—and the rest of our gang—later . . .

We all played together in our crazy, creative sandbox and delivered a fresh, Broadway-like musical comedy review each week, and boy did we have fun . . . *for eleven years!*

Going gaga over Lyle.

VARIETY SHOWS IN THE SEVENTIES

I t was a great decade for variety. Some amazing shows were aired
during our run: *Rowan & Martin's Laugh-In*, *The Sonny and Cher
Comedy Hour*, *The Smothers Brothers Comedy Hour*, *The Dean
Martin Show*, *Flip Wilson*, *The Glen Campbell Goodtime Hour*, *The
Jim Nabors Hour*, *Van Dyke and Company*, *The Andy Williams Show*,
and many more. I remember that some of the writers from *Laugh-In*,
wanting to write longer sketches, would come on our show, while
some of our writers, after a few seasons, opted to write for *Laugh-In's*
shorter form. There was a plethora of talented sketch writers, and
that was one of the prime reasons it was a good time for comedy-
variety hours.

As I've said, we premiered Monday night, September 11, 1967, at
10:00, opposite *I Spy* and *The Big Valley*, both immensely popular
shows. We did well in that time slot, but in the fall of 1971, CBS moved
us to an earlier slot, 8:00 p.m. on Wednesdays, opposite *Adam-12* and
Bewitched. I always felt we were a "ten o'clock show" and shouldn't
have been moved. A year later, CBS moved us again, to where we became part of a powerhouse Saturday night lineup at 10:00, following
All in the Family, *M*A*S*H*, *The Mary Tyler Moore Show*, and *The
Bob Newhart Show*. We happily remained there until the network
moved us, yet again, to Sunday nights at 10:00 in December of 1977.
During all those years, our ratings fluctuated from terrific to not so
terrific, but CBS had faith in us and we held our own.

We taped our show on Fridays, in Studio 33 at Television City in Hollywood. Sonny and Cher were taping in the studio next door to us. The ladies' and men's rooms were shared by both studios, and sometimes during a tape stop, I would sneak through the ladies' room to their set and watch them do a number or a sketch. Once in a while they would see me on the sidelines and call me out on stage to kid around in front of their audience. A couple of times, both Sonny and Cher (separately and together) would do a surprise walk-on while I was doing "Questions and Answers," much to the delight of our audience. The Smothers Brothers also taped on Fridays, across the hall. During breaks, sometimes one of their young writers would come over and watch us block a musical number or a sketch—Steve Martin. Fridays at Television City was like one big dorm, buzzing with activity and unbelievable talent.

Sonny and Cher were our next-door neighbors at Studio 33.

Speaking of studios, as far as I'm concerned Studio 33 was the *gem* in Television City. Hands down, it was the best television studio I ever worked in, because the audience seats were arranged below the stage, like in a real theater, and the cameras didn't come between the performers and the audience . . . whereas other studios featured bleacher seats—tiers—where the audience would be looking down on the stage and the actors, while the cameras blocked their view. Whenever I've worked in one of those venues, I've likened it to "the Christians vs. the Lions." Also, some television shows prefer to rehearse in their sets from the get-go, and so many sitcoms have permanent sets that spread horizontally across the floor of the studio, like a choo-choo train. Some of these sets are spread out so far away, the audience has to watch the action on monitors to see what's going on. They might as well have stayed home.

And when it comes time for a run-through, the writers and producers have to stand or sit facing the darkish, unlit set to watch the actors do the first scene. Then they have to get up and walk or scrape their chairs across the floor to watch the second scene, and when *it* is over, they have to walk *yet again* to the next set to watch the next scene, and so forth and so on.

I hate that way of doing things. Coming from Broadway rehearsals, and then from variety show rehearsals, I like working things out in a rehearsal hall *first*. Then when it was time for our run-through, the writers, the producers, and the crew would come into the main rehearsal hall, take their seats, and be able to watch all the sketches and musical numbers without having to interrupt the proceedings by getting up and *moving* after each bit!

We'd be in the rehearsal hall through Wednesday, and then be on our stage Thursday to block the show in the real sets for the cameras. Years later, when I was doing an anthology show for Disney, I asked them to let us do our rehearsals in a nice large sunny room on the lot. The first week's run-through was attended by several studio "suits," something that never happened when we were doing my variety show. It was a little intimidating, but that was the norm for Disney, so okay. However, to make matters worse, they took their seats in the front row and proceeded to bury their noses in the script—*while we were performing*—never looking up from the printed word to even watch what we were doing!

I politely halted the rehearsal. "Gentlemen, could you do us all a favor and sit on your scripts? That way, you can see the actors' faces and watch what we think are some funny pieces of business that you'd otherwise miss, because they just might *not* be on the written page. Thanks, a lot!"

Looking somewhat chagrined, one by one they stood up, placed their scripts on their chairs, and sat back down again. It worked. We had their undivided attention.

What did they think we were doing? A radio show?

A TYPICAL WEEK

Our schedule never varied, week to week. It was like a "school schedule." We always knew what "class" was next and when to report.

MONDAY

10:00–11:00 a.m. Script reading with principals and guests. Notes afterward.

11:00 a.m.–12:00 p.m. Music rehearsal with special material writers in music room.

12:00 p.m.–1:00 p.m. Lunch. *(I would watch my favorite soap opera,* All My Children—AMC.*)*

1:00 p.m.–3:00 p.m. Sketch rehearsals with director in small rehearsal hall.

(Dancers with choreographer in main rehearsal hall.)

(Finished for the day.)

TUESDAY

10:00 a.m.–12:00 p.m. Sketch rehearsals with director in the rehearsal hall.

12:00 p.m.-1:00 p.m. Lunch. (AMC)

1:00 p.m.–3:00 p.m. Principals and guests learn dance routines with choreographer and dancers in main rehearsal hall.

(Finished for the day.)

WEDNESDAY

10:00 a.m.–11:30 a.m. Costume fittings for Carol at Bob Mackie's workplace.

Fittings for guests and dancers at other times.

12:00 p.m.–1:00 p.m. Lunch. (AMC)

1:00 p.m.–3:00 p.m. Sketch and dance rehearsals with principals, guests, and dancers.

3:00 p.m.–4:00 p.m. Run-through of entire show for writers, producers, and crew in main rehearsal hall.

4:15 p.m.–5:00 p.m. Notes with Carol, producers, and writers in producer's office.

(Finished for the day.)

THURSDAY

2:00 p.m.–6:00 p.m. Blocking in Studio 33 with camera crew and scenery. No costumes.

6:00 p.m.–7:00 p.m. Dinner.

7:00 p.m.–8:00 p.m. Orchestra rehearsal with principals and guests (as needed).

(Finished for the day.)

FRIDAY (TAPE DAY)

11:00 a.m.–1:00 p.m. Complete run-through (stop and start) in studio with orchestra and costumes. No makeup.

12:00 p.m.–1:00 p.m. Lunch. (AMC)

1:00 p.m.–2:00 p.m. Notes. Any changes since the run-through are gone over with the principals.

2:00 p.m.–3:00 p.m. Hair and makeup.

(Audience arrives for the dress rehearsal, which will be taped.)

4:00 p.m.–5:30 p.m. Dress rehearsal. *(My daughters would come when they were old enough, and after the show they often had their picture taken with our guest stars!)*

6:00 p.m.–7:00 p.m. Notes. Any line changes or cuts made since the dress rehearsal are gone over with the principals, plus final touch-ups for principals and dancers.

(Audience arrives for the air show.)

7:30 p.m.–9:00 p.m. Air show, with Carol's Q&A at the top of the show.

We were usually out early enough, so that after the show Joe and I would take our guest stars to dinner at Chasen's restaurant.

This schedule often allowed me to take my kids to school most mornings, and even pick them up after school if I finished rehearsing early enough. With the exception of Thursdays and Fridays, we'd have dinner at home every night at 6:30.

We averaged one week off every four weeks. Two weeks off at Christmas. One week off at Easter. Summers off. It was *THE* perfect schedule.

Many people in our business can't believe that we could tape our entire show, with all the sketches, musical numbers, scenery, and costume changes, plus special effects, in less than two hours. We did very few retakes because I wanted our show to have a spontaneous feel. I used to make bets with our crew that I could make a "skin-out" costume change (complete with different wigs and makeup) before they could change the scenery, because I didn't want our studio audience to have to sit a long time between scenes. We needed their energy and enthusiasm! Their positive responses made us better. It was as close as we could get to live theater.

I have been a guest on a few sitcoms where they took as many as four hours to tape twenty-two minutes! *AND* in front of a captive and increasingly bored audience! Needless to say, that drove me nuts.

One time when I was a guest on a sitcom, I actually wanted to kill the director. This is why: The other actors and I were in the middle of a scene and the audience was howling with laughter. I mean we were definitely on a roll, when out of the blue, we hear from the director's booth, "CUT!"—totally killing the momentum of the scene. We had no idea what had gone wrong. And then we found out. It seems a picture on the wall behind us was a bit crooked, and the stage manager was told to come out and straighten it!

Lord!

LET'S BUMP UP THE LIGHTS!

U sually a television show hires a comedian to warm up the audience before the cameras start turning, telling jokes to get the audience excited and happy. However, Garry Moore would have none of it because he wanted to be the warm-up guy himself, and he was wonderful at it. He would go out on stage and ask the folks in the audience if they had any questions. They always had plenty, and Garry would answer them, getting lots of laughs . . . *without having any plants.* No questions were planned. It was entirely off the cuff. He was funny, accessible, and always genuinely warm. His homey approach made the audience feel like they knew him. I would hang backstage and listen in awe.

In the summer of 1967, Joe, Bob Banner (our co–executive producer), and I were playing around with some ideas for our show over dinner. We were premiering in a few weeks and we were trying to nail everything down. We had already determined that we wanted music, dancing, comedy sketches, a rep company, and guest stars each week. We also knew the value of returning characters like Sid Caesar's German Professor, Red Skelton's Clem Kadiddlehopper, and Jackie Gleason's Poor Soul and Ralph Kramden.

Bob Banner suggested that I do the warm-up just like Garry did . . . only we would actually *tape* it and show it on the air! I balked at the idea big-time, feeling that I would be at a loss to come up with any kind of a snappy answer and wind up with egg on my face.

We did know how we'd close the show: The cast, the guest stars, and the dancers would all be on camera taking bows. I would sing our theme song, "I'm So Glad We Had This Time Together," which Joe wrote (having been a songwriter and musician before becoming a producer). I would then have my guests for that week sign an autograph book, and after having pulled my left ear as a signal for Nanny, my grandmother who raised me, we'd all wave good night.

Put me in a fat suit or a fright wig or black out my two front teeth and I'm in hog heaven. But Bob was convinced that I should be myself and let the audience get to know me first before I jumped into the various characters who would dominate the rest of the show. He kept saying that interacting with the audience would be "the perfect opening," and I kept saying that I was only comfortable hiding behind a character. I didn't have a clue as to how I could "be myself." But Bob was like a dog on a bone. He wouldn't give up. Finally, and very reluctantly, I gave in and agreed to try it a couple of times. I made him promise that if it didn't work, we'd deep-six the idea—forever!

The First Q&As.

I came out on stage that first show and I was absolutely scared stiff. It wasn't stage fright exactly; I had been on stage lots of times before a live audience, but this wasn't scripted! I looked out at all of those people, sitting in their seats waiting for me to say something that would amuse them, and I felt *naked*. What if no one had a question? Or worse, what if they did and I didn't have an answer?

"Hi, and welcome to our show. Um . . . let's see if you have anything to say . . . I mean, if you have any questions . . . er . . . about our show . . . or whatever. Let's bump up the lights . . ."

The lights went up and the audience was staring at me politely.

"Anything at all? Just raise your hands."

No hands. Nada.

"I mean whatever you have in mind . . . Anything?"

(Hello, flop sweat.)

FINALLY, a hand shot up. "Yes?" I squeaked, relieved beyond measure.

"Who's on?" a kind soul asked.

I told them about our rep players, Harvey and Vicki and Lyle. Jim Nabors, my buddy and the godfather of my daughter Jody, was our premiere guest star that night, so when I mentioned this, the audience went wild! Jim was one of the most popular performers in the country then. They were warming up and I was breathing again!

I did the same opening again the next week and things went a little better. By the third week the audience had seen the first two airings and knew what to expect and were not nearly so shy about raising their hands. The questions got funnier and I began to have fun. Some people thought we should have some "planted" questions occasionally, but I didn't want to do that. I figured it would be more fun if I flew without a net.

Naturally it was a little different from week to week and season to season—but after that first night it became a tradition that would last for the entire eleven years.

SOME OF MY FAVORITE Q&As

A boy in the audience wants to read a poem he wrote. I ask him what his name is.

"Danny Kruger."

I'm in love with a wonderful girl,
But there's a catch, oh brother!
The girl I love, this glorious girl,
Is old enough to be my mother!

I scream with laughter, and then say, "Sit down, Danny!"

A LADY IN pink asks, "What has been your most embarrassing question?"

"I think my most embarrassing question was whether or not I'd had a sex change.

(Laughter) "Yep, I think that takes the cake." (Immediately pointing to another audience member) "Yes?"

"Did you?" (*Much* laughter)

"DID YOU EVER take acting lessons?"

"Yes, I did . . . when I was at UCLA, I studied for a while."

"Think it did you any good?"

. . .

A WOMAN ASKS, "What kind of soap do you use to clean the floor?" I tell her, "I think that's a little personal." Over the laughter from the audience, I ask a stagehand, and he says "vinyl cleaner."

I ask the woman where in her house does she have vinyl, "In the kitchen? Bathroom?" The woman nods and I say, "You have vinyl all over your house?"

The woman replies dryly, "Just on the floor."

A KID ASKS, "Is this a repeat show?"

"No, no . . . actually, we're live here."

A MAN ASKS, "Do you enjoy being TV's new sex symbol?" Before I can answer, our cameraman, Pat Kenny—on Camera 4—pipes up, "She paid him to ask that question." The audience laughs and the very next question comes from a little girl, who asks (*about our funny camera-man*), "If he's such a smart aleck, why don't you fire him?" The audience erupts in laughter, along with Pat and me. Pat says, "She doesn't pay me enough!" I come back with "I'll pay you when you're sober enough to count it!" (*I might add that Pat Kenny was with us the whole eleven years, and many times during the Q&As he would come up with some pretty funny zingers, which I always loved. He and I had a great rapport.*)

Our funny cameraman, Pat Kenny.

· · ·

A QUESTION IS asked about my preference for long or short hair on boys. (*Remember, it's the sixties.*) "I don't mind the long hair on boys, but their hair is longer than mine!" (*In looking back at my VERY short haircut, what in the world was I thinking? I look like I'm about to join the Marines. The haircut is atrocious!*)

I BRING OUT a very shy and giggly Vicki Lawrence (*with the same bad haircut I have*) to answer any questions. When asked how old she is, she responds with "I don't know."
    Question from a man in the audience: "How old are you?"
    "How old do you think I am? And be careful."
    The man replies, "Twenty-six."
    "Right!" (Grabbing my chest) "Right here." (*This became a running gag about being flat-chested. If I could go back in time, these "jokes" would never have seen the light of day. The flat-chested and homely jokes were a holdover from my Garry Moore Show days. The all-male writers used them for easy laughs, and I went along with the concept. Shame on me. However, as I've mentioned, that changed as our show—and I—"matured" over the years.*)

ELIZABETH MONTGOMERY IS in the audience. I introduce her, telling the folks in the studio that we were in a movie together starring Dean Martin (Who's Been Sleeping in My Bed? *which was pretty bad*). Elizabeth jokes that when she saw the movie on an airplane, "There were seventeen walkouts!" I bring out our guest, Jonathan Winters, who's asked if he was ever in the service. "I was a Marine. Yep, and I was a hero. I kept walking and looking through bushes, y'know, and I killed a Japanese gardener."

I'M WEARING A "maxi-length" dress and ask the audience their opinion—long vs. short. They wholeheartedly applaud for shorter skirts. I introduce a lady in the audience who "never needed any clothes," Gypsy Rose Lee *(the famous striptease artist)*. Gypsy comes up on stage and comments on all the "lovely bald men" in the audience, saying, "I built a career on heads like that!" *(She was very cute.)* Guest Soupy Sales is on stage and says to Gypsy, "I read your book and every time I picked it up the jacket fell off!"

I'M ASKED, "HOW many hours does it take to put your face on?"
    "Well, the makeup man comes in on Tuesdays."
    A man asks, "How long does it take you to get ready?"
    "For what?"

AN AUDIENCE MEMBER comments on my peculiar-looking limp hairdo. "I always wash my hair before we do a show, but tonight I goofed and washed it with the *conditioner*, instead of shampoo!" *(Joe thought I should wash my hair again before the show, because it looked so awful, but the audience was coming in and I wasn't about to keep them waiting. I figured, "What the heck and who cares?")*

TAPE DATE: APRIL 26, 1968 (my thirty-fifth birthday).
    I'm pregnant with my third baby, due in August, and starting to show. Bob Mackie's costumes are cleverly trying to hide my "baby bump," but I still looked pretty pregnant. This particular episode would be aired at a later date. *(What's funny is that when it aired* five months later, *in September, I had already had my baby in August, but because this show was pretaped, I looked pregnant all over again!)*

THE AUDIENCE WAS into it and I loved their questions. *I'll share more of these later in the book.*

OUR GANG

I n the early days of television, all of the great comedy-variety shows I watched had a repertoire of amazing comic actors. *The Jackie Gleason Show* had Art Carney and Audrey Meadows; *Your Show of Shows* starred Sid Caesar with Carl Reiner, Imogene Coca, and Howie Morris; *Caesar's Hour* included Nanette Fabray; and dear Garry Moore had his own special band of merry players. So it was only natural for me to follow in those sacred footsteps when I set out to create a variety show. I wanted my own TV family and that's just what I got.

Vicki Lawrence

O ne mid-January afternoon in 1967, I was not only two weeks overdue with my second child and a mite cranky, but looking and feeling like I had swallowed a watermelon. As I sat going through the mail, I noticed an envelope that had been forwarded from CBS (they had been forwarding fan mail to me since Garry's show). I sliced it open. A seventeen-year-old high school senior from Inglewood, California, wanted advice on how to get into show business. Everyone told her she reminded them of me, and to prove it she had included a photograph that looked more like me than I had at seventeen.

My jaw dropped. She had also sent an article from her local

newspaper that said she was talented, a member of the Young Americans singing group, and a good student.

Coincidentally, ever since CBS had given us the nod, just before New Year's Day, we had been working on the idea of a recurring sketch with a husband, a wife, and her kid sister. I thought this girl might be right for the kid sister role. The newspaper piece mentioned that she was a contestant for the annual Miss Fireball contest. I checked the date, and the contest was going to be held that very night! It was complete serendipity, but there was something about all of this that seemed somehow fated. Her parents' names were mentioned, so I picked up the phone and asked the operator for the number of a Howard Lawrence in Inglewood.

A woman answered on the second ring.

"Hello?" A sweet, pleasant voice.

"Hello . . . is Vicki there?"

"This is her mother. May I ask who's calling?"

"Hi, this is Carol Burnett. I just received—"

"VICKI!" A shout heard round the world. *"VICKI!"*

I heard whispering and shuffling and then Vicki came on the line, her voice laced with ennui: "Oh, hi, Marsha."

Obviously she and Marsha played telephone games.

Once Vicki realized I wasn't Marsha and she pulled herself together, I asked her if Joe and I could come to the contest that night. I told her we wouldn't want to disrupt anything, so we would slide in after the lights went down and sit in the back. She gave me the details of where and when and we hung up.

I duckwalked into the kitchen, where Joe was eating lunch, and told him we were going to Inglewood that night.

"We're what?"

"To catch the Miss Fireball contest at Hollywood Park. There is an auditorium there."

"Why?" he asked calmly, putting down the rest of his sandwich.

"*BECAUSE* I'm fourteen months pregnant and I want to see the Miss Fireball contest!" I shrieked.

"Are you nuts?"

I showed him the letter, the newspaper article, and the photograph. We went. Vicki did a comedy routine, accompanied herself on the guitar, and even played the kazoo. She wound up winning. The man who ran the contest had spotted me in the back, and asked me to come up and crown the winner. I waddled up and put the crown on Vicki's head. The audience gave her thunderous applause. We had pictures taken, congratulated the new Miss Fireball, and went home.

Miss Fireball and a very
pregnant me.

My daughter Jody Hamilton, whom I named after my dad, finally arrived on January 18, 1967, weighing eight pounds, eleven ounces. Vicki came to the hospital and brought me flowers—apparently the nurses thought she was my kid sister and ushered her right in. I hugged her, thanked her, and told her I'd stay in touch. I didn't say anything about the show.

A few months later we were still thinking about the kid sister part. We decided to do a screen test with Vicki and another young actress CBS had recommended. When Perry Lafferty, a CBS executive, saw them both, he was a little worried about Vicki's lack of experience. He called her "rough." I said, "So are diamonds, at first." We hired her.

Vicki developed into a marvelous comedienne over the next eleven seasons, but it didn't come naturally to her at first. She was eighteen and really, really shy—so shy she often didn't speak unless spoken to. She played my kid sister in a sketch called "Carol & Sis," which was a little ho-hum, as it turned out. Beyond this, Vicki wasn't on the show that much.

This was when my beloved colleague Harvey Korman worked his magic and helped her with everything from character development to accents. You name it. He was a selfless mentor and we started using her a lot more. The more she was on camera, the better and more confident she became.

An interesting aside: in 1973, Vicki had a major hit record with "The Night the Lights Went Out in Georgia," and we presented her with her gold record on our show. We were all very proud of her.

Then along came Mama, but more about that later.

In 1979, the Television Academy interviewed Vicki, and what follows is her own description of our crazy but momentous first meeting and her work with Harvey.

"That night at the contest, I said to the guy that was in charge of the publicity, 'I'm going to need two seats way in the back for Carol Burnett, and he's like 'Yeah, right.'

"And I said 'No, really, she's going to come to the contest and she doesn't want to be seen, so please don't tell anybody.' And (again) he was like 'Yeah, right.' I remember standing backstage peeking through the curtain, thinking, 'Well, why on earth would Carol Burnett come to this contest?' She and her husband sure enough did show up. It was at the racetrack in Hollywood Park, in some big old huge hall, and we girls did two can-can numbers 'cause they had something like an 1890s firehouse theme going, and then there was a little individual talent segment and I remember singing 'Won't You Come Home, Bill

Bailey?' with my guitar and a kazoo strapped around my neck. That was my individual talent and I wound up winning.

"Then that same fellow who had promised to get the seats and *not say a word*, got up on the stage at the end of the contest and said 'We have a very special guest in our audience this evening and will she please come up on stage and crown the winner!' And, I thought, you know, 'Great, my career is over before it even got started.' But she did come up on stage and crown me Miss Fireball. And we took pictures. I still have pictures of her; she was very pregnant, in this huge red cape, and she wore this hysterical black turban smooched down over her bangs, and she and her husband took pictures with the mayor and whoever, and it was in the newspaper.

"And after that night I didn't hear from her. It was like a dream. Later in January, I came home from school and my mom's got the radio on and they announce that Carol has finally had that baby, thank goodness, and that she's at St. John's in Santa Monica. So I'm on my way to a Young Americans rehearsal and recording. We were doing one of those old Firestone Christmas albums. On the way there, I said to the guy that I was sharing the ride with, 'Let's stop and get some flowers and run by the hospital and say hi to her.' And he said, 'You can't get in to see Carol Burnett.' And I said 'Well, I know her married name now and I think I'm going to try,' 'cause I had not heard a word from her.

"So yeah, I get my little flowers, I go into St. John's. Maternity is on the third floor and I go up there, and two nurses are sitting behind the nurse's station, not doing much of anything, it's very quiet. I walk up and in my most polite voice say, 'I'm here to see Mrs. Hamilton.' And they said 'Oh my God, you must be her sister Chrissy, wait till you see her, wait till you see the baby.' And they took me right into her room. And I mean, in hindsight she was very, very sweet, 'cause I mean how incredibly pushy of me to do such a thing, and she said, 'I haven't forgotten you. I promise we're going to call you as soon as I get my stomach back.'

"And it was, oh gosh, several months after that that I heard from her husband, Joe Hamilton, that they were auditioning for someone to play her kid sister on her new variety show that they were putting together and would I care to come down and audition to play her sister!

"An interesting little side note to that story is that Carol, sitting at home, recuperating after having the baby, gets a call from her manager, who was in New York. He was watching *The Andy Williams Show* that the Young Americans had appeared on, and in the body of our number, I had a little ten-second solo of my own. So he calls her and says, 'You're not going to believe this but I have found the kid to play your sister!' And Carol says 'Who is it?' And he says, 'I don't know, but she sings with the Young Americans, and she looks just like you.' And Carol says, 'I've already met her.'"

(Recalling her audition for the show.) "The audition was with me and one other girl. She was an actress and I think on a soap opera at the time, and I remember walking into CBS all alone and being taken to my little dressing room. The other girl was there with her agent and her manager and flowers everywhere. At the time it was a very traumatic decision for me. I remember going to the director of the Young Americans, Milton Anderson, and telling him that I was going to drop out of the summer tour because I was going to go do this audition. And he said, 'You listen to me, young lady, what are the odds that this is going to pan out? If you drop out of the tour, you're not coming back in the middle. You're off the summer tour.' I remember at the time that it was a very, very difficult decision for me to say I'm going to roll the dice, and go do this audition.

"The audition [itself] is a blur. It was a little short scene. I don't remember the rehearsal. I remember being nervous when we shot it, and I remember thinking the actress is going to be a shoo-in because I'm such a geek.

"Joe Hamilton's assistant, Charlene, called me, I don't know, shortly after we'd done the audition, and I remember her on the phone saying, 'Hi, sweetie, it's Charlene,' and her voice sounded like it was going to be bad news. 'Joe would like to speak to you, sweetie.' And I thought, 'Oh, you don't have to break it to me gently because really, I get it,' and he came on the phone and said, 'You know, we've looked at your audition.' And I am like, 'Just drop the bomb.' And then he said, 'We've decided that we're going to give you a shot.' Now there you have it.

A very "sixties" Vicki and me.

"It was just sort of surreal that this whole thing happened because she was just *happening* to be putting *The Carol Burnett Show* together, just *happening* to be looking for a person to play her kid sister. It was all very surreal.

"But then when I started on her show, I was such a geek. I was pitiful. Harvey used to get mad at me when I would say that, but he took me under his wing and it was either kill me or train me, one of the two; he would say, 'You forget stage right and stage left and you can't even find the ladies' room!' So he's the one who took me aside and trained me, 'cause Harvey was nothing if not a team player and probably the best, I would say arguably the best, sketch comedian ever, and how fortunate for me that I feel like I got to go to the Harvard School of Comedy in front of America.

"So, I don't know. Carol kind of thinks that we were meant to be together, and that one way or the other we would have found each other. I always say she sidetracked me and I was not going into show business. I was going to be a dental hygienist. She thinks it would have happened somehow . . . it would've happened regardless."

Harvey Korman

J oe and I had been big fans of *The Danny Kaye Show* and his incredibly talented second banana, Harvey Korman. "Second banana" is a term that has been used in comedy from as far back as I can remember and probably originated in vaudeville. I was never crazy about the term, because the distance between the star and the "second banana" was almost illusory, and frequently he or she walked away with the laugh—if the star would allow that to happen. My view was always to let everyone shine, the way Sid, Jackie, and Garry did. They were never afraid to let someone else score the touchdown. They knew it only made their show better.

We were premiering in the same year that Danny Kaye's show went off the air, but the lightbulb didn't light up, the penny didn't drop, and we just kept thinking, "We need a Harvey Korman!" *Finally*, we arrived at the brilliant conclusion that we could actually ask *the* Harvey Korman to come on board.

As I recall we had phoned his agent and were waiting to hear back when I saw Harvey in the CBS parking lot one afternoon at Television City. He didn't see me, but I shouted, "Harvey!"

He turned vaguely in the direction of the sound and smiled. I waved wildly. We hardly knew each other, but I swear I practically jumped him. I could be misremembering this, but I think I had him pinned against the hood of his car.

"Please, *please* be on our show! You're the very best! PLEASE?"

It was unorthodox, but hey, it worked! Harvey recognized me, started laughing, and said yes. I was in heaven! Honestly, I don't think there is anyone, anywhere who can top what he did—he created hysterically funny characters with different accents and looks—in only four days of rehearsals!

Personally, I've always felt that you need to play tennis with a better player, because your game only improves every time. That's what Harvey did for me as an actor; he made me better. *He made all of us better.*

Lyle Waggoner

When CBS gave us the green light to do our show, Joe and I got in touch with Carl Reiner, hoping he might become our main producer. He said that he would have loved to be with us, at any other time in his life, but he had just signed to write and direct his first film, *Enter Laughing*. He said he was thrilled for us, and predicted that our show would be a big success. He then offered a suggestion: hire an announcer who would be more than someone simply saying, "We'll be right back after this commercial break."

Carl had seen me in a sketch once, on Garry's show, where I played a goofy teenager who fawned, fainted, and went ballistic over a handsome matinee idol. He loved that bit so much that he said we should hire a "to-die-for" handsome announcer whom I could interact with. He would be someone I could swoon over, as a running gag, because I was still relying on the kooky, loudmouth, ugly-duckling character I had played on Garry's show (and, before that, as the man-hungry princess in *Once Upon a Mattress*).

We took Carl's suggestion and held auditions in 1967. Dozens of gorgeous men showed up, all looking like Adonis. But when Lyle Waggoner walked in, the contest was over.

He, too, was gorgeous, of course, but there was a lot more to him than that. He was funny. He had a sly, tongue-in-cheek delivery that let you know he wasn't taking himself or the situation he was in too seriously. He was perfect.

In fact, we came to trust Lyle's comedic instincts so much we wrote him into more and more sketches as time went on.

He had lots of other talents, too. After we had been on the air for just a few weeks, he was getting piles of fan mail from swooning girls and women all over the country. He got a card table and a chair and set up an "office" in the hallway outside the writers' room. He would sit there when he had time and answer his mail. One day as I was walking past I saw him open an envelope and add a dollar bill to a growing stack of cash on the card table.

"What's all this?" I asked.

He produced a copy of *How to Audition and Get the Job*, a very professional-looking brochure he had written, filled with advice for would-be actors and performers, which he was selling for a dollar a pop!

I read it and it was really well written and, I thought, a pretty good value for a dollar. It also provided me with new insight into Lyle's impressive entrepreneurial nature!

Another one of his talents: He was a very good carpenter and builder. One week our set designer, Paul Barnes, created a cruise ship for a sketch Tim Conway and I were doing about a nerdy couple who couldn't quite keep their footing on the high seas. The deck was designed so that it rocked back and forth and Tim and I would slide around, trying to hang on for dear life.

After the taping, Lyle asked Paul what he was planning to do with the huge cruise ship set. Paul told him it would be cut up and burned as rubbish, because it was too big to store. Lyle asked if he could have it. After the show the crew took the set apart and Lyle hauled it home in a big pickup truck. A bunch of us went over to the Waggoners' for a party some weeks later, and Lyle and his beautiful wife, Sharon, were showing us around, when we walked into a cozy, nicely furnished room.

"Recognize anything?" Lyle asked, grinning. "It's the cruise ship. I used the wood and built another room!"

In looking back now, I regret the whole "Going Gaga Over Lyle" routine. It worked at first, but after a while it became a tiresome gag. I was a married woman with two children who was forced to act like a lovesick silly teenager whenever Lyle was around. We finally dropped the bit (*whew*), and Lyle, along with being our announcer, became much more than a foil for me. He became a true rep player.

Today, Lyle has a hugely successful business furnishing movie studios with his Star Waggons (motor homes), which house actors working on films and/or on television shoots. I've been in a few of his motor homes, and they're definitely the best, no question about it. He's a man of all trades. Smart, funny, and as gorgeous as ever, silver hair and all . . . (and still someone easy to swoon over).

Tim Conway

Even though it seemed like Tim was a regular performer on our show from the get-go, he was just a guest once or twice a month for the first eight years. He was hysterical—with a comedic mind so brilliant that it was downright scary—and we loved him, but for some dumb reason it took us all those years to wake up and ask him to be on the show with us every single week!

His work with Harvey alone deserves a spot in the comedy hall of fame!

We always taped two shows on Fridays, with two different audiences.

The first one was basically a dress rehearsal and everyone performed everything *just* as it had been written, "to the ink." The second show was looser, especially when Conway was involved. He would always check with our director, Dave Powers (Clark Jones was with us for only the first year), to be sure he had gotten every shot in the first pass. Dave had always gotten the shots, which left Tim free to go crazy.

Whatever he had been cooking up all week was about to burst into the scene in the second taping. When this happened, Tim's ad-libs and improvisations were *always* funnier than what we'd had before.

Part of what makes Tim so brilliant is his fearlessness. If the audience didn't get it right away, he would keep upping the ante until they did, and we were caught in the middle. I dare anyone to be on camera and be able to hold it together when Conway gets on a roll. We really tried *not* to break up, but when we did, it was honest.

*The very first time Tim was
on our show.*

I AM FREQUENTLY asked what Tim is like in "real life." The answer: he is sweet, kind, considerate, thoughtful—*and gloriously nutty!*

I've told the next story every chance I get since it happened, because it is so typical of Tim's genius and the way his mind works!

Joe and I went to a party one night in the Valley, at Ernie and Edwina Anderson's home. Ernie was the top announcer for ABC programming and had worked with Tim when they were both starting out in the business on a local TV show in Cleveland. The whole gang was there: our dancers and writers and Tim and Harvey. When Joe and I got there, Tim was sitting on the couch with his whole head wrapped tightly in toilet paper. He had punched in holes for his eyes and his mouth, but that was it. He was definitely not drunk, but beyond that I don't know how or why he had decided to become Claude Rains in *The Invisible Man*.

He never broke character the entire evening, and we didn't even seem to notice his getup after a while. Our host took a Polaroid of Tim, and his face came out the size of a postage stamp. Tim carefully trimmed it and inserted the Polaroid over his regular driver's license picture—no lamination in those days, folks!

As Joe and I were leaving, we saw Tim get in his car still looking like the Invisible Man. What happened next is pure Conway. He knew there was one particular street in this San Fernando neighborhood where a cop liked to lie in wait behind some bushes near a four-way stop. Tim intentionally eased on through and saw the red light come to life behind him. He pulled over and rolled down his window. The policeman looked at Tim, still wrapped in toilet paper, and, in a stern voice, asked for his license. Tim handed it right over.

Fortunately, the cop had a sense of humor.

THE TELEVISION ACADEMY interviewed Tim a while back, and he talked about his childhood, among other things. I think the following is funny and endearing, too, and gives his fans—me included—valuable insight into where he got his cockeyed view of life.

He was asked, "Was there a lot of humor in your house?"

Tim: "Humor that nobody knew about. Yeah, my parents were hysterical, but had no idea that they were. One time my father hooked up a doorbell in our house. He always did his own work and he hooked it up *backwards* so it rang all the time *except* when you pressed the doorbell. So we would sit around at night and listen to this (buzzing noise) and I would say to my dad, 'You know I think that it's hooked up backwards.' He would say, 'Leave it alone.' And when it would stop he'd go, 'I'll get it.'

"A tornado came through town one day, on a Sunday afternoon, about three o'clock in the afternoon. All of a sudden everything went red and this tornado came right up the river we were living close to, and it was a like a bomb went off. It took the roof off the house next door and took a tree out of our yard and just threw it down the street, and wires were crackling and everything. My dad got up, went to the screen door, looked out, and saw this house, no roof, this tree down, the street wires, and everything, and he looked outside and he said, 'Damn kids.' So as you can see it was humor that they really didn't know they had, but I, I truly enjoyed it. I wish I had stories about them beating me and things of that nature, but it never really happened. So it's unfortunate, but I had a very pleasant childhood."

Perhaps Tim's most popular character
was the Old Man.

After he graduated from college:

"I volunteered for the army and defended Seattle from '56 to '58. As you know they were not attacked in Seattle during that time period!

"I was court-martialed. No sense of humor in the army. I was on guard duty one night and didn't have my rifle. They're very touchy about keeping your rifle close to your body in case of an attack and everything, but I was guarding a service club with pool halls and Ping-Pong balls and cards and things, and I didn't think anybody would be stealing those, it wasn't even wartime. A lieutenant came around the corner, and you're supposed to say, 'Halt! Advance and be recognized,' with your rifle, and I didn't have mine 'cause I'd lost it, so I picked one of those large white neon tubes out of the garbage, and I held it on the lieutenant, and I said, 'Halt! Advance and be recognized,' and he said (pointing to my 'weapon'), 'What is *that*?' and I said, 'It's a lightbulb and if you come any closer I'll turn it on!' You know they just didn't understand my sense of humor in the army, but that's their responsibility."

THOSE BEHIND THE SCENES FOR THE ENTIRE ELEVEN-YEAR RUN

Bob Mackie

W hat can you possibly say about a brilliant and clever genius? Plenty. This man designed as many as sixty to seventy costumes *a week* for eleven years! Our variety show would have been a sadder, less vibrant, and less hilarious one without him.

Joe and I knew from the beginning that costume design would be as important as writing for our show. On a comedy-variety show the designer is creating looks for every character in every sketch, not to mention the musical numbers—both serious and silly. And it is a *huge* job!

Joe and I were already fans of Bob Mackie's. We had watched the *Alice in Wonderland* special on TV and also Mitzi Gaynor's show and we had marveled at the brilliant mind that had created those outfits. We had checked the credits and made note that it was Bob Mackie's skill and flair at work. Who else would we possibly call?

At the appointed hour the doorbell rang, and I opened the door on a handsome young lad (he looked to be about twelve) claiming to be Bob Mackie. It turned out he was in his early twenties, and he was charming and funny and offered us several clever ideas as we talked, so we hired him on the spot!

It was one of the smartest things we ever did, and my wonderful relationship with Bob lasts to this day. His wit and sharp eye for detail saved many a sketch. In fact, after the third week, I stopped asking to see his drawings of the characters I'd be playing and waited for him to surprise me in my weekly fittings.

We would give Bob the script for the next week's show on Fridays, and he would begin to design every outfit worn by the regular cast, our guest stars, and our singers and dancers. He would design the wigs and often the makeup, too, and do all of this in less than a week. I was constantly amazed. I still am!

Bob and me in 1967.

Speaking of wigs, I wore a ton of them as different characters during our eleven years. They were made by a wonderful woman, Roselle Friedland. As for my own hair, it changed constantly, sometimes from show to show. Because, as I've said, I hated sitting in a beauty parlor, I dyed my own naturally brown hair at home with Miss Clairol, which resulted in my color varying from dark red to strawberry blond any given week. During the ninth season, I made the huge mistake of getting my hair cut even shorter than it was on our first show. It was so awful I wore a baseball cap during the day and a wig during questions and answers until my hair grew out!

Wednesday was my costume-fitting day, and I looked forward to it every week. I never knew what Bob would have in mind for me until I arrived at his workplace, and sometimes I wouldn't have a clue as to how I planned to play a character until I got dressed in the costume Bob had created for me and looked in the mirror.

It still makes me laugh to remember the Wednesday I went in for the *Gone With the Wind* fitting. I was "Starlett" O'Hara and our takeoff was called "Went With the Wind." It was a brilliant send-up, with Harvey as "Rat" Butler. There's a classic scene in the film where Scarlett, desperate for a new dress to impress Rhett, takes down the green velvet drapes at Tara, with their golden tie tassels, and has Mammy make her a dress. In our version I was to appear at the top of the stairs with the drapes simply hanging on me, while Rat waited below. Funny enough. That might have gotten a good laugh, but what did Bob do?

When I walked into the fitting room, he said, "I have an idea for the drapery bit."

He brought out THE DRESS. It was a green velvet gown *still attached to the curtain rod*. It would fit across my shoulders, with golden curtain tassels at the waist. He had even made a hat out of the tassels.

I fell on the floor laughing.

That Friday taping has gone down in history. When Starlett appeared at the top of the stairs in that getup, the audience went crazy. It has been called one of the funniest moments in the history of television comedy.

And it was all because of Bob.

Today his spectacular creation is on view at the Smithsonian.

WHEN WE TAPED our very first show, Bob dressed me in a yellow-and-white polka-dot "cover-up" robe, which we planned to repeat every week so that, with me still wearing the same outfit, we could "bank" any Q&As for a future show. After the first five shows, this idea was abandoned so I could wear a different Bob Mackie opening gown every week. A very smart decision. At times, I didn't know what to do with my hands, so Bob (cleverly) designed my gowns to have pockets!

The first time I was to do a very physical sketch, I suggested to Bob that he put me in slacks. He said, "It'll be funnier if you're in heels and a tight skirt." He was so right. Wearing a skirt and heels forced me to move in a much more awkward way than I would have wearing pants. From then on, I usually wore a tight skirt whenever I had to jump out of a window or even swing on a chandelier.

A few years ago, Bob was interviewed by the Television Academy about his brilliant body of work, spanning from the early sixties to the present, doing costumes for specials, movies, and television shows. Here are Bob's own words about "The Dress" from that interview:

Q: "How would you present your [costume] ideas?"

MACKIE: "Drawings usually . . . and very often just a pencil drawing, in a weekly TV thing. It would be a pencil drawing like when Carol wore the *Gone With the Wind* curtain rod dress. That [drawing] was on the back of a script. I tore off a page and I went, 'Well we could do this, this and this,' you know, and that was one of those that I couldn't figure out what to do. It said, 'Scarlett takes the drapes off the window, goes upstairs and comes down with the drapes just hanging off of her.' Well, that wasn't very funny. I mean that was kind of like . . . so, what does that mean? And I was trying to think, 'Well maybe I should make it really into a dress.' And I thought, 'Well no, that isn't funny either, we've seen that. We saw that in the real movie *Gone With the Wind*.' So, actually I called the art director and said, 'Can you get me a curtain rod and some of that velvet? I want the real curtain rod like you're gonna use.' And I just made it on a mannequin. And I didn't even put it on her really until the day of the show. It was so heavy and she had to [make the change] way up on top of this staircase and her dresser was this little tiny woman. And they had these terrible steep getaway stairs in the back of the set. And I said, 'Annette, I'll go up there. I'll help you with this change because you're not gonna be able to do it and there's no room for anybody else up there but us.' And there was just a little space for Carol to go off and then come back. And we had to do the change live while Harvey and Vicki were doing a little scene. She ran up the stairs. We put it on her, got her ready, and then she walked down the stairs. And I've never, *never* heard laughter like that in my life. I mean people were just . . . it just hit! Everybody had seen that movie and it just made people laugh. And it still does. Every time I talk to anybody, they bring up this silly curtain rod outfit, with the velvet drapes attached to it. I had an exhibit in New York of my whole career and what was in the front window? That outfit. You know it just doesn't make one bit of sense, but anyway it's fine. (*Laughing*) It'll be on my tombstone one day."

(*Let's add up all of Bob's creations during the 11 years: 60 to 70 costumes a week. Splitting the difference, say 65 costumes per week. Okay, 65 × 276 shows equals: 17,940 costumes!*)

Ernie Flatt

I can't dance. Never could. Then I met Ernie Flatt, the brilliant choreographer of *The Garry Moore Show*. I was hopeless, but he didn't give up on me, and even though he intimidated the hell out of me, he somehow made it look like I didn't have two left feet, so when my show got the go-ahead, Ernie was our natural first choice to stage the musical numbers. The Ernie Flatt Dancers were a major part of our show. When the show went into syndication long ago, it was cut to a half-hour format, because of costs. All of the wonderful musical numbers were lost to our audience and only the sketches aired, but I am delighted to report that there are now several DVDs available showing the full hours, so finally his amazing dances *and* dancers can be enjoyed all over again.

A younger Ernie Flatt danced in Gene Kelly's *An American in Paris* and *Singin' in the Rain*. After he became a choreographer, he won several awards for his choreography, including Emmys, a Christopher Award, and a Golden Rose. He was one of the most versatile people I've ever known. Aside from the work we had done together on Garry's show, Ernie staged the dances for two of the specials I did with my chum Julie Andrews, plus several others.

Every week for *The Carol Burnett Show*, he created incredibly original dance numbers for our finales, and also for the guest stars who danced, such as Gwen Verdon, Juliet Prowse, Chita Rivera, Rita Moreno, Bernadette Peters, Ken Berry, and many more. After our show, Ernie went on to stage and direct various Broadway shows including *Sugar Babies*, *Honky Tonk Nights*, and others. Ernie retired to Taos, New Mexico, where he died in 1995.

Don Crichton

I met Don when he was one of the Ernie Flatt Dancers on *The Garry Moore Show*. He was so gifted that he soon became the lead male dancer. He was also very tall and handsome, so Ernie had him "partner" every dancing female guest star. Don and I hit it off immediately, and often ate together on our lunch breaks. He, too, followed us to California and became the lead male dancer on our show for the entire eleven seasons. As talented as he was as a dancer, he could sometimes be an absolute klutz. The big joke was that when he simply *walked*, he would often trip! In Studio 33 at CBS Television City, there were steps that led up to our stage from the audience. Whenever Don had to run up onto the stage from the audience when we were rehearsing, he would inevitably *trip*! One time, I said,

"Don, why don't you try *dancing* up the stairs?" And it worked! Nary a stumble. Also, he had one whale of an appetite. He could pack it away and never gain an ounce. The female dancers, who lived on lettuce, wanted to kill him when he showed up for rehearsals scarfing down a hero sandwich and polishing off a couple pints of ice cream for dessert.

Don was also the lead dancer on several specials I did. After our show went off the air, he became a successful choreographer. We met fifty-seven years ago, and to this day, he remains one of my closest friends.

Artie Malvin

Artie was the first special musical material writer we hired, and he was with our show for the entire eleven seasons. He arranged not only the vocal numbers for already existing songs but also wrote original lyrics and music.

During World War II, Artie performed with Glenn Miller as part of the Crew Chiefs. Recordings of his performances with Miller and the Army Air Force Band were released as V-Discs.

After World War II and Glenn Miller's death Artie became heavily immersed in the popular music of the 1940s and 1950s, everything from children's music, to the beginnings of rock and roll, to jingles for commercials. In the late 1950s he worked in television as the music arranger for *The Pat Boone–Chevy Showroom*.

He had a gold-plated résumé when we asked him to come on board. I just loved him. He was always smiling and eager to contribute.

Artie collaborated with other writers, Buz Kohan and Bill Angelos the first few seasons, and then Ken and Mitzie Welch when they came on board for seasons five through ten. He also worked with Stan Freeman during our eleventh year.

Artie used to make a tape of the music I had to learn for the following week so I could take it home on Fridays and listen to it over the weekend. I didn't read music, but after listening to the number several times, I was ahead of the game when Monday rehearsals rolled around. When Ken and Mitzie were writing on our show, and I had a number to learn that week, I would listen to Mitzie sing my part, which made it that much easier for me to learn, and Artie would sing the other part. Depending on the guests that week, he would be Steve Lawrence, Bing Crosby, Ray Charles, etc., etc., and sometimes even Eydie Gormé! Always a delight, Artie welcomed working with other creative musicians and lyricists. There never was any ego involved. After we went off the air, Artie, along with Ernie Flatt, created the wildly successful Broadway musical *Sugar Babies*, starring Mickey Rooney and Ann Miller. He also wrote a number for me (as Miss Hannigan) and Albert Finney (as Daddy Warbucks) to sing in the movie *Annie*, called "Sign." He wanted no credit. Artie died in 2006.

Music

Since my first show business love was musical comedy, it was a given that we would have lots of music in our variety show. And what music! We had a live twenty-eight-piece orchestra (unheard of today!), conducted and orchestrated by Harry Zimmerman (who had been the musical director on *The Dinah Shore Show* and *The Garry Moore Show*) for our first three years, and then Peter Matz (a composer and conductor for stage and screen, also famous for his work on Barbra Streisand's early albums) for the final eight years. I couldn't wait for orchestra rehearsals on Thursday nights.

All week long we would be rehearsing with just a piano and drums, and then Thursday would roll around, and we'd all be thrilled to hear the beautiful sounds that came out of the band shell. Since I never learned to read music, the only way I could learn a medley where I had to sing harmonies was to look at the lyrics printed in my script, and pencil in "squiggles," which was my own personal invention, a sort of shorthand. If a note went "up," I would draw a line over the lyric that swooped *up*, or I would draw a line that swooped *down* if the note descended. If I had to look at the cue cards for a lyric, our cue card guys would copy the squiggles from my script! For instance, here is a sample of how the squiggles would work with "Row, Row, Row, Your Boat."

Row, row, row your boat,

Gently down the stream.

Merrily, merrily, merrily, merrily,

Life is but a dream.

I never liked singing alone, *as myself.* I was okay with it when I was doing a character, but singing a straight solo always scared me. However, I was fearless when it came to singing duets with our musical guests. (Some might say I was *too* fearless, but I didn't care because I was in "medley heaven!") Our special material writers would brilliantly weave several different songs together that usually had a theme. There were some amazing singers who graced our show over the eleven years: Ella Fitzgerald, Steve Lawrence, Eydie Gormé, Bing Crosby, Perry Como, Mel Tormé, Ray Charles, the Carpenters, and Marilyn Horne, to name but a few. The medleys we sang were so well written that I can remember a lot of them to this day.

We wrote our own musical takeoffs on *Show Boat* with Hal Linden, *Cinderella* with the Pointer Sisters as the evil stepsisters, a Fred and Ginger movie ("Hi-Hat" with Ken Berry and Roddy McDowall), and many more. All of them had original music and lyrics by our special material writers over the years: Ken and Mitzie Welch, Artie

Malvin, the team of Buz Kohan and Bill Angelos, and Stan Freeman, and all of them won Emmys for their creations. Then there were the solo performances by our many musical guests.

In 1968, there was a musicians' strike that lasted three weeks, and guess who our guest was the first week? Ella Fitzgerald! *Great timing.* Ella lip-synched her recordings of "Day In, Day Out" and "Skylark." I lip-synched a recording I did of "The Trolley Song," where our director Dave Powers bet me a dollar that he could foul me up by randomly speeding up and slowing down my voice from his perch in the booth. It was a hoot, and I won the dollar. The wildest part of these shows was that our singers replaced the missing orchestra by *humming* everything, from the opening theme song to all the play-ons and play-offs! It was pretty funny and we had a blast making do without the band, but I sure was happy when everything was settled and we got our orchestra back.

Our Sound Effects

I was somewhat obsessive when it came to sound effects. It began when I was on Garry's show. We had a sound effects man (I wish I could remember his name) who was a throwback to radio. Back in the day, so many radio shows depended on sound effects to help tell the story—and generate laughs. I remember listening to Jack Benny when I was a kid. The sound effects were so important that you could almost say they were another "character" on the show. I remember Jack's footsteps walking down to his basement where he kept his money in a vault, and the sound of him removing the heavy chains wrapped around the safe, and then the creaking noise as he opened the vault's very heavy door: hysterical.

In doing Garry's show, the sound effects man would simulate a body fall whenever one of us fell down. If a gunshot sound was required, he'd provide it at that *very* moment. If we fell out of a window, you'd hear a slide whistle denoting the fall, followed by the sound of garbage cans being banged into, and maybe the loud meow of an angry alley cat.

When I got my own show, we hired the brilliant Ross Murray, who was blessed with perfect timing and a terrific sense of humor. He had a small booth upstairs, behind the audience, that looked out over our stage and was filled with various recordings and tangible objects he invented to create the effects that were needed in whatever sketch we were doing. We did a *LOT* of physical stuff, and he never once missed a cue in eleven years.

Lots of times we would do something that required an effect that we hadn't even rehearsed. For instance, the first time I was asked in a Q&A if I ever got nervous when performing, I said no and then, out of the blue, pretended to faint and fall on the floor. Ross was right there with a "body fall," and the audience screamed with laughter. They wouldn't have laughed as hard without the added benefit of the sound of my body hitting the ground. I always preferred "real" sound effects, as opposed to comic ones. To me, the real ones were funnier. Alas, today this is a lost art. If sound effects are required in a television show that's being taped or filmed before a studio audience, they are added later in the editing room. The studio audience never hears them, and the spontaneous laughs they would have generated are lost. It's really too bad. Ross Murray always made our sketches funnier with his live inventions.

CBS Censorship

Over the years we had a great censor, Charlie Pettyjohn, who came to every run-through and taping and never gave us any grief. Maybe because we never gave *him* any grief. However, one week, in 1968, Harvey and I were doing a sketch where he was interviewing my character, who was a nudist in a nudist colony, standing behind a fence showing bare shoulders and bare legs, with high-top sneakers on my feet. Harvey asks, "What do you nudists do for recreation?" My reply was "We have a dance every Saturday night."

"How do nudists dance?" he asks. My answer was "Very carefully." Charlie was okay with that line, but somebody higher up who was with CBS Program Practices (and Charlie's boss) considered the line to be too risqué, so we had to come up with a different joke. We came up with a different one, all right. And CBS bought it.

"How do nudists dance?"

"Cheek to cheek."

Go figure.

Actually, the network pretty much left us alone. Besides Charlie Pettyjohn, there was always a CBS representative around who never said much and who also didn't do much, for which we were grateful. One of our writers said once, "Looks like his job is to warn us when an iceberg's heading down Fairfax Avenue."

The Writing Staff

During our show's long run, I often didn't know who took the lead in writing each of our sketches, with a few exceptions. I wish I could name those exceptions, but it wouldn't be fair to single out any writers from within the different groups while not being able to give credit to others whom I'm in the dark about. There were a number of factors that reluctantly led me to this decision, one of those being the credit guidelines of the Writers Guild of America, an institution I greatly respect.

But for some reason, there was never a "byline" when I was handed a sketch to read. I suppose Joe felt that if I knew who wrote it, I might start to favor a particular writer or writing team over others. I wasn't like the "boys"—i.e., Gleason, Caesar, Berle, etc.—who were joined at the hip with their writers and spent hours with them in the writers' room kicking around ideas and throwing out one-liners.

So, later on in this book, when I describe certain sketches where I actually know who did have the initial idea, I can't give those writers credit, even though I would like very much to do so, out of a concern for fairness to all the others and a desire to be 100 percent accurate.

Join me in celebrating the immensely talented and hilarious writers who graced the show with their fine work over our eleven years by turning to page 299, where you will find a comprehensive list.

I was like Lucy, when her husband Desi Arnaz was at the helm. She and her cast were simply the performers who brought the writing to life. Joe was my "Desi." He had run Garry's show, overseeing the writers, sketches, and musical numbers, so I was comfortable letting him do the same for me. I trusted his judgment. Joe hired our head writers and producers, Arnie Rosen, and later Buz Kohan and Bill Angelos, and after them Ed Simmons—all terrific at their jobs. They would assign certain sketches to the writing staff, or if a writer turned in an idea of his/her own, it would either be approved and make the cut or be deep-sixed without seeing the light of day.

I did have a say in many sketches, such as which particular movies I wanted to parody, and occasionally I would propose other ideas. In rehearsal, I had no hesitation in suggesting changing a line here or there, and I encouraged the cast, and those of our guests who were seasoned sketch performers, to speak up if an idea occurred to them. To their credit, the writers had no objection to our input if it helped make the sketch better. I wonder how it would've been different if I had been in on *everything* from the ground floor up.

In thinking about it over the years, I realize that this schedule allowed me to have a normal *life* all those years. I wasn't burning the midnight oil working with the writing staff—I was raising a family—so I can't say this way of doing it was wrong. Besides, we did wind up with a pretty successful show.

Our writers were brilliantly funny, on the page and off. There was one particular time that stands out from early on in our run, when Arnie Rosen was at the helm. Arnie's office was across the hall from mine, and often during our lunch break Arnie and the rest of the writers would watch kinescopes of the all-time television greats— Berle, Gleason, Caesar, etc.—on a portable screen set up at the end of the room. Some of our writers had started out with these shows, and stories would fly back and forth about the good old days. Lots of times I would cross the hall to watch some of the sketches for a few minutes. Those sketches held up and were still as funny as they were back when.

During this one lunch break I went into his dark office to question Arnie about a particular sketch we were doing that week. Not looking at the screen, I bent over to whisper in his ear. I heard moaning and grunting and turned around to look at the screen. Ohmigod! They were watching porn! They had set me up, and were howling at my reaction. I had never seen a porn film in my life, and I sputtered, "Ohhh! Ohmigod! That's just AWFUL!!!"

Arnie said, "Well, gosh, Carol, he's doing the best he can!"

"LIFE ONCE REMOVED"

A Conversation with Larry Gelbart

S everal years ago, I found myself sitting next to Larry Gelbart
at a dinner at the State Department in Washington, D.C., celebrating the Kennedy Center Honors. Larry was right up there
with Neil Simon when it came to writing comedy.

He began as a writer at the age of sixteen, for Danny Thomas's
radio show, after his father, who was Thomas's barber, showed Thomas
some jokes Larry had written. During the 1940s he also wrote for Jack
Paar and Bob Hope. In the 1950s he wrote for Sid Caesar on *Caesar's
Hour*. He worked with writers Mel Tolkin, Michael Stewart, Selma
Diamond, Neil Simon, Mel Brooks, Carl Reiner, and Woody Allen on
two Caesar specials.

Larry was one of the main forces behind the creation of the television series *M*A*S*H*, writing the pilot then producing, often writing, and occasionally directing the series for its first four seasons.
He earned a Peabody Award and an Emmy for *M*A*S*H*. His movie
work included the screenplays for *Tootsie* and *Oh, God!* and he received Oscar nominations for both.

There are a lot more of his credits to add, but you get the picture.
At the dinner we got into a conversation about the "dumbing down"
of America when it came to television.

ME: "I don't know, but when I watch a comedy show on TV
today, I know exactly what's coming as far as the writing goes.

No surprises. No originality. Usually it's the 'setup' first, and then comes the obvious joke, and then you hear that awful laugh track. It's as if all the shows are alike and repeating themselves."

LARRY: "I think it's because most of the writers today grew up watching television. That was their childhood, so they're writing about life *once removed*."

ME: "What do you mean?"

LARRY: "They never played stickball in the street."

EXPLAINING A PUNCH LINE

Joe and I were at a dinner party at the producer Jennings Lang's home in Beverly Hills. Walter Matthau and his beautiful wife, Carol, were there along with a lot of other movie folks. Some I knew, and some I didn't know. During cocktails, I got into a conversation with a nice young man about writing. He said he was a fan of our show, but he kept asking, "Why can't there be funnier endings to the skits? They start out great, and then they usually peter out." Obviously, this guy wasn't up on how difficult it is to write anything, especially comedy. I asked him what his name was. Edward. I tried to explain, "Well, Edward, writing a terrific punch line for a comedy sketch (I prefer that word to 'skit') isn't as easy as some folks, who don't write, might think." As I'm sitting there attempting to give a simple lecture on the difficult art of putting words down on paper, our host comes up to us and says cheerfully, "Carol, I see you've met Edward Albee."

OUR RECURRING SKETCHES
OVER THE YEARS

Audiences love the recurring sketch—provided the characters are likable and funny, of course. They look forward to their favorites and get particular pleasure when those characters show up in that week's episode, whether we're talking about Jackie Gleason's Ralph Kramden or Steve Martin and Dan Aykroyd's Wild and Crazy Guys. We were lucky to come up with a group of comedy sketches that we loved doing, and characters that our audiences looked forward to seeing again and again. Here are some that were an important part of our show. I hope you'll enjoy spending more time in the company of these characters.

The Charwoman

In 1962, one of the top-selling instrumental recordings was "The Stripper," which was composed by David Rose. It had a definite jazz influence, with especially prominent trombone lines, and felt just like the music that was often used to accompany striptease artists. I remember listening to it on the radio, and hearing the disc jockey say that since its release, it had turned out to be "a favorite of housewives across the country." I visualized a woman with a broom, listening to the sexy music as she did bumps and grinds across the kitchen floor, sweeping up crumbs from breakfast.

I was preparing to do a special for CBS called *Carol and Company*, with the wonderful Robert Preston, who was the Tony-winning star of *The Music Man*, a smash hit on Broadway. I was going to do an opening number, written by Ken Welch, about my childhood and how I was always "Nelson" to my beautiful cousin's "Jeanette," which featured me as a thrilled Jeanette surrounded by twenty gorgeous mounted policemen as a bunch of Nelsons. Robert and I would sing a duet next, and then do a sketch. And he would do a special material solo singing about all the death scenes he played in the movies he had made.

And then I would do a final solo.

The Charwoman never spoke or had a name.

I thought about "The Stripper," and came up with the idea of putting a charwoman on the empty stage of a burlesque house after hours. She enters with a mop and a bucket and starts to mop the stage, when out of nowhere she hears a drum. The drum begins to catch her every move, much to her delight, and as she peels off one of her work gloves, we hear a slide trombone that introduces "The Stripper" song in all its glory. The charwoman morphs into her version of Gypsy Rose Lee and bumps and grinds, pretending to strip when all she actually removes is her mop cap and ratty sweater. The number ends as she skips into the wings. She then returns and, finding herself all alone again, sits on the bucket and sings a sad song, "Nobody."

I didn't realize at the time that the Charwoman would become somewhat of an icon. She caught on with the viewers, and later when we started my variety show, she was the cartoon figure in our opening credits. Often during the season, she would appear in a pantomime, always winding up sitting on the bucket and singing the blues. At the end of every season, I would do a Charwoman bit and then sit on the bucket and sing the entire version of "I'm So Glad We Had This Time Together."

In looking back, there were some Charwoman pantomime bits that weren't up to par, premise-wise. She would enter a scene, do a little dusting here and there, and then sit on the bucket and sing for no particular reason.

She never spoke. Only sang. I never gave her a name. I don't know why. I just never did.

"Carol and Sis"

We decided we would feature a sort of "mini-sitcom," every so often during the season, in the way Jackie Gleason introduced "The Honeymooners" on his hour-long variety show. The only *slight* difference was that "The Honeymooners" was brilliant, something you couldn't accuse "Carol and Sis" of being. Some of these sketches were amusing, but this concept wasn't a particular favorite of mine.

We used my real first name and my real kid sister's name. Harvey became Roger Bradford. Carol and Roger Bradford along with Carol's kid sister, Chris, played by Vicki, live in a modest home in "Anywhere, USA." He works for a "Company" (we never really identified his job) and Carol is a housewife. The set consisted of a living room, a kitchen with a swinging door and stairs leading to offstage bedrooms, bathroom, etc. Close to the kitchen, in a corner of the living room, sat a tall potted plant. Lots of times, when we were stuck for an ending, we'd finish with one of us barreling out of the kitchen and slamming into another one of us on the other side of the door, sending that person sailing into the potted plant. It was a total cop-out, but it always got a laugh.

Vicki (as Chris) was often in the first few minutes of the sketch and then she'd leave the scene, usually to go over to her friend Marcia's house. She was still pretty wet behind the ears, and we were careful not to throw too much at her. After a few months, CBS suggested that we let Vicki go; they didn't feel that she was contributing anything to the show. We said no, and to their credit, the network backed off. Harvey was terrific with her and gave her a lot of tips on such things as how to "make props your friends," and how to listen to the other actors and not just wait for your cue to speak, etc. She was like a sponge. She *got it*. We slowly started giving her other roles in other sketches, and when we did, she blossomed.

Eventually, around the eighth season, "Carol and Sis" faded into the ether for good.

George and Zelda

These characters were born out of a short takeoff Harvey and I did on the movie *A Place in the Sun*. We were in a rowboat on a lake (like the scene featuring Montgomery Clift and Shelley Winters). I play Zelda, who is nagging poor George in a kvetching, high-pitched nasal voice that defies description. The camera (from George's point of view) keeps zooming in closer and closer on my mouth, whining and whining, until it practically fills the whole picture. George winds up jumping in the lake to get away from me.

We decided to do more with these characters because we enjoyed doing them so much. There was one sketch where poor George is on death row, and Zelda pays him a final visit. Ignoring the fact that he's a goner come dawn, she whines on and on and on about the bumpy bus ride and the fumes that made her sick to her stomach. She asks George to ring for room service to bring her an aspirin. George, at his wit's end, says, "There's no room service!" How she can be so heart-less! He's going to die!

When a guard comes in to ask George what he'd like for his last meal, a miffed Zelda says, "I thought you said there was no room service!"

I loved doing Zelda at first, but then I made the mistake of trying to "improve" the character, a common error some actors make, and unfortunately I was one of them in this case. I kept adding to her un-attractiveness by going way over the top with the nagging whine, so much so that I almost gave myself a headache. After several of these sketches, Zelda bit the dust.

"The Old Folks"

Harvey's character kept trying to get lucky.

The set is a front porch featuring two rocking chairs. Harvey and I, as Bert and Molly (probably in their late eighties), always entered from a screen door, heading for the rockers. They would sit and rock and usually talk about their age and sex. Bert was an old geezer, always wanting to get it on, and Molly was forever putting him down.

*He's bragging about a new pretty young nurse in his
doctor's office in one sketch and this miffs Molly,
of course, who turns away from him.*

BERT: "Oh, c'mon, Molly, don't be jealous. I find *you* mighty attractive!"

He puts his hand on her knee.

BERT: "Does that remind you of anything?"
MOLLY: (Thinking it over) "Atheism."
BERT: (Confused) "Why?"
MOLLY: "You haven't got a prayer."

Bert is reading the travel section in the newspaper.

BERT: "Say, why don't we go on vacation?"
MOLLY: "Oh, that'd be nice. Y'know, I've always wanted to see them pyramids in Egypt."
BERT: "Naw, I saw 'em once when I was a kid."
MOLLY: "Yeah, but they're finished now."
BERT: (Hot to trot) "I'll get into my pajamas, an' we'll watch some television, an' I'll hold your hand, an' then *maybe* . . . " (Chuckles) "who knows?"
MOLLY: "That's my favorite program."
BERT: "What is?"
MOLLY: (Sizing him up and down) "*Mission: Impossible!*"

We got some mail from senior citizens who thought Bert and Molly were too risqué, but the majority of them got a kick out of "The Old Folks" and liked the fact that these characters could kid around like that.

Sample letter: "Just because there's snow on the roof doesn't mean there's no furnace in the basement!"

(I think he was quoting an old joke, but the sentiment was there.)

"As the Stomach Turns"

T hese sketches were an homage to daytime soap operas, and they were over-the-top fun to do. They were also an audience favorite, so we wound up doing around thirty of them. The setting was always Marian's living room in the fictional town of Canoga Falls, and I always played Marian, single and forever horny. Marian continually talks to the camera to give her interpretation of the plot. Often, the offstage organ music drowns her out, and she always shoots the offender dirty looks. In Marian's life, there are constant problems to deal with, much to her delight. The sketches would end with a voice-over announcer posing silly questions about the future fates of the characters while the camera panned to each actor for a facial response.

The first time we did one of these sketches was February 12, 1968, and our guests were Betty Grable and Martha Raye. In it, Betty is the Town Amnesiac, who finally remembers that she gave birth to a child many years ago.

"I had a beautiful baby girl!"

Marian corrects her. "No, dear, you had a son. You just dressed him funny."

Betty Grable and I socialize with Martha Raye and Lyle in Marian's living room (the very first "As the Stomach Turns").

Lyle enters with his fiancée, the Town Rich Lady, played by Martha. He turns out to be Betty's long-lost son. We learn that Betty's amnesia was a result of Martha's pushing her over the "Canoga Falls falls," only because: "You were a little prettier and a little younger."

Betty, consoling her, responds, "That's not true, dear . . . I was a *lot* prettier." Betty had great comedic timing, and Martha was absolutely hysterical as the rich lady, causing Betty, at times, to try to stifle a laugh. Vicki was always Marian's long-lost daughter, turning up each time as a different character and always with a baby, which she left with Marian (who would usually deposit the infant in the umbrella stand).

In one bit: Vicki enters, with a baby in her arms, as Marian's long-lost daughter who ran away to join the circus. Handing the infant to Marian, she tells her the father was the "Half-Man, Half-Woman." Marian asks the baby's name. "Irving Elizabeth," Vicki says. She tells her mother that she has a new boyfriend who is the sword swallower, but they won't get married because "He's stuck on himself." (*Rim shot from the drums.*) Harvey and Lyle would be various characters, and the guest stars would be Marian's acquaintances who always had dire problems.

The first time I saw Harvey in drag. I am
desperately trying to hold it together!

The first time Harvey did Mother Marcus was in one of these sketches. I hadn't seen him in the character's costume until the dress rehearsal; the same went for the crew. As Marian, I got up to answer the doorbell, and there is Harvey in full drag, padded to the hilt with humongous boobs. He was in a flowered dress, a gray wig, hose, and heels, and holding a pocketbook. He was wearing lipstick and rouge. The audience screamed for about a minute. Looking at him, I tried to keep it together, but I wound up slamming the door while he was standing in the doorjamb. When I opened it again, he had a hurt look on his face and his hands were cradling his boobs.

Speaking of Martha Raye . . .

Tuesday, February 17, 1959, was a very important day for me. The previous Sunday afternoon, I had received an urgent call from the producers of *The Garry Moore Show* saying that Martha Raye, who was to have been the guest that week, couldn't do the show because she had come down with a bad case of bronchitis, and could I come over to the rehearsal hall right away and learn her sketches and songs and fill in for her when the show went on the air—live—on Tuesday night. Could I?! (I had appeared on Garry's morning TV show several times, and Garry had enough faith in me to give me this break.) I got to the rehearsal hall as fast as I could, and tried my best to learn everything that had been written for Martha. The following Tuesday night was like a dream. I had been well rehearsed, had learned everything, and was lovingly supported by Garry, Durward Kirby, Marion Lorne, and the entire staff. During the bows, Garry told the studio audience all about how I was filling in for the ailing Martha, and there was a standing ovation. All I could do was blubber. As I was leaving to go home, there was a bouquet of one dozen red roses waiting for me at the stage door guard's desk. They were from Martha, who was also calling me on the backstage phone. "Hey, kiddo, you were terrific!"

A side note: In 1956, I got a job as an extra in a sketch on *The Martha Raye Show*. I had no lines. Another extra and I were a couple in a Tunnel of Love boat. The joke was that Martha was the only one in the boat without a partner. I remember laughing at her outrageous antics during rehearsals, never dreaming that she would be the reason for my big break in television three years later . . . or that she would eventually be a frequent guest on my own variety show. She was a very special lady.

The Queen

When you saw me, I was dressed to look like Queen Elizabeth, even though we referred to Harvey's character as the King and there was no King of England. Obviously, we were not trying to be historically correct, but the audience loved seeing me as Elizabeth and howled. Tim's character was known as the Hollow Hero, earning that moniker because he had saved his whole platoon by swallowing a live hand grenade, leaving the poor lad with no internal organs! The Queen proves it by opening his mouth and saying, "Hello," which results in a loud echo . . . "Hell-ooo-ooo-ooo!"

In these sketches, the King and Queen are constantly frustrated by Tim's character, who is not the least bit impressed with royalty and can be downright rude. Harvey and I did English accents, and Tim opted to sound like he came from the Midwest. Actually, my English accent was highly exaggerated, while Harvey's was dead-on.

In one sketch, as a Buckingham Palace guard, armed with a rifle, Tim refuses to let the Queen and King enter unless they can give him the correct password.

"But young man, I am your Queen."

Looking carefully at his notes, he says, "That's not it."

The King appeals to him: "Young man, the Queen has to get to the throne."

No dice.

The King tries to bribe the Private with a nice shiny new shilling. He'll have none of it. "Stick it in your ear."

The King says, "I beg your pardon?"

"I *said*, 'Stick it in your ear.'"

The Queen beckons to the King. "Pssst! What did he say?" The King answers, "He said stick it in my ear." There's a pause while she thinks for a moment. She then says, matter-of-factly, "Don't do it."

We are amused, but we can't show it!

When the Queen asks the Hollow Hero what he *does* want, he says, "A popsicle."

"A what?"

"A *popsicle*. You know, a frozen thing on a stick . . . Jeez."

The King beckons to the Queen. "What did he say?"

She repeats the odd request. "He said he wants a popsicle."

"A what?"

"A *popsicle*. You know, a frozen thing on a stick . . . Jeez."

The Private finally says he'll settle for an ice cream cone. The Royal Couple are quite relieved when an ice cream truck just happens to pull up. The Queen asks the Private what flavor he'd like.

"Buffalo."

The Queen informs him that there is no such thing as buffalo-flavored ice cream, and he says he'll settle for a double-decker cone, which pleases the Queen until he adds, "One scoop of antelope sherbet and one scoop of goat hoof ice cream."

The Queen loses it and screams, "They got VANILLA! They got CHOCOLATE! They even got COCONUT PAPAYA! But there's no such thing as *ANIMAL*-FLAVORED ICE CREAM!" (Forcing his mouth open, yelling into it so we hear a loud echo) "YOU HOLLOWED-OUT LITTLE CREEEEEEEP!!!!"

Another sketch had him requesting "A pony." When he is presented with one, he says he doesn't want it.

"But why?"

"I want a blue one."

In each sketch we did, Private Newbury thwarted the Queen at every turn with ridiculous requests, and the Queen always wound up having a hissy fit and calling him a "hollowed-out little creep!" These sketches were as funny as they were ridiculous. Because of my resemblance to Queen Elizabeth, people in Canada and Australia weighed in with opposite opinions. I'm not sure anymore which country got a kick out of these sketches and which country was "not amused."

Stella Toddler

Cary Grant once told me that Stella Toddler was one of his favorite characters on our show. She was also one of mine. The first time we introduced her was in the fifth year, and our guests were Tony Randall and Jack Klugman, who had the hit television show *The Odd Couple*. In the sketch, Stella was a very, *very* old retired acting teacher who was just this side of the Pearly Gates. The idea for this sketch was to do a takeoff on *This Is Your Life*, a television show popular in the fifties, sixties, and seventies. It was originally hosted by its producer Ralph Edwards. In the show, the host surprises a guest and proceeds to take them through their life in front of an audience, including special guest appearances by colleagues, friends, and family. In our version, Harvey is the unctuous emcee, who surprises the doddering and very frail ninety-four-year-old famous acting teacher Stella Toddler, who wants to be anywhere else but where she is (and she's not even sure where *that* is!).

The unctuous emcee surprises Stella.

The emcee (Harvey) introduces Gaga Gabor (Vicki), one of Stella's acting students, who enters and hugs Stella so hard that she cracks the poor old lady's ribs.

The next student is Buster Weisscrab (Lyle), wearing a loincloth, swinging in on a vine doing the Tarzan yell, and accidentally knocking Stella over the couch, after which he picks her up and generally throws her around.

Tony Randall enters as a famous Broadway director, sporting a walking cane, who constantly keeps hitting and knocking Stella down accidentally with his cane while talking to Harvey.

This was the first time I did Stella, but it wouldn't be the last.

This sketch has tons of physical shtick, with me being pummeled at every turn. Poor old Stella wound up being put in harm's way in several sketches after this first one. In future sketches she would be buried in wet cement, blown through a wall by a huge wind machine, ride a wrecking ball, etc., etc., constantly being beat up, and all the time just wanting to "go home."

Ever since doing *The Garry Moore Show,* I opted to teach myself how to do stunts. Stella wasn't the only character to get knocked around during our eleven-year run. I haven't counted the times I fell down, jumped out of windows, walked into walls, and so forth, but I'm guessing more than two hundred. I'm amazed I never broke a bone, or even sprained a body part. A few bruises here and there. Sheer luck, and I might add, I loved doing it!

I have to tell you an embarrassing story here . . . before every run-through for our crew on Wednesdays at 3:00, I would slip into the ladies' room across the hall for a few minutes. I'd close the door to a stall, sit on the toilet seat lid, and go over the show in my mind. Earlier in the week, while rehearsing and trying to "find" Stella's character, I had been using a kind of wobbly high-pitched old age voice. I wasn't satisfied because I had used that same voice when Harvey and I did "The Old Folks" sketches.

I wanted to come up with something different, when suddenly, out of the blue, the old character actor Gabby Hayes, who was Roy Rogers's pal in those cowboy movies in the forties, popped into my head. I remembered his comically distinctive voice, which was low-pitched and much slower than the one I had been doing in rehearsals. So there I was, sitting on the toilet seat, behind the closed stall door. Not sure whether or not this would be the right way to go, I decided to try this new voice out *loud* before the run-through. I remember saying to myself, "Yes, this is good, this is *very* good, much better than what I've been trying to do all week!" Satisfied with my new take on the character, I opened the stall door and there were two women standing at the sinks, who had heard the whole thing. They just stared at me, not saying a word, as I slunk out of there and reported for the run-through, red-faced to the max.

Mrs. Wiggins and Mr. Tudball

*Trying to keep it together as Tim adds one
of his unexpected zingers.*

These loopy characters appeared often in our show. I was Mrs. Wiggins and, as Mr. Tudball, Tim Conway spoke in an accent that was a cross between a Romanian native and someone from outer space. The setting was Mr. Tudball's office, and Mrs. Wiggins's little outer office. Mrs. Wiggins was originally written to be a doddering senior citizen, but Bob Mackie had other ideas for her character. I went to my costume fitting for that week, and Bob said, "You've done so many old ladies, let's try something different." The "something different" was that a much younger Mrs. Wiggins would be dressed as a blond bimbo, complete with a Farrah Fawcett wig, a low-cut flowered blouse (with a padded push-up bra), a tight black skirt, and stiletto high heels. The skirt was an old one Bob had in "the great closet in the sky" (a term I always used to describe his vast inventory), and it bagged in the behind. Instead of taking it in, Bob suggested, "Stick your butt out." I did, and that's how the "Wiggins Walk" was born. Mrs. Wiggins was the epitome of laziness, always filing and painting her nails, becoming exhausted after sharpening a pencil. She was fun to play, but sometimes tricky when Tim, as Tudball, would go off script (naturally) in front of the audience and come up with some one-liners that weren't in our rehearsals. I say tricky, because Mrs. Wiggins was a person whom the IQ Fairy had never visited, which means that she could have no sense of humor at all, and therefore couldn't possibly laugh at Tudball's insulting remarks. It was no easy feat for me to keep a straight face, so more often than not, I would appear to be chewing on one of my fingernails, when in reality I was biting my finger to keep from breaking up.

There was the time when Mrs. Wiggins was walking past Mr. Tudball's desk, and he asks her to halt. She stops dead in her tracks, and he ad-libs, "You know, Misses-ah-Wiggins, from-a da waist down, you look-a like-a Africa!" Another time (still referring to her large posterior) he said, "That's a novel idea to walk around pointing to places you've already been!" I almost drew blood from my pinkie.

"*Mary Worthless*"

E ven though we did this sketch only one time, it's worth talking about. We had planned to make Mary Worthless another one of those characters we'd do every so often. The whole concept was based on the comic strip *Mary Worth*, who is an elderly and wise "do-gooder." She is a compassionate widow who advises friends, neighbors, and acquaintances. She is always helpful and loving.

Our version was intended to be a satire in which I played the title character, who is determined to "help" people "whether they like it or not."

In the sketch, Harvey and Vicki are the world's happiest married couple. He has just been promoted in his job, and the boss is coming over for dinner to celebrate. They've hired a maid to help with the festivities. Mary Worthless shows up and proceeds to throw a monkey wrench into the plans while being as sweet as sugar. Passive-aggressive to the max, she manages to turn the lovebirds against each other by insinuating that the wife is cheating on the husband with the boss and slyly intimating that the husband is an alcoholic, all the while behaving as if she is a loving and kind soul, out to help them solve their marital woes. Her meddling interference causes the couple to have a big fight. Lyle enters as the boss, and the husband socks him. Mary enters with a cake she has baked, and Vicki takes it and lets Harvey have it in the face before she leaves him. He wants to kill himself and proceeds to jump out the window. Mary then turns to the camera and sweetly says, "Don't be surprised if I show up on *your* doorstep someday!"

Okay. Well . . . not okay.

SAYING "BYE, BYE, MARY!"

The sketch wasn't really all that good, but we gave it the old college try. However, things totally went south when Lyle arrived. First of all, Harvey jumped a cue and went to open the door before the doorbell rang. Lyle accidentally dropped something and as he bent down to pick up whatever it was, Harvey swung wildly, slammed the door too soon, and started to crack up. I came in with the cake, and Vicki smashed it into his face. Harvey, still laughing, headed for the window and jumped. His jump didn't clear the window, and on the way out he clunked his shins on the sill, prompting me to gasp and start laughing.

I was totally embarrassed by the whole mess, so when I turned to the camera—instead of just saying what I was supposed to say, I said, "Don't be surprised if I show up on *your* doorstep someday," and then added, "Better yet, *be* surprised, because I'm not ever doing this again!"

Mary Worthless bit the dust.

Another One That Bit the Dust

I recall another sketch featuring Harvey, Vicki, Tim, and me, in which Tim and Harvey were crooks and Vicki and I were their molls. We were in a seedy hotel room planning our next caper, a robbery. It wasn't the least bit funny, and all week I kept trying to deep-six the sketch, but Joe and the writers insisted it was worth trying to save.

I wasn't alone. Harvey, Tim, and Vicki felt the same way, and every time we tried to tackle this turkey, we'd just look at each other and roll our eyes.

Friday came around, and it hadn't been cut from the show in spite of my misgivings. During the dress rehearsal the audience, watching this debacle, just sat there and stared at us. They looked like an oil painting. Joe wouldn't give up, saying we should give it another shot on the air show. I contemplated filing for divorce. The second show rolled around, and we plunged in all over again, giving it our all. It was still bombing when, about four minutes in, who should appear on stage walking *onto the set* . . . Joe! I thought I was in the Twilight Zone! What the hell was he doing out here? Why wasn't he in the director's booth? Then he said what I thought were the most beautiful words I had ever heard: "Stop doing this."

We did, and happily went on with the rest of the show.

A Bad Idea for a Number

I never wanted to have the reputation of being a "diva," so I would bend over backwards not to warrant it, much to my disadvantage at times. Looking back, I realize that this wasn't the best tactic. One particular show comes to mind. It was 1968, and our choreographer, Ernie Flatt, got the not-so-brilliant idea for a number where I would be dressed as a Spanish dancer, singing "You Don't Have to Say You Love Me," while my clothes are being whipped off, little by little, until I'm left only in my underwear at the tail end of the song.

Being whipped!

I wasn't too thrilled with this idea, but the consensus was that this would be a very funny bit and I was wrong to be nervous for no reason at all. This had to be one of the dumbest sketches I ever let myself be talked into. A professional "whip artist" was hired, and believe me, he was anything but an artist. I think he was more nervous than I was, because during the dress rehearsal he totally missed whipping a piece of my costume off and nicked me in the shoulder instead, causing it to bleed. Not wanting to seem like a bad sport, I put a flesh-colored Band-Aid on and reluctantly went back for more on the air show.

This time, he goofed and whipped off every bit of my costume at the beginning of the song . . . *way* before he was supposed to . . . leaving me standing there to sing the *entire* song in my underwear. How stupid was I? *Very.*

Fred and Marge

Thesese two characters were the creations of our orchestrator and conductor, Pete Matz. He always felt that the Midwest was shortchanged when it was compared to the "hipper" East and West coasts. He told me he imagined Fred and Marge living on the outskirts of Omaha, or beyond. They watch a lot of television and read *TV Guide* religiously. They're up on just about everything they see on their TV set. Nestled snugly in their Barcaloungers, they wisely comment on everything from the choreography to the camera shots and the use of microphones.

As I've said, on my show, we usually sang live. The microphones ("boom mikes") were operated by our soundmen just above our heads, and we seldom had to prerecord anything, unless the booms were in danger of being seen on camera for some shots.

Pete came up with an imaginary example of an evening with Fred and Marge. Picture the two of them watching a finale on *The Carol Burnett Show*. Eydie Gormé and I are singing a tribute to Cole Porter's music and lyrics. At the end of the number, the camera pulls way back and up while we're rendering "You're the Top."

FRED: "That was a nice wide shot . . . their director Dave Powers pulled the camera back, showing us the entire set."
MARGE: "Yeah, but they weren't singing live in that shot. They had to lip-synch those last eight bars."
FRED: "Right. That camera shot was way too wide to get a boom in there."

"The Family"

It was our seventh season when "The Family" was born, a sketch about a totally poor, ignorant, and dysfunctional family, consisting of Eunice (the wife), Ed (the husband), and Mama, Eunice's cranky mother. I loved it because it was all about character and situation, without any written jokes. What made it funny was the way we played it. In fact, if we had played it straight there wouldn't have been many laughs. The sketch was more like a one-act play. At first, we thought I'd play Mama, but I leaned more toward Eunice. Harvey, of course, would be the hapless Ed. We were thinking of hiring an older actress to come in and play Mama, when Bob Mackie, our costumer, suggested Vicki. Why not give it a whirl? We thought this would only be a onetime thing. We sat down to read the script and I tore into Eunice with a kind of "South Texas" accent. I just *saw* these three coming from that part of the country. It felt right. Harvey and Vicki followed suit with the accent, and "The Family" was born.

Our guest star that week was Roddy McDowall, who played Eunice's brother Phillip, returning home to Raytown for a visit. Phillip is a highly successful author who has appeared on the cover of *Time* magazine and has won the Pulitzer Prize and the Nobel Peace Prize for his most recent book about India. His accomplishments don't mean diddly-squat to Eunice, Mama, or Ed.

Mama advises him: "Well now, you can't coast on them forever, baby."

Eunice says, "Lord, I can't remember the last time I read a book clean through. I mean now, what with our brood, I'm lucky if I get time to read the *TV Guide!*" Ed asks Phillip if he's going to stick with "this writin' game," saying it really isn't "steady." Eunice pipes in, "I bet if you wanted to, you could wrangle yourself a column right here on the *Raytown Morning Star,* an' then you wouldn't have to keep gallivantin' all over the world and buryin' yourself in places like India, of all the godforsaken places!" Mama asks him, "Why do they let those cows just run all over the street and just do anything they want?" Phillip tries to explain that the cows in India are sacred, but Mama, Eunice, and Ed keep interrupting, either to argue with each other or to brag about Mama's poodle, Topaz. They are much too interested in talking about themselves and Topaz, and arguing about anything and everything, to really engage poor Phillip in any meaningful conversation. When he explains that he can't stay because he has to fly to London to interview Princess Anne, Mama undercuts him with "Why aren't you interviewin' the Queen? She too uppity to talk to ya?" A disheartened Phillip is about to leave for the airport, and asks Mama if she'd like him to send her a copy of his book. She replies, "Oh, you don't have to do that, Phillip. Besides I've got so many books now I don't know where to put 'em."

Roddy was a wonderful actor, and he played Phillip in subsequent sketches, even though it seemed odd that coming from this family, he had an English accent! Eunice wound up having four siblings in all. One time Alan Alda played Larry, a successful artist who pays the family a Christmas visit. Another time, Tommy Smothers was Jack, who is in the hospital for minor surgery, and when the doctor tells him his family is in the hall wanting to visit, he begs the doctor to "Tell them I died!" Betty White appeared several times as Eunice's snooty sister, Ellen. After a while, we settled for Eunice having only two siblings, Phillip and Ellen.

Mama lighting into Eunice.

"The Family" was so successful, our writers wrote a full-length play, *Eunice*, that CBS aired as a special in 1982. It featured Eunice, Ed, Mama, Ellen, and Phillip (this time played by Ken Berry). It chronicled several years of their lives, and ended up in the last act with Eunice, Ellen, and Phillip coming home from Mama's funeral.

A quote from John J. O'Connor of the *New York Times*:

> *EUNICE, played by Carol Burnett on a 90-minute CBS-TV special tonight at 9:30, is a troubling television character. She was created by Dick Clair and Jenna McMahon and was a regular part of "The Carol Burnett Show" for five seasons. Eunice could be very funny, in a ridiculous sort of way. For that very reason, she could also be sad, even quite pathetic. She represented a departure from Miss Burnett's usual brand of clowning. She was closer to the more ambiguous creations favored by Lily Tomlin.*
>
> *This is not, clearly, the stuff of standard Carol Burnett sketches. There are laughs here, to be sure, primarily in the form of insult humor. And there are intermittent efforts to endow Eunice and the Higgins family with what might be regarded as an admirable spunkiness. Once in a while, even a distant note of tenderness can be detected. But, for the most part, "Eunice" is preoccupied with the overwhelming dreariness of their hopelessly narrow little lives. The underlying bitterness of this "comedy-drama" is little short of startling.*

I loved Mr. O'Connor's take on the show, and it reminded me that the first time we performed "The Family" in our weekly run-through, the writers were horrified that we were portraying the family as "Southern trash" and felt that we would be alienating a huge section of the United States. I didn't feel we were doing that at all. I just liked giving Eunice, Ed, and Mama those accents and, as it turned out, the South didn't object at all.

Bob dressed Eunice in a god-awful flowered-print dress, white patent-leather shoes, and a sad dark brown wig that looked like it had been fried to death. She always wore the same outfit. Ed wore an old shirt and baggy mismatched pants with suspenders. Bob put Vicki in a padded dress, a gray wig, and spectacles. She narrowed her eyes and jutted out her chin, and laced into her character with a vengeance. She was hysterical. However, there were a few times when we did "The Family," where you can see that Vicki had wiped off her lipstick but still had on her full eye makeup! Can you just picture Mama with fake eyelashes?

All our characters were over-the-top, and the audience screamed with laughter.

Eunice and Ed had two boys, whom we talked about but never saw. I remember one afternoon when we were rehearsing a "Family" sketch where Eunice, Mama, and Ed had been called in by their son's schoolteacher, played by the wonderful Maggie Smith. It seems their son Bubba is the school bully and impossible to deal with. Maggie discovers, during her meeting with Eunice, Ed, and Mama, the reasons for the little boy's bad behavior: his home life.

During the course of the interview, Eunice, Ed, and Mama scream and blame each other for the way Bubba has turned out. Eunice shrieks and cries, "I wasn't meant to have boys!" She cries that she had wanted pretty little girls that she could dress up, and instead she got these awful *boys*!

Ed says, "What that boy needs is a good wallopin'! That's what my daddy did to me! It made a man out of me!" Mama says, "I think he was a couple of wallopin's short!" Ed shoots back at Mama, "You're on thin ice, old woman!"

Bubba's teacher produces a drawing he made depicting his family. It shows Ed and Eunice as huge stick figures with their faces twisted into ugly snarls, and in the background, Bubba has drawn himself as a tiny insignificant dot. Completely missing the point of the drawing, Eunice blurts out, "Is that supposed to be my *hair*? My hair don't look like that!"

One day, and I'm not sure who suggested it, we decided to experiment just for the heck of it and play it one time "straight" during a rehearsal without using the accents and/or "going overboard" with the characters as we usually did. We would simply be an ordinary family, without the histrionics. The result was . . . devastating. Because there were no jokes in the scene, we were able to play these people as the damaged goods they were, without going for laughs. The very same material could be played for comedy *or* tragedy, and it turned out that this was the stuff of high drama. In playing it straight, we could've had a serious one-act play on our hands, but when we added the comedic overtones, it was hysterical. That's what I call great writing. It was also a great acting experiment.

In fact, when I read the first "Family" sketch, I was blown away by the quality of the writing. This was definitely not the norm for a variety show. Eunice, Mama, and Ed were perfect examples of a dysfunctional family, and the mail we got reflected that. "My sister is just like Eunice, she drives me nuts!" "My mother is like Mama. I hate the holidays, because we always wind up fighting!" etc., and all the while it was becoming one of the most popular recurring sketches we ever did.

People identified.

The "Family" sketches became a running feature of our show and aired once every month or so. We did about thirty-five of them before we went off the air. With each one, Vicki got better and better. Here she had started out playing my kid sister and wound up brilliantly acting the part of my mama. I was incredibly proud when Vicki was awarded an Emmy in 1976. And after our show ended, she starred in her own successful sitcom: *Mama's Family.*

Betty White

I first met Betty in the early sixties in New York when she and I were frequent guests on the game show *Password*, hosted by Allen Ludden.

She and Allen married in 1963, and Joe and I became close friends with the newlyweds. After we moved to California, we often got together with the Luddens at their home in Los Angeles. Those were great evenings. We were all "game nuts," and we'd play games like Charades and Win, Lose, or Draw. I remember a frequent guest of theirs was Fred Astaire. He was as good a game player as he was a dancer.

Back then, Betty's persona was that of Miss Goody Two-Shoes, but those of us who knew her were in love with her wicked sense of humor. It wasn't long before she was able to bury that early (and wrong) perception, especially with her hysterical appearances on talk shows like Johnny Carson's *Tonight Show*.

And then along came the man-hungry Sue Ann Nivens on *The Mary Tyler Moore Show*. The running gag was that Sue Ann's bitchy private personality was the complete opposite of how she presented herself on her "Happy Homemaker" show. When they were going to cast Sue Ann, Mary wanted someone "who can play sickeningly sweet, like Betty White." Voilà! She got the part! (Along with a couple of Emmys to boot.)

During this time, when Betty was going to guest on our show, we got the idea to have her play Eunice's equally bitchy sister, Ellen, in the "Family" sketches. I loved our scenes together. She was sugary sweet around Mama, but would lace into Eunice with her "velvet hammer" delivery every chance she got.

One of my favorite "Family" sketches took place in Mama's attic, where Mama has asked Eunice and Ed to help her clean out a bunch of old stuff in boxes she has stored up there for years. Eunice is none too thrilled when Ellen shows up and starts poking around and finding some hidden treasures that she stakes a claim to. Ellen also gets a perverse pleasure out of insulting the hapless Ed.

ELLEN: "How's the plumbing business, Ed?"
ED: "I ain't in no plumbin' business. I'm in hardware!"

*Betty joined "The Family" as Eunice's
snooty sister, Ellen.*

ELLEN: (Sweetly) "Oh, of course! I don't know why it is, but whenever I see you I always think of septic tanks!"

Looking through some of the boxes, Eunice discovers a drawing she made, as a little kid, of her pet rabbit, Fluffy. She recalls how much she loved Fluffy, and how devastated she was when she came home from school one day to find his cage empty. Mama says he probably ran away because Eunice didn't clean his cage and she played too rough with him. Even though it was years ago, the Fluffy wounds are still raw as far as Eunice is concerned.

Mama opens a box that contains a lampshade she has no interest in and says to Eunice, "You got any use for this god-awful thing?" Eunice is interested in it, but Ellen jumps the gun and discovers it's a real Tiffany lampshade! Oblivious, Mama says she can have it because "I wouldn't even keep my garbage in it." Eunice is furious that Mama gave the lampshade to Ellen, and loses it even more when Ellen latches on to a box of china. "It'll be perfect for my bridge club."

EUNICE: "You sailin' off with that china, too? Why don't you just hire a van and have 'em come over here and cart off the entire attic! You've got a whole closet just chock-full of china, and I don't even have one dish without a crack in it. You already got that Tiffany lamp, you do *not* need that china!"

ELLEN: "And just who do you ever entertain? I mean just how many big parties do you and the *plumber* here give, in that little cracker box you live in?"

They tear into each other, and in the heat of the argument, Ellen lets loose with a bombshell: "Eunice, I think it's time you knew . . . You remember that Friday when Fluffy the rabbit disappeared? Well, Toots, that wasn't fried chicken we had for supper that night!"

Stunned, Eunice begs Mama to tell her that isn't so.

MAMA: "For pity sake, how do you expect me to remember what we had for supper thirty years ago?"

EUNICE: (Going ballistic) "MURDERERS! CANNIBALS! Oh my God! I'm a cannibal, too! Oh Fluffy, Fluffy, Fluffy!"

She collapses and sobs uncontrollably.

MAMA: "Eunice, will you look at it this way, if we hadn't eaten the damn thing up he'd be dead by now of old age."

Ellen starts to leave with the lamp, and Eunice knocks it to the floor, breaking it into pieces. She then sits down and bounces up and down hard on the box of china. Furious, Ellen accuses Eunice of being crazy and tells her she should be locked up. Shouting, she says, "AND I'LL BE HAPPY TO SIGN THE PAPERS!" (*Betty exited to huge applause from the audience.*)

After she leaves, Mama says, "Eunice, was that really necessary?"

EUNICE: (Deadly quiet) "Shut up, you rabbit killer."

Betty was brilliant as Ellen. We featured her in musical numbers and other sketches as well, where she was equally wonderful.

Betty and me.

Allen Ludden died from stomach cancer in 1981. In an interview with Larry King, when asked whether or not she would remarry, Betty replied, "Once you've had the best, who needs the rest?"

Betty hosted *Saturday Night Live* in 2010, at the age of eighty-eight, garnering terrific ratings and another Emmy for her appearance.

I had the pleasure of working with her twice on her hit series *Hot in Cleveland*. I also had the pleasure of saluting her in a TV special honoring her on her ninetieth birthday. I plan to do the same thing when she hits one hundred.

Cary Grant and "The Family"

In the mid-seventies, Joe and I were at a small dinner party at Dinah Shore's home in Beverly Hills. After cocktails, I found myself sitting next to Cary Grant at the dining room table. Even though I had met him several times before and we were on a first-name basis, I was still in awe of him. He was, of course, as charming as ever, so I was thrilled when he reminded me of how much he liked our show, *with one major reservation*:

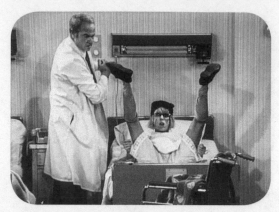

"You look like a taco!"

CARY: "I wish you wouldn't do those awful people in those 'Family' sketches. What are their names? 'Eunice'? 'Ed'? And that nasty mother?"

ME: (Gulp) "Gee, I'm sorry you don't like them."

CARY: "Don't like them? I hate them. They're ugly characters, yelling and fighting all the time, and utterly without any redeeming qualities! They give me the willies!"

ME: "Oh, gosh, I'm truly sorry . . . Sometimes we get negative comments about 'The Family,' but more often we get lots of positive fan mail from people all over the country, saying they make them laugh."

CARY: "Well, there's no accounting for taste, now, is there?"

ME: (Changing the subject) "What are your favorites?"

CARY: "Well, I love it when Tim goes after Harvey, and I get a kick out of that old lady you do . . ."

ME: "Stella Toddler?"

CARY: "That's the one! You're always getting beat up, falling down, and running into walls. I loved the one where you were in a hospital bed and Harvey was your doctor and he pressed the wrong controls on the bed and you were folded in half,

and Harvey says, 'You look like a taco!' I loved that! I've always
loved slapstick!"
ME: "Me, too! And I love to *do* it!"

I remembered seeing him in a couple of his early movies, before
he became the suave Cary Grant we later saw with Grace Kelly, Audrey Hepburn, Eva Marie Saint, and so many others. In those films
he showed off his athletic abilities by doing backflips, cartwheels, and
all-around tumbling. I understood where he was coming from, and
we had a lively chat about how to fall down a flight of stairs or jump
out of a window without breaking our bones. The rest of the evening
went smoothly. As we were leaving, he kissed me on the cheek and
said, "I hope I didn't upset you earlier." That was the nicest apology
I ever got. Look up "class" in the dictionary and there's a picture of
you-know-who.

A few days later, I was getting a manicure and the manicurist happened to be Russian.

MANICURIST: "I vatch your show all da time."
ME: "Thank you!"
MANICURIST: "You know, dat fam-i-ly you do vit dat daugh-
ter and her mama?"
ME: "You mean Eunice and Mama?"
MANICURIST: "I love dem! Dey remind me of my own fam-
i-ly in Russia. Dey make me laugh and be homesick."

There's no accounting for taste . . .

Eunice

I was drawn to Eunice from the get-go. I'm not a high-strung person
by any stretch of the imagination, so I got a kick out of being able

to vent as Eunice. I actually felt very sorry for her. Underneath all that screaming was a sad soul who was frustrated and angry because not one of her high hopes had ever been realized. She had a mother who constantly pissed on her dreams and a hapless dolt of a husband who was dealing with his own personal misery.

In a weird way, Eunice reminded me of my own mother. My mama, however, was a beautiful woman. She looked nothing like Eunice, and she was well read and educated. What was it then?

Like Eunice, Mama had high hopes. In the early forties she left Texas and headed out to Hollywood, dreaming of being a famous columnist like Hedda Hopper or Louella Parsons who interviewed movie stars. Nanny and I followed her shortly afterward. Mama was mildly successful in landing a couple of freelance interviews with the likes of Bob Hope and Rita Hayworth—people I would later know and work with—but she was never able to land a real job. Her head was always in the clouds. She and Nanny had one doozy of an argument after another about our lack of money and Mama's "pipe dreams." Mama railed against life. "I could've been *somebody*, but the cards were stacked against me!"

That was the connection, of course: Eunice and her "pipe dreams." I wish Mama had lived to see my pipe dreams come true.

THE FAMOUS BLOOPER

As I've said, I never wanted to stop and do a retake, because I liked our show to be "live," so when the "Family" sketches came along, I was adamant that we never break up in those scenes, because Eunice, Ed, and Mama were, in an odd way, sacred to me. They were real people in real situations, some of which were as sad and pitiful as they were funny, and I didn't want any of us to break the fourth wall and be out of character.

Then one week, in the eleventh season, Tim was appearing as Mickey Hart, Ed's hapless helper in the hardware store, and the family was playing Password, with Mickey as Eunice's partner and Dick Van Dyke, playing a boarder named Dan, as Mama's partner. Eunice wants Mickey to guess the password "ridiculous," and gives him the clue "laughable." Mickey responds with "elephant!" Eunice is obviously pissed as hell at this dumb answer, and is lacing into Mickey about his stupidity, when Mickey starts to explain why he thought the word was "elephant."

Okay, now it's the early show and Tim, as the dim-witted Mickey, starts riffing about how he once saw a "laughable" elephant in the circus, whose trainer dressed him in a tutu, etc., etc., and there was a rumor that they were lovers, etc., etc. None of us had ever heard these lines until that dress rehearsal. The audience was hysterical, and much to my grief, *so was I*, after all my pontificating about not breaking up in the "Family" sketches!

I was determined not to break character on the 7:30 show. Between shows, our director, Dave Powers, gave us the note that "the elephant story will be different on the second show, and good luck." Period.

Sure enough, Tim talks about a totally different elephant on the air show. He's on a roll with his new tale about these (oh my God!) *Siamese elephants* (!) joined at their trunks, and how a monkey would show up and dance up and down on their trunks doing the merengue, and that when one of the elephants would sneeze the other one's eyes would get real big, etc., etc.

Again, the audience is screaming with laughter, and I'm practically burying my head in Vicki's lap trying to hide the tears streaming down my face. As Eunice, I keep saying to Mama, trying to keep the sketch going, "Go ahead, Mama . . . Go ahead Mama . . . ," and then Vicki, as Mama, delivers her classic ad-lib, "Are you sure that little asshole's finished?"

The entire studio audience (and the cameramen) exploded. The laughter went on for days. I don't know if it was because it came out of Vicki, or because it was the perfect line coming out of Mama. I think it may have been a bit of both. We edited out that line when the show aired, but somehow Dick Clark got ahold of it and it made the list as his favorite blooper of all time.

It was a delicious moment. Vicki later said that after Dave had given her the note that the story would be different on the second show, she said to her husband, Al Schultz, who was our makeup man, "How does Tim keep getting away with doing this stuff?" and Al simply said, "Get him." She sure did.

CRACKING UP

It seems only natural to follow my initial foray into all of these funny sketches with a disclaimer of sorts that I swear is completely true:

Some people think we *constantly* cracked up during our eleven-year run, and it's just not so. Yes, we were guilty of breaking character at times, but not as often as you would think. It's just that when it did happen, it stands out in people's minds because it was so very real and often created even more hilarity. In fact, we did our best *not* to break up. Coming from theater and live television, I never wanted to have to redo a scene if something went awry. Occasionally we had to, but it didn't happen often. I loved rolling with the unexpected. I still do.

Most of the breaking up was Conway's fault, anyway.

One week, we were doing a takeoff on the TV series *Columbo*, where Harvey and I are a wealthy couple in our mansion nervously waiting for Detective Cobumble (guest Steve Lawrence) to arrive to investigate a murder that took place in our home. Tim is our butler, James. When Cobumble knocks on the door, Tim is supposed to answer it and is ordered by Harvey to use his gloves on the doorknob so as not to disturb any possible incriminating fingerprints. Okay. Simple enough.

However, Tim went to Dave between shows to talk about a specific camera shot: "When I go to answer the door, don't be on a waist shot. Instead, be on me from head to toe, and stay there."

Period. That was the only hint he gave Dave. Dave and the cameramen would have to wing it. We already had it in the can the way we'd rehearsed it, from when we taped the first show, so we would usually let Tim go crazy on the second taping. And usually it was pure gold.

On the air show, Tim walks to the door, but is unable to turn the knob with his gloves on, because it's too *slippery*!

HARVEY: "Open the door, James!"
TIM: "Sorry, sir, but I just waxed the doorknob!"
HARVEY: "Open the door!"

Another brilliant piece of shtick!

Going off script, Tim produced a small rope, wrapped it around the doorknob, and used the rope like the pull cord on an outboard motor! *At this point, Harvey and I were beginning to lose it.* Still unsuccessful, Tim pulled himself up holding on to the top of the doorjamb and tried, unsuccessfully, to turn the knob with his feet. As a last resort, he lowered his whole body and wound up with the huge doorknob between his legs, and proceeded to use his torso and legs as a *wrench*!

By this time, everyone in the studio was in hysterics (including the cameramen).

We figured he had to have rehearsed this bit of business on the set when it was in the shop, where no one could see him. It was a brilliant piece of shtick.

WHENEVER THERE WAS a Tim and Harvey sketch in the show, we would start a pool where we all put in a dollar, not to bet whether Harvey would break up, but to bet *how far into the sketch* they would get before Tim got him.

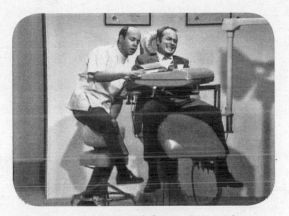

Harvey is utterly helpless and, according to Tim, wetting his pants.

The dentist sketch with Harvey as Tim's hapless patient is one of the funniest pieces of comedy ever performed. It should go in the time capsule. It started out with the premise that Tim, as a nervous new graduate fresh out of dental college, would accidentally stick himself in the hand with the Novocain needle. Tim took it from there and added several bits of business by sticking himself in his hip, his leg, and finally his forehead while Harvey was stuck in the chair helplessly losing it. I was watching the sketch on the monitor in my dressing room and screaming with laughter. I ran to the backstage area and watched the rest of it from the wings where I could also see the audience. They were exploding. Our cameramen were howling. There was not a dry eye—or seat—in the house.

I looked over at Harvey and he couldn't move. Lying in the dentist's chair, he was utterly helpless and laughing hysterically. He tried to keep it together, but tears began rolling down his cheeks. Tim was relentless, and swears Harvey wet his pants.

But that wasn't the norm. Out of 276 shows, I'd say we cracked up around 7 percent of the time. Honest.

"THE PIGEON LADY" GETS BACK AT TIM

I absolutely loved doing her. She was this crazy old lady in the park who liked to feed the pigeons. She had a snaggletoothed smile, stringy gray hair peeking out from under an old torn brown felt hat, a ragged sweater, a faded dress, gloves with fingers missing, sagging stockings, and worn-out sandals.

The sketch usually started with Tim, a trim, wealthy-looking, spiffy old man, Mr. Purdy, being wheeled into the park by his nurse, Leona, who helps him get settled on a bench, leaving him there for a few minutes to enjoy reading his newspaper in the sun. This peaceful scene is always interrupted by an old bag lady, who shuffles in with a sack full of birdseed, tossing the food to the pigeons, and calling to the birds, "Here pigie, pigie, here pigie." She plops herself next to the hapless Mr. Purdy—who is bench-bound and can't get away from her—and strikes up a bizarre conversation. This was a sketch where I did all the talking, becoming crazier and crazier. Mr. Purdy hardly spoke, except when he looked off camera and weakly called to his nurse for help.

After Tim's outrageous ad-lib about the Siamese elephants during a "Family" sketch earlier that season, I decided that I was going get back at him with my own unrehearsed and outrageous elephant story. This would be the perfect revenge as Tim's character had very few lines and was stuck sitting there with nowhere to go. He was at my mercy this time. Here's how it went . . .

The Pigeon Lady enters and sits on the park bench next to a wary

Mr. Purdy. She says she has just come from a lecture at the civic auditorium on past lives.

(The first part of what follows is what we rehearsed all week. You'll know when I go off script.)

> **PIGEON LADY:** "They had this psychic today givin' this lecture on reincarnation, y'know, how ever' body lived a bunch of different lives, things like that. Shoot . . . you know Sylvia Armbruster, that big heavyset woman, whose husband is in the escrow business?"
> **MR. PURDY:** (Warily) "No . . . no I don't."
> **PIGEON LADY:** "That's the one. Well, right in the middle of this *throng* of *thousands* of people, Sylvia Armbruster stands up just as big as you please and she says, 'In a previous lifetime, I was Cleopatra, Queen of Egypt!' (Cackles) "I 'bout died! Boy, was she sucked in! Can you imagine Sylvia Armbruster, Cleopatra, Queen of Egypt?" (Cackles) "NO WAY . . . *I* was!"
> **MR. PURDY:** (Weakly calling out) "Leona!"
> **PIGEON LADY:** "Egypt was nice. It was a little bit like Idaho, but without the mountains and the Winnebagos."

She goes on to describe her life with Julius Caesar.

> **PIGEON LADY:** "Boy, for a guy who used to run around all day in the forum in a dress, at night he made Burt Reynolds look like Mr. Whipple."
> **MR. PURDY:** "Leona . . ."

Making matters worse, she rattles on that in yet another lifetime she was married to Attila the Hun.

> **PIGEON LADY:** "I met old Attila in a singles bar. He made me a charm bracelet once out of genuine 'people teeth.' An'

ever' time we had an anniversary, he'd add another little
charm to it."

By this time, Mr. Purdy is desperate and weakly tries whistling for
Leona, to no avail.

PIGEON LADY: (Continuing) "He gave me a rock once. It
must've been yea big. It wasn't your ordinary rock at all. It happened when he was pillaging through Italy. Got it at Gucci's.
Yep, he was a swell little provider."

(Now I go off script.)

PIGEON LADY: "An' then for transportation once, he gave me
this pair of elephants. They was Siamese . . ." *(The crew starts
to laugh, and Tim begins to realize he's in for it. The audience
catches on right away because they remember the time Tim had
us at his mercy with his elephant story.)* "They was joined at the
trunk, an' when one of 'em had to go somewhere, the other
one would have to run backwards! Then one of 'em caught a
cold, and sneezed, an' blew both their brains out!"

We did another one of these sketches the following season, and
I decided I would come up with yet a different elephant story to get
Tim.

> Mr. Purdy's nurse, Leona, helps him onto the park bench
> before she exits. He's calmly reading his newspaper when
> the Pigeon Lady enters and plops down next to him.

PIGEON LADY: "Here pigie, pigie. Eat all yer corn an' I'll
tell you where there's a new statue." (She looks at Mr. Purdy)
"Nice day, isn't it?" (He nods politely) "What's yer sign?"
MR. PURDY: "Sagittarius."

PIGEON LADY: "Oh." (Grins at him happily) "I hear tell that a 'Sage' makes a good lover!" (He's becoming uncomfortable) "I'm a Leo, y'know, like the lion? Grrrrr!"

Mr. Purdy looks off for Leona.

PIGEON LADY: "You married?" (He shakes his head no) "Well you're all alike. I lived with this guy once, named AR-MAN-DO. I lived with him an' he split on me without so much as leavin' me a dime. I moved in with him one morning. I gave him everything I had . . . an' he split that afternoon."

While Mr. Purdy is looking off for Leona to come save him, the Pigeon Lady rattles on about how she met Armando when he was in the navy and how she used to play the trumpet for all the "gobs" on the ship, "the SS *Burgoyne*." She shows him a snapshot of her, Armando, and the gobs.

PIGEON LADY: "That's me there. You can tell by my smile." (Flashes her snaggletoothed grin) "One time I played 'Boogie Woogie Bugle Boy from Company B' for three solid hours! Yep, I blew enough wind to sail that sucker to Guam!"

She calls his attention to Armando's little sister,
Alexandra, who is also in the snapshot.

PIGEON LADY: "She was a gob, too! All the other gobs called her 'Alexandra the Great!' She was a little bitty thing, no bigger'n a milk bottle. All of us used to go up on deck and play with her. We'd play 'Spin the Gob!'"

(At this point, I went off script and started to spin a whole other story.)

PIGEON LADY: (Continuing) "Then after she got out of the navy, Alexandra went into the circus." *(Tim starts to catch on and stifles a grin. The audience, along with our crew, is in on it, too.)* "She became the world's littlest elephant trainer. She'd play 'Spin the Trunk!' Well, this big ol' elephant got real mad at her an' one day he *stepped* on Alexandra, an' he killed her! She was just a spot in the sawdust. An' that elephant was charged with *murder* . . . an' he went to trial . . . an' the jury came back with a verdict of 'Guilty, of premeditated murder' . . . an' they *hung* that elephant . . . as a deterrent to other elephants!"

At this point, Tim looked into the camera, shook his head back and forth, and rolled his eyes to heaven, all the while stifling a laugh. I had a ball doing this to him!

"There was this pair of elephants."

CHARACTERS AND AURAS

In the mid-seventies a close friend of mine asked me to attend a lecture at UCLA on parapsychology being given by a woman named Thelma Moss. She spoke about "Kirlian photography," which claims to be able to photograph the "auras" of various plants and even inanimate objects such as coins. More interesting to me was the claim that this technique can photograph human auras. After her lecture, I was introduced to Ms. Moss, who asked me if I would take part in a little "experiment" in her lab at the university.

Sure, why not? I showed up at the appointed time the next day, and she said she was going to photograph my hand using the Kirlian method. She asked me to relax, and I placed my hand on a flat plate of some kind. A photograph was taken, and she showed me the results. There were shooting lights surrounding each finger. Okay . . . but what did that mean? Then she explained the experiment she had in mind.

"I want you to imagine some of the characters you portray when you do your show, and I'll photograph them individually. Don't tell me which ones you're doing. Just write down the character's name and the order in which their pictures are taken, so you'll remember." Okay. The first one I thought of doing was Eunice from the "Family" sketches. Ms. Moss said, "Try to conjure up the way you feel when you're acting as the character . . . Take your time, and when you're ready, place your hand on the plate." I put myself in Eunice's shoes, thinking of her frustrations and her temper tantrums and the constant disappointments in her life . . . and put my hand on the plate.

The next character I conjured up was Charo, the bubbly, outgoing, and happy Latin bombshell I often had fun doing. Hand on plate. Then I did Nora Desmond, the over-the-top crazy-as-a-loon silent screen movie star. Hand on plate.

Ms. Moss and I looked at the three photographs, and each one had totally different "auras" surrounding the fingers. Okay . . . but *then* she described each character's personality and nailed each one. Looking at the Eunice photo, she said, "This is a very angry and sad person who is closed and hampered by her own doing." (Eunice's aura was close to her fingers, no "shooting lights" to be seen.)

She described the second character (Charo) as a free soul, happy and perhaps "musical." Charo's aura was shooting out all over the place.

Nora was described as someone who was somewhat "unhinged." The fingers of her aura were uneven and kind of spikey.

Pretty amazing, huh?

Kirlian photography has been debunked by science, but it sure was a fun experiment.

THE MOVIE PARODIES

I was practically raised in a movie theater. My dad managed a small one for a while in San Antonio, Texas. In April 1933, my mother was sitting in the back row, watching a second run of *Rasputin and the Empress*, when she went into labor with me. One of my first memories is sitting in the dark and watching cartoons when I was about three. When the grown-up movie started, Daddy would pick me up and I'd take a nap in his small office. Years later, in the 1940s, when I was living in Hollywood with Nanny, we would save our pennies and hit Hollywood Boulevard, sometimes seeing as many as *eight* movies a week! In those days, we would go to the "second-run" houses, where they would be showing a double feature, along with cartoons, newsreels, and coming attractions. (*More bang for your buck.*) Actually, the ticket prices were twelve cents for me (under twelve years old) and a quarter for Nanny IF we got in before the prices went up at 6:00 p.m. So, going to four theaters in one week . . . Bang! Eight movies! That was when I fell in love with the likes of James Stewart, Betty Grable, Mickey Rooney, Judy Garland, Joan Crawford, Bette Davis, Humphrey Bogart, and Rita Hayworth, to name some favorites.

My best friend, Ilomay, and I would often pretend like we were these stars and act out the movies. Little did I dream that one day I'd have my own show and *REALLY* get to "act out" and lovingly satirize these films, complete with gorgeous costumes, sets, and a twenty-eight-piece orchestra, on television! Of course not! How could I? There *was no* television in those days!

Fast-forward to our variety show. It was a given that I'd want to send up the films I grew up on, plus others that impressed me as I got older.

I have to stress here that we never intended to satirize the actors *personally*, even though we would be dressed and made up to look like them, wigs and all. We only wanted to kid the movie itself, or the *genre*. However, there were a few actors who weren't too happy with our takeoffs.

"Mildred Fierce" and "Torchy Song"

In 1976, we did a spoof of the famous Warner Bros. movie *Mildred Pierce*, starring Joan Crawford, for which she won an Academy Award in 1946. The original movie is the story of a hardworking mother, the long-suffering Mildred, who adores her selfish daughter, Veda, and spoils her rotten. Veda goads her mother about their lack of money, and in response, Mildred proposes opening a small restaurant, which disgusts Veda even more. Mildred is introduced to the oily Monte Beragon, a wealthy playboy. Mildred marries him for Veda's sake even though she doesn't love him.

The story is basically a triangle involving a loving mother, her two-timing husband, and her self-centered daughter, which leads to tragedy.

We called ours "Mildred Fierce" and stuck pretty close to the original screenplay. As Mildred, I wore a brunette wig and heavy black eyebrows made of *real hair*, which we glued on, and every outfit was fitted with huge shoulder pads just like those Joan Crawford wore in the movie. Harvey was a brilliantly smarmy Zachary Scott (Monte), and Vicki was equally brilliant as Mildred's scheming money-hungry daughter, Veda, played by Ann Blyth in the film.

We open with Mildred in a police station confessing a murder she committed to the captain (Tim). She's told to wait her turn because there's an old lady ahead of her reporting her lost parakeet.

My glued-on "Joan Crawford" eyebrows were truly expressive.

The captain calls Mildred to his desk and she begins to tell her story . . .

In a flashback throughout the sketch, we see Mildred spoiling her "precious" daughter rotten. Veda rules the roost, and Mildred is a wimp where her daughter is concerned. Veda hates her mother and insults her at every turn.

At one point, determined to run away, Veda rifles through Mildred's purse for money. "I belong in a mansion! I'm not hanging around this dump any longer!" Mildred pleads with her rotten daughter to stay, and before she walks out the door, Veda hauls off and slaps her mother silly.

MILDRED: (To herself, still reeling from the slap, but *forever* forgiving Veda) "I know a little girl who got out on the wrong side of the bed this morning!"

Enter Monte Slick (Harvey), a lecherous millionaire
playboy who makes a play for Mildred.

MONTE: "Why don't you come out to my beach house and I'll show you the ocean."
MILDRED: "I've seen the ocean, chum."
MONTE: "Not my hunk of it."

As Mildred asks him to leave, Veda returns wanting more money.

VEDA: "Honestly, Mother, these are only twenties!" (Seeing Monte, she lays on the sweetness) "Oh, hi, sir."
MONTE: (Coming on to Veda) "Well hell-o! Don't tell me this enchanting child is yours, Mrs. Fierce."
MILDRED: "Yes, she *is* enchanting, isn't she?"

Mildred introduces them. Veda is very impressed.

VEDA: "*The* Monte Slick? The irresponsible, lecherous playboy and owner of the Slick Mansion?"
MONTE: "In the glorious flesh." (Turning to Mildred) "Let's stop playing games. How about that little jaunt to my beach house?"

Mildred rebuffs his advances and
Veda takes her mother aside.

VEDA: (Baby talk) "Mommy, you want your wittle baby Veda wif you forever, don't you?"
MILDRED: "Of course I do! You know that, my darling!"
VEDA: "Well, this is your big chance, dimwit! This is your chance to get your wittle Veda a mansion and a beach house and furs and jewels . . . and a new daddy!"
MILDRED: (Stunned) "You mean . . . ?"

VEDA: "That's right. Marry this joker quick before he gets a real good look at you."

Mildred thinks that wouldn't be forthright because she doesn't love Monte.

VEDA: "Mother, 'forthright' does not buy Ferraris!" (Bordering on a tantrum) "Can't you just do me this one little favor?"
MILDRED: (Giving in) "All right. I'll try."

She turns back to Monte and says she'll accept his invitation but that she "plays for keeps."

MONTE: "Marriage?"
MILDRED: "Yes."
MONTE: "One of those decent dames, eh?"
MILDRED: "You make 'decent' sound 'indecent.'"
MONTE: "I can also make 'indecent' . . . pretty 'decent.' But let's get down to cases. You're saying that no marriage, no beach house?"
MILDRED: "That's right. No hanky, no panky."
MONTE: "No contract, no contact?"
MILDRED: "No ring, no ring-a-ding-ding."

Monte says marriage is not for him. Veda takes the bull by the horns and comes on to him.

VEDA:"I don't blame you, Mr. Slick. You'd be taking on a wife *AND* a daughter . . . *in the flower of her youth*, both living there in the same mansion with you!"

Monte changes his mind. This is a great suggestion. As he hugs Mildred, he reaches over her shoulder and plants a kiss on Veda.
Time passes, and Mildred, now a rich and successful business-woman, returning home to the beach house, discovers Monte and

Veda in a passionate embrace. Veda hits Mildred with the news that she and Monte are in love and will marry after he gets a divorce! Humiliated, Mildred accepts this news and exits, saying, "All right. I don't need a brick to fall on my head." As she's walking out the door, a brick falls on her head.

"No hanky, no panky! No ring, no ring-a-ding ding!" The sketch Joan loved.

Monte then tells Veda he'd never want to be with her, calling her a "little twit." Veda shoots him. Mildred reenters, telling Veda that it's okay if she wants Monte. Upon seeing Monte's dead body, she asks, "You still want him?"

VEDA: (In her "little girl" voice) "Mommy! Mommy! Monte fall down and go boom! You've got to help me! I can't go to the big bad jail!"

MILDRED: "I don't know what to do, this is a real lulu, Veda! I think it's time for a little discipline." (Picks up the phone to call the police)

VEDA: (Desperate) "You can't turn me in! I didn't spoil me, YOU did!"

MILDRED: (Stung by this accusation, hanging up the phone, her bottom lip quivering) "You're right. I'll take the blame." (Pause) "But, Veda, I think you'd better skip the prom."

Mildred tells Veda she'll have to lay low for a couple of days: "Here's fifty thousand dollars, that should hold you for a day or two."

The scene ends with Mildred saying to herself, "Kids . . . they sure keep you hopping!"

BACK TO THE police station. The captain tells Mildred that they've captured the real killer. Veda is brought in, but Mildred convinces the captain to let her daughter go, because "Monte was a letch and deserved what he got!" As she and Veda are exiting, the girl starts bad-mouthing her mother. We hear a gun shot. Mildred has let Veda have it and, reentering the police station, begins another confession.

THE END

My Joan Crawford to Harvey's Michael Wilding in our spoof of Torch Song. *The sketch Joan didn't love.*

After the sketch aired, I got a call from Joan Crawford herself! "Carol, I absolutely *loved* it! You guys gave it more production value than that f——g Jack Warner!" I howled with laughter and, of course, I was thrilled with her response.

A year later, we spoofed another one of her movies, *Torch Song*.

In it, Joan is a tough Broadway musical star, Jenny, alienating her colleagues with her neurotic demands for absolute perfection, who then winds up falling for her blind rehearsal pianist (Michael Wilding). We called our version "Torchy Song," and Harvey's character, instead of being blind, was written as a myopic piano player saddled with Coke-bottle eyeglasses, who keeps walking into walls. Though the actual movie itself wasn't a hit, our audience got a kick out of it.

Joan didn't.

I heard through the grapevine that she didn't care for my interpretation, thinking it was mean. That wasn't my intention at all. Again, I wasn't doing Joan Crawford, I was doing her *character* in the movie. I always felt bad that she wasn't happy with that sketch.

"The African Queen"

Steve Lawrence is in the Humphrey Bogart role, as Charlie the uncouth, drunken boat captain, and I'm in the Katharine Hepburn role, as Rosie, a prim and virginal spinster. They are trapped together in his rickety boat, *The African Queen*.

Steve Lawrence was one of my
favorite acting partners.

Dirty, greasy Charlie comes on to Rosie, and she fights him off at first. After a while, she begins to like the idea of romance, and a "dance" begins, where she kisses Charlie and then resists her sudden passionate urges by throwing him overboard. He climbs back on board, and Rosie begins the routine over again: kissing him, getting herself all dirty and greasy in the process, and resisting him by throwing him overboard. Every time he climbs back into the boat, Rosie starts kissing him and throwing him overboard again, getting more and more grease and dirt on her clothes and face, until finally, resisting him no longer, she jumps into his arms, saying she will give in to his "debauchery" and will be all his to love.

Charlie says, "Y'know, Rosie, I learned somethin' from a lady like you . . ."

"What, Charlie? What?"

He replies, "This Rosie, this . . ." and throws her overboard.

I remember this sketch wasn't working during rehearsals, but Steve and I came up with the idea of tossing each other overboard again and again . . . getting filthy dirty in the process, and it worked! It was one of our most physical sketches, but miraculously neither one of us was the worse for wear. Also, this is just more proof that Steve Lawrence is a brilliant comedic actor and why he was one of my favorite guests.

Steve Lawrence and Eydie Gormé

Eydie Gormé and hubby Steve Lawrence were two of my dearest buddies, dating back to 1960, when we all met when I was doing *The Garry Moore Show* and they were his guests. As a result, because of their talents and our friendship, they became regular guests on my show, not only as singers, but also as sketch performers, with Steve appearing twenty-five times and Eydie thirteen.

They never appeared together on my show because they saved

their act for their nightclub appearances and the television specials they hosted.

Steve was one of my very favorite sketch partners. He and I did several takeoffs on classic movies such as *The Postman Always Rings Twice, Double Indemnity, Laura, The African Queen, Gilda, The Godfather, From Here to Eternity,* and *The Roaring Twenties,* to name a few. He's as great a comedic actor as he is a singer . . . and that's saying *plenty*! If our show was running long, I remember he said to me several times, "Hey, cut my song, but don't cut the sketch!" One time after our show had been in syndication, showing only the sketches and not the musical numbers, Steve and Eydie were approached by some teenagers in an airport, and one of them said to Steve, "Hey, you're that funny guy on the Burnett show!"

STEVE WAS DRIVING to Television City in Los Angeles for our rehearsals once, when he was pulled over by a cop for making an illegal turn on Fairfax Avenue. He and Eydie were still living in New York at the time and were staying in a hotel and renting a car that week, while he was a guest.

The cop got off his motorcycle and approached the car.

COP: "Lemme see your license."

Steve reached for his wallet, and . . . oops! He had left it in the hotel room. Apologizing profusely, he tried to explain to the officer who he was, and that he was just in from New York. It was pretty evident the officer didn't recognize him.

STEVE: "Officer, please believe me, I'm here to do *The Carol Burnett Show!*"
COP: "Yeah, and I'm on Carson tonight. This your car?"
STEVE: "No, sir. It's a rental."
COP: "How do I know you didn't steal it?"

STEVE: "No, really!" (Seeing his script binder on the seat) "Look, see? Here's the script in a binder with my name on it! 'STEVE LAWRENCE'!"

COP: "Yeah, so where's your identification?"

STEVE: "*In my wallet in the hotel room!!!!*" (Brilliant idea) "Look, I tell you what . . . here's the script. Turn to page eleven. That's where I do a sketch with Carol." (Hands the script to the cop) "Now, I'll say my lines, and you read Carol's . . . that way you'll know it's me because I *know* the lines!!!" (The cop turns to page 11)

STEVE: "Ready?" (The cop nods) "*Hi, honey, I'm home.*"

COP: (As Carol, "rote-like") "*Why-didn't-you-call-and-tell-me-you-were-going-to-be-so-late?*"

STEVE: "*Gee, I meant to, honey, but I got sidetracked by an old army buddy, and . . .*"

COP: (As Carol) "*And-you-expect-me-to-buy-that-lame-excuse?*"

This had gone on for a while, with the cop and Steve acting out the sketch on the sidewalk at Beverly and Fairfax, at ten o'clock in the morning, when the cop abruptly stopped, handed the script back to Steve, and said, "This ain't funny."

AND THEN THERE was Eydie Gormé. Eydie, of the glorious voice and fantastic range. We sang several duets together, one time ending a medley saluting Hollywood songs at the foot of the Hollywood sign. As the medley came to an end, the camera, in a helicopter, pulled back, showing the sign and the two of us getting smaller and smaller, until we were dwarfed by its huge letters. As a "joke," our director, Dave Powers, had the helicopter keep going until it was out of sight, and Eydie and I were left stranded on the hill under the hot sun for about twenty minutes. Looking back, it was funny . . . but at the time neither one of us laughed very much. What's that old saying? "A lot of comedy is tragedy plus time." In other words, slipping on a banana peel isn't funny as it's happening, but telling about it later can be hilarious. Now, looking back on the two of us stranded beneath the Hollywood sign, strikes me as (somewhat) funny . . .

Eydie was fearless and fun.

Eydie was fearless when it came to expressing an opinion. I remember a duet with her that ended with our walking downstage toward the audience on a two-foot platform that came to a halt several feet before the rest of the stage ended. Our instinct was to step down off the platform, walk further downstage, and belt out the ending so we could be a lot closer to the studio audience than the platform would allow. We both felt that ending the medley that way was much more exciting. We were blocking the number on Thursday in the studio before the actual taping on Friday. As usual on Thursdays, Dave was directing the cameras and talking to us over a microphone from his perch in the booth. As Eydie and I stepped off the platform, Dave's voice boomed from the booth: "Ladies, don't step off the platform. Let's take it again." Eydie and I obediently backed up and began to sing the last few phrases from the medley, while walking downstage on the platform. Yet again, our instincts won out and we both automatically stepped down and walked to the end of the stage.

DAVE: (Over the microphone) "Ladies!!! Please stay on the platform!!"

Once again, we tried and once again, we couldn't help ourselves.

DAVE: (Losing patience) "C'mon, *girls* . . ."

I have to explain something here. At that time back in the seventies, if a woman had her own show on TV and "spoke up," she could be labeled a bitch, whereas if a man (such as Gleason, Berle, Caesar, etc.) did the same thing, he was labeled assertive, strong, smart, etc. Hence, I seldom ruffled feathers. I would somehow find a way to ease into expressing an opinion and still be "ladylike," thus avoiding being a "bitch." For instance, when a particular sketch was "lacking," so to speak, instead of saying to the writers, "We have to fix this, it's not funny," I would tap-dance around the criticism by saying, "Gosh, you guys, I don't know what's wrong with me today, but I'm having trouble making this work, can you help me?" Yep, that's how it was back then. At least, that's how I was.

Back to the duet. Eydie whispered to me: "Hey, what'sa matter with you? It's *your* show! You can walk wherever you damn well please!"

ME: (Nicely to Dave) "Hey, Dave . . . is there a reason you don't want us to walk downstage more?"
DAVE: (Loudly) "YOU ARE NOT LIT FOR DOWNSTAGE!"
EYDIE: (Loudly back to Dave) "Well then, why can't you hit us with a *spotlight* . . . *LIKE IN REAL SHOW BUSINESS???*"

I wanted to kiss her feet.
We lost our beloved Eydie in 2013. Thank God her glorious voice can be heard on all the beautiful recordings she made. I miss her . . . a lot.

"Went With the Wind"

The classic 1939 movie *Gone With the Wind* was making its TV debut in 1976, so . . . I introduced this sketch by saying, "For those of you who ran out of Kleenex, and were unable to watch it for the whole five hours, we've put together our own mini version to let you know what you missed!"

We called our takeoff "Went With the Wind," and it's mostly famous for the brilliant "curtain rod dress" Bob Mackie came up with for my character, Starlett O'Hara. The costume is now in the Smithsonian. When I made my entrance at the top of the stairs in that outfit, the studio audience went wild. It was one of the longest laughs we got in our eleven years and is listed by several critics as one of the funniest sight gags in the history of television.

Added to that, the sketch was beautifully written. It was over twenty minutes long and managed to cover every key element in the movie.

During rehearsals, Harvey was concerned and worried about doing Clark Gable's iconic Rhett Butler, Rat Butler in our version. He didn't want to give in to a common imitation of Gable, and was in a bit of a tizzy all week, until . . . he got into the costume Bob created for his character. Added to that was a great wig, and the mustache, and voilà! Harvey walked, talked, and even *looked* like Gable!

The sketch opens with a sour-sounding orchestra playing an out-of-tune version of the movie theme over a picture of an old Southern home and the words "Alabama Terra Plantation. Somewhere in Georgia." There's a party going on and Starlett O'Hara is eagerly waiting for the man she loves, Brashley (Tim Conway), to arrive. Vicki as Starlett's slow maid, Sissy (doing a great Butterfly McQueen imitation), enters jumping up and down and screaming, "Miss Starlett! Miss Starlett! Miss Starlett!" Starlett slaps her silly to calm her down, and Sissy tells Starlett that Mr. Brashley has arrived! Starlett excitedly starts jumping up and down, but is dismayed when Brashley shows up with his new bride, Melody (Dinah Shore), who is sweetness personified . . . an absolute angel. Furious, Starlett suggests to Melody that she stick her head in the punch bowl: "I'm sure it could use a little more sugar!" Sweet Melody happily obliges, "All right!"

Alone and distraught, Starlett picks up a large vase and hurls it across the room, only to be caught by Rat Butler, who makes a play for Starlett and is rebuffed. The party fizzles when it's announced that war has broken out. As the guests are leaving, the self-centered Starlett is upset and tries to get everyone to stay and have fun because, "Fiddle-dee-dee! It's the shank of the night!" Rat and Brashley go off to join the army, leaving Starlett, Sissy, and Melody . . . who announces that she's going to have a baby!

STARLETT: "A baby! Shoot!"

Sissy confidently assures Starlett that she knows all about "birthin' babies!" When Melody promptly goes into labor, Sissy goes berserk and Starlett slaps her silly. While Melody is giving birth behind a sofa, and Atlanta is burning, Starlett delivers a dramatic monologue about survival: "As God is my witness, I won't be defeated! If I have to lie, cheat, and steal, I'll never go hungry again! If I have to make *tuna casseroles and go without my grits*, this war won't get the best of me! I ain't down yet!" During all this, the music swells louder and louder, and Sissy is lazily circling Starlett and the sofa singing and drowning out Starlett's harangue.

(In the heat of the moment, instead of saying, "If I have to lie, cheat and steal," what came out of my mouth was "If I have to lie, steet and cheal"! This goof is alive and well on YouTube.)

The second act finds Terra in shambles and the women in rags. Starlett owes $300 in back taxes. The war is over and Brashley returns. Both Melody and Starlett are thrilled to see him. Starlett asks if he has money to pay the taxes with. "No." However, he informs them that Rat Butler made a fortune during the war. Melody takes

Brashley upstairs to meet his son, "Brashley Jr." Slightly disappointed, Brashley says, "I was hoping you would name him after *me*."

Starlett sees a way out of debt by getting the money from Rat, who is approaching Terra. Starlett doesn't want him to see her so poor and "looking like the insides of a goat's stomach!" Sissy suggests she hide behind the drapes and a lightbulb goes off in Starlett's head! She pulls the draperies down and heads up the staircase, telling Sissy to keep Rat occupied. "I've got me a *dress* to make!"

There's a knock on the door and Sissy hysterically screams, "What'll I say? What'll I say?" She slaps *herself* silly in the face and says, "I'll think of somethin'!" Rat enters, looks around at the war-torn room, and says, "I really like what you've done with the place."

SISSY: "So how are you, Captain Butler?"

RAT: "How am I? You ask that of a man who's just returned from battle? Who's seen brother pitted against brother, who's seen the world he loved crumble beneath his feet? And you ask" (Angrily raising his voice), "'HOW ARE YOU?' 'HOW ARE YOU?'"

SISSY: "Oh, purty good, thanks, and you?"

Starlett and Rat and "The Dress."

Starlett appears at the top of the staircase in her green velvet dress with the curtain rod intact, and slowly walks down to meet Rat. (Because of the huge audience response, I had to bite my cheek to keep from laughing myself!)

STARLETT: "What brings you to Terra?"
RAT: "You, you vixen, you. Starlett, I love you and that gown is gorgeous."
STARLETT: "Thank you. I saw it in the window and I just couldn't resist it." *(A great line to follow a brilliant sight gag.)*

After Rat provides the tax money, even though Starlett rebuffs his advances, he picks her up and carries her kicking and screaming upstairs. *(Harvey had a rough time, because he kept stepping on my hoop skirt, but we kept going.)* When they arrive at the landing, Starlett is impressed with Rat's strength and tells him, "I'm yours." Panting, he responds, "Not now, Starlett, I'm pooped!"

Brashley enters the landing and Starlett comes on to him. An angry Rat takes a swing at Brashley and misses, socking Starlett, who falls down the entire staircase, landing in a heap on the floor. Both men rush to her, and Melody appears on the landing saying she's going to "That Big Plantation in the Sky" and collapses. Brashley runs up to her, and she asks him to send Starlett up to see her. Starlett rushes up the stairs to be with Melody, who sweetly says she thinks of her "darlin' Starlett as her sister."

"I've been thinkin' about our friendship all these years and I want you to know how I really feel." Melody then puts her hands on Starlet's shoulders and shoves her down the stairs, where she lands in yet another heap on the floor.

(I tumbled down those stairs six times that day! Two times in the morning run-through, two times in the dress rehearsal, and twice in the air show. Oddly enough, I didn't hurt myself at all. It's somewhat of a miracle, because, as I said before, I was never taught how to do all

the crazy stunts I did over the eleven years. I just did them. Once in a while, I'd wind up with a bruise or two, but that would be the worst of it. I remember this particular one clearly because I instinctively let my body go "loose" when I was tumbling down those stairs, knowing that if I stiffened up, I would probably cause some damage. Also, I fell slowly, so maybe that's why I came out unscathed. The comedy was enhanced by our sound effects man, Ross Murray, producing several brilliant "tumbling" and body fall sounds right on the spot.)

Melody blows a good-bye kiss (the way Dinah always did on her shows) and goes to That Big Plantation in the Sky. Brashley is grief-stricken and leaves. Starlett finally wants to be with Rat, but he wants nothing to do with her, heading for the door to leave as she cries, "But, Rat, what'll I do? What will become of me?"

RAT: "Frankly my dear, I don't gi—"

Starlett slams the door in his face before he can finish the sentence. Sissy enters.

SISSY: "What did he say?"
STARLETT: (Echoing Rat) "'Frankly my dear, I don't gi—!'" (Hysterically crying) "Oh Sissy! Without Rat, what'll I do? What'll I do???"
SISSY: "Frankly, Miss Starlett, I don't give a damn." (She exits after slapping Starlett silly)

THE END

OUR TRIPS TO ENGLAND, IRELAND, AND ITALY

We were asked by the BBC to tape a show in London. Harvey, Lyle, Vicki, and I flew over in April 1970, along with key members of our staff and our guest star, Juliet Prowse.

One of the questions I got was "Why did it take you so long to come to London?"

"I swam."

It was all pretty exciting, and we had a good time. (Unfortunately, it wasn't one of our best efforts. I don't remember how many of our shows were aired in England after that, but they weren't as successful as we had hoped.)

After our week in London, several of us had made plans to travel to other parts of Europe. Harvey, his wife, and some of our staff members opted for Rome. Joe and I had a very different and detailed itinerary: For four days, we would stay at the historic Dromoland Castle Hotel (built in the sixteenth century) in County Clare, Ireland. Then we would go to Scotland for another few days and stay at another historic hotel (the name of which I can't remember), where Joe would play golf.

We flew into Shannon (a very tiny airport) and were met by a driver, Derry O'Keefe (how Irish can you get?). We piled into his Mercedes-Benz, where he proceeded to put the pedal to the floor, speeding like crazy down country lanes, slowing only for cows, who happened to be crossing the dirt roads every so often. Looking out the window, I realized why Ireland is called the Emerald Isle. Green has never been so green. The countryside was breathtaking. We arrived at the majestic Dromoland Castle and were escorted to the registration desk. The carpet had to be a foot high. "Plush" was the word for the furnishings and draperies. Our large, comfortable room was awash in brightly colored wallpaper and bedding. We unpacked and took a walk on the grounds. Everywhere you looked there was eye candy.

Gorgeous, simply gorgeous.

And quiet, simply quiet.

We got the feeling that we were the *only* guests. We had arranged with Derry O'Keefe to pick us up in an hour and take us to the "best department store in Limerick." Once again, Derry could've set a re-cord at the Indy. The best department store, which happened to be the *only* department store, reminded me of the dime store in Hollywood where my grandmother used to shop when I was a kid, or today's version of a Kmart. I'm sure it's a different story now, but there wasn't much to choose from in the way of souvenirs that day. We drove back to the castle, and around 5:00 p.m. Joe and I went into the hotel pub for a drink.

Quiet, simply quiet.

Again, we saw no other guests. After a few minutes, Joe and I looked at each other and, without saying a word, went up to our room, packed our bags, and had the concierge book us on the next flight to Rome (which was in about an hour and a half!). We called Derry to drive us to the Shannon Airport, saying that an emergency had come up and we had to leave right away. A helicopter couldn't have gotten us there any faster than good old Derry O'Keefe behind the wheel.

We landed in Rome after midnight . . . *with no place to go.* What were we thinking? We had no hotel reservation, nothing. While Joe was getting our luggage, I was making frantic calls to various hotels. The first one I called was the Hassler, where Harvey and the rest of our gang were staying. Everything was solidly booked. I made a weak

joke to Joe saying we might have to sleep in a stable. After about another hour of trying, we finally booked a room at a hotel outside of
the city. When we registered, we were informed that we could only
stay overnight as the room was going to be occupied the next day. The
room was so small . . . how small was it? "If you dropped a Kleenex,
you'd have wall-to-wall carpeting!" (Forgive me.) In order to get to the
bathroom, you had to walk on the bed. We didn't care. Exhausted, we
passed out and woke up to a telephone call from the manager telling
us we had to vacate before noon. We called Harvey at the Hassler
Hotel.

Harvey answered and said, "I thought you guys were in Ireland
and Scotland!?"

US: "It's a long story. Can you see if you can get us a room
there?"
HARVEY: "I'll see what I can do. It's pretty full. I'll introduce
myself to the manager. Nobody knows who we are over here. I
can't promise anything! Where are you?"

We gave him our number and sat on the bed waiting for Harvey
to call back, keeping our fingers crossed that he could come up with
a miracle. At about 11:45 a.m., the phone rang.

HARVEY: "I told the manager that you had your own TV show
in America, and needed a room. He doesn't know you, so he
said they could put you up for two nights only. Get on over
here!"

We checked into the Hassler and happily unpacked, trying to forget that our time there would run out in forty-eight hours.

It was great having dinner with the gang that night and laughing
about our aborted trip, but we realized that in order to stay longer, I
would have to impress the manager somehow . . .

It is not in my nature to call attention to myself—except when I'm on stage, that is—but desperate times call for desperate measures . . . The next morning, I took root in the hotel lobby. The intention was to make myself highly visible to any and all American tourists who would (hopefully) ask for my autograph in front of our Italian hotel manager. Nothing was happening. People were passing in and out of the lobby, not looking in my direction. I began toying with the idea of doing the Tarzan yell to get attention. Thinking better of that idea, I moved away from the corner chair I was sitting in and plopped myself down on a pouf in the middle of the lobby. It worked! A family (Mom, Dad, and four kids) from Kansas City was checking in and spotted me. I smiled and said, "Hi there! First trip to Rome?" They couldn't have been more *beautiful*. They not only had me sign several autographs, but I posed for pictures with all six of them, with flashbulbs popping all over the place. Other American tourists took notice, and I wound up signing and posing and signing and posing . . . *AND* the hotel manager saw it all!

Our stay at the beautiful Hassler was extended, and Joe and I and our gang had a wonderful Roman week together. Oh, yes, and we took the Kansas City family to dinner. Bless them.

"AND THEN SOMEBODY ASKED ME . . ."

M any times I would get the same questions during the Q&As. For instance:

"Why do you pull your left ear at the end of the show?"

"I was raised by my grandmother, Nanny, and when I got my very first job on television in New York, I called her in California to give her the good news, and she said, 'Well, say hello to me!' I explained that the network probably wouldn't be too keen on me saying 'Hi, Nanny!' so I came up with the idea that I'd pull my left ear for her as a 'signal.' From that time on, whenever I was on TV I'd send Nanny the signal, which meant, 'I'm fine and I love you.' As the years went by and I got more and more work, the signal grew to mean, 'I'm fine, I love you—and your check's on the way.'" (*Years ago, a reporter from* Life *magazine measured my left ear, and it was one millimeter longer than my right ear.*)

There's a request to do the Tarzan yell (*the first of many over the course of the show*). I comply, and explain how the yell came about. "When I was little—around nine or ten—I had a beautiful cousin, Janice, and we used to act out the movies we saw, like Nelson and Jeanette and Tarzan and Jane. Naturally—because she was the pretty one—I was Nelson and, naturally, it follows that I was Tarzan." I introduce my beautiful cousin Janice, who is in the audience.

AN AUDIENCE MEMBER wants to know, "Have you ever had training in learning how to fall down and did you ever hurt yourself?"

"No and yes."

*The Q&As became one of my
favorite parts of the show.*

"ARE YOU GOING to be a *Playboy* centerfold?" asks another.
"No, but I'm the centerfold in *Field & Stream* this month."

A WOMAN WANTS to know, "Do you cook?" I give a detailed recipe for
my meatloaf, ending with "Cook it for about forty-five minutes, and
then go out to dinner."

I'M ASKED, "WERE you ever shy?" I tell the story of when I was around
fourteen and got a penicillin shot in the rear end. "It just so happened
that I had an adolescent crush on the doctor, and I was so embarrassed that, as I was leaving, I accidentally walked into a closet . . .
and *stayed* there!"

"IS YOUR MOUTH insured?"
"There's not enough money."

A WOMAN IN the audience wants to know where the ladies' room
is. I call her up on stage and lead her to one backstage. When the
woman returns, the entire audience and I sing, "We know where
you've been!"

A very shy Vicki before she blossomed.

I WOULD DO several public service announcements at the end of our show, encouraging all of us to do something about air pollution. I read a poem sent in by a little kid:

Someday I want to grow up
And live in a great big town.
Do you think I'll ever grow up?
'Cause blue skies now are brown.

A LADY SAYS, "You look much nicer in person." I tell the story about a man who stopped me on the street one time in New York, having recognized me from *The Garry Moore Show.* "He looked at me closely, and then yelled down the street to his wife, 'Hey, Mae, it *is* her!' He then turned back to me and said, 'You ain't such a dog!'"

"WHAT WAS ONE of your most embarrassing moments?"
I tell about the time when I was in the ladies' room in a restaurant and heard tiny footsteps approaching. A little girl about five years old bent down, peeked under the door, looked up at me sitting there, and asked, "Are you Carol Burnett?"

. . .

THESE OFF-THE-CUFF MOMENTS during the Q&As were some of my favorites. I would usually do about fifteen minutes and we'd choose the best ones to air. Also, the Q&A segments provided us with a cushion in case the show ran short or long. For instance, if we ran long, we would "bank" a sketch and save it for a future show.

A MIRACLE MOMENT

One of the zaniest moments in the history of the Q&As came about when a woman in the audience asked me when I was going to do another takeoff on Shirley Temple. Now, I could have called on a lot of other people that night. It was a miracle I called on her, and it all worked out so perfectly—*this is my favorite!*

We had developed a character named Shirley Dimple earlier in the season, and Harvey had played a newsman who interviewed me as Shirley on a couple of shows. When the lady asked the question that evening, the cameramen and the rest of the crew burst out laughing! Why? Because *in that very show that very evening* we were doing a send-up of Shirley Temple movies that we had been rehearsing for the entire week! It was going to take up the whole last half hour and be our big extravaganza finale!

There were four elaborate sets, dozens of amazing costumes, and our own original music and lyrics. The guest stars were Anthony Newley and Bernadette Peters, appearing along with Harvey, Vicki, Lyle, and our dancers, all supported by our twenty-eight-piece orchestra led by Peter Matz.

So, her question was a *total coincidence*, but I decided this was too good not to have some fun with, so I asked, "Do you like it when we do Shirley?" She smiled enthusiastically and nodded. "Gosh," I said, "I'm not sure, but maybe we can whip up *something* before the end of the show. I can't promise, but we'll try."

The first half hour was our usual formula of some sketches interspersed with musical numbers by Anthony and Bernadette. Then it was time for the second half of the show.

There was the overture and Lyle's deep-voiced announcement: "Ladies and gentlemen! Tonight we present our movie of the week, LITTLE MISS SHOWBIZ! Starring Shirley Dimple!"

As Shirley with Anthony Newley and
Bernadette Peters.

The curtains open and Shirley and other little girls in pj's are dancing in an orphanage dormitory room. Shirley is the only one with taps on the bottoms of her pj's feet. The story involves Shirley's two uncles: the rich Scrooge-like Uncle Meany (Harvey) and his younger brother, the kind, out-of-work, but aspiring Broadway musical playwright, Uncle Miney (Anthony Newley), who wants to write a big Broadway show starring his beautiful girlfriend, Trixie (Bernadette Peters). Each uncle is determined to adopt Shirley, whose father, Moe, died in an accident. Naturally the rich uncle prevails, and Shirley sings a sad farewell song to her friends and leaves with the unpleasant Uncle Meany, much to the dismay of good-hearted Uncle Miney, who sings a sorrowful lament with the remaining orphans.

In the next scene Uncle Miney is in his cold-water flat with Trixie trying to write a hit show tune, which they sing as Trixie taps her way around the room. Shirley bursts in, a runaway from Meany, and begs Miney to let her stay. The girlfriend thinks Shirley's a brat, and Shirley's not too crazy about the girlfriend, either, so she tries to come between the pair by writing and singing her own song (a takeoff on Shirley's "On the Good Ship Lollipop" and "Animal Crackers"), which Miney loves. He says her song will make them a major hit on Broadway if Shirley stars in the show. After they sing it together, Uncle Meany thunders through the door and demands that Shirley come back with him. They finally agree to take this custody problem to the highest court in the land!

In the next scene Shirley's fate is being determined in a courtroom before a jury. The two uncles and the girlfriend are there when Shirley enters and sings her plea to the judge. Soon she has perched herself on Uncle Meany's lap and is singing to him, the lyrics asking him not to be so mean. The title of the song is "Don't Be a Grouchy-Wouchy."

Uncle Miney and Trixie enter, dancing, in formal clothes. Miney asks Shirley to sing and tap-dance for the court.

She removes her coat to reveal a sequined costume with dozens of petticoats. Suddenly the set revolves, the judge and jury remove their outer garments, and we find ourselves in a Broadway show with everyone singing and tapping their hearts out, including Uncle Meany, who agrees to invest in Miney and Shirley's show.

TA-DA! The end.

Just before we all took our bows, I asked the lady in the audience how she liked the show.

She said, "Oh, thank you so much for going to all that trouble!"

DOWN MEMORY LANE WITH
SOME OF OUR GUESTS

W hat great guests we had! At the end of this book there is a list of everyone who got into the sandbox with us for the whole eleven years. I wish I had enough pages to write about each and every one of them, but here are some highlights.

Jim Nabors

I loved *Gomer Pyle: USMC*. I watched it every week, along with millions of viewers. I didn't know Jim Nabors personally, but his portrayal of Gomer was not only downright funny, it was touching at the same time. In one show Gomer pulled out a guitar and softly sang a beautiful folk song to his girlfriend as they sat in a porch swing. It was a lovely moment. I wrote him a fan letter the next day. The year was 1965, and Jim and I met for the first time shortly after that, when he was in New York on business. We hit it off immediately.

When Joe and I moved to California, I had the chance to see a lot more of Jim, and my fondness for him only grew. In a funny way, I felt he was the brother I never had, and as if to prove it, I asked him to be my daughter Jody's godfather after she was born.

We thought it would be fun to perform together in the summer months, when my show was on hiatus, so we wrote an act and took it on the road. We did sketches and sang and danced. After each show, we would set up a table and a couple of chairs and autograph our personal eight-by-ten photos for the folks who came to see us. One time, after Jim had signed one of his pictures, a very excited fan clutched it to her bosom and blurted out: "THANK YOU! THANK YOU! THANK YOU! AS SOON AS I GET HOME I'M GONNA HANG THIS UP ON MY WALL RIGHT NEXT TO JESUS!" Jim literally fell out of his chair.

My buddy, the versatile and
amazing Jim Nabors.

Jim loved Hawaii and went there as often as he could, so I wasn't surprised when he decided to split his time between performing on the mainland and farming on the beautiful spread he bought in Maui. He also bought a lovely home in Honolulu.

One summer we were performing at the MGM Grand in Las Vegas and, as usual, Jim had brought down the house with his beautiful rendition of "The Impossible Dream." As he came offstage, he saw me waiting in the wings, gave me that great big grin of his, and said in his Gomer voice, "Well, I just bought me another tractor!"

When my variety show was about to premiere, I asked Jim to be our very first guest. I had no idea if we were going to be picked up by CBS for a second season, and when we were, I thought, "Jim's my good-luck charm!" He was our guest on the first show every year for the entire eleven seasons.

Jim liked teasing me about my being hooked on *All My Children* (AMC), my favorite soap opera, which I watched every day in my office during our lunch break. One Monday when he was my guest that week, I invited him to have lunch with me and watch the show. He said, "I'd love to have lunch with you, but do we *have* to watch that dad-gummed soap opera of yours?" I told him it was a deal breaker: "no AMC, no lunch." He laughed, and showed up at noon. I turned on the TV. It was an episode where the wily, beautiful Erica Kane was in a load of trouble (although, when wasn't she?). Jim watched and rolled his eyes a few times between bites of his ham on rye, indicating how silly he thought the whole thing was. We finished our sandwiches and reported back to the rehearsal hall at 1:00.

The next day (Tuesday) at noon, Jim walked into my office with his lunch, sat down, and said, "What kinda trouble do you think Erica's gonna go through today?"

In 2015 I flew to Honolulu to celebrate Jim's eighty-fifth birthday, along with my daughter Jody and her husband. The party was held in his home that overlooks the ocean. It was quite a shindig. Several tables were set up around the swimming pool, and the food was delicious homespun Southern cooking as a salute to Jim's home state of Alabama. Over two hundred guests attended, including a past governor and the present one. A Marine Corps band serenaded the throng and ended it with everyone joining in for a rousing rendition of "Happy Birthday." Jim is so very much loved in the Aloha state that I'm sure if he wanted to, he could run for governor and win in a landslide.

He is still in Hawaii, so we don't get to see as much of each other as we'd like, but we talk often. He remains my good-luck charm, whom I love very much.

Ken Berry

When I was still doing *The Garry Moore Show*, I flew to Los Angeles to visit my grandmother while we were on a break.

One night I attended the popular *Billy Barnes Revue*, which featured comedy sketches and musical numbers performed by several new talents. That was the first time I saw Ken Berry, and I fell in love with him. There was nothing Ken couldn't do. He was a terrific dancer, singer, and comedian, *and* he was sexy.

When I got back to New York, I told Garry about Ken and convinced him to give him a shot on the show. Ken was booked and flew to New York, where he performed a spectacular tap routine.

He and his wife at the time, Jackie Joseph, became good friends of mine, and when my variety show was on the air, Ken was my guest nineteen times. He was also a guest on a special I did for CBS and costarred with me in a television version of *Once Upon a Mattress*, as Prince Dauntless to my Princess Winnifred.

Ken has always been extremely shy and unassuming about his talent. Totally "egoless." I don't think he has ever been aware of how brilliant a performer he is. He would be fairly quiet during rehearsals, quickly learning his lines and the complicated dances Ernie Flatt cooked up for him, with nary a comment. He was totally cooperative and an absolute doll, but still kind of shy. However, come showtime and with the cameras rolling, he absolutely "lit up" in front of the audience and was gangbusters in every sketch and musical number . . . a powerhouse of an entertainer! No wonder we had him come play with us nineteen times!

In a way, Ken was born too late. He could've had a fantastic career in the heyday of those great MGM musicals, which starred the likes of Gene Kelly, Fred Astaire, and Donald O'Connor. He possessed all their qualities, and yet was uniquely original.

I'm just happy that our show was able to show him off to great advantage. Added to that, he was and is one of the nicest human beings I've ever known.

Bernadette Peters

·······································

My husband Joe and I first laid eyes on a nineteen-year-old wonder by the name of Bernadette Peters when we went to see the
show *Dames at Sea* (a campy takeoff on those old Busby Berkeley
movie musicals). She was being managed by a mutual friend of ours,
Lou Kristofer, who told us, "You *have* to see this girl, she's fantastic!!"
That was an understatement. Not only was she beautiful, and could
dance and sing up a storm, but she was also hysterically funny. (Later,
in other roles, she also proved she could elicit tears from an audience
with her dramatic abilities, as both a singer and an actress.) After seeing her in *Dames at Sea*, Joe and I went backstage and introduced
ourselves. Our show was going to start airing that coming September,
and we asked Bernadette then and there if she would be a guest. She
was the very first guest we asked. She wound up being one of our
most frequent guest stars.

Bernadette Peters was the first guest we
ever invited to appear on the show.

We had a great time being villains together, along with Tim Curry,
in the movie *Annie*. She also played the role of Lady Larken in our
1972 television version of *Once Upon a Mattress*.

Of course, she went on to become the Queen of Broadway, where she continues to reign supreme. To this day, I consider "Bern" one of my closest friends.

Alan Alda

E ven though we don't see each other, living on different coasts, I consider Alan and his terrific wife, Arlene, good friends. I had the pleasure (joy!) of working with Alan three times. The first was when he came on my show in 1974, and in the same year, we acted together in the television version of the Broadway play *6 Rms Riv Vu*, which he also directed. Then in 1981, I played his wife in the highly successful movie *The Four Seasons*, which he wrote, directed, and starred in.

We kept him pretty busy the week he got into the sandbox with us, by using him in every sketch and musical number. He also happens to be a very good singer.

Alan Alda was a great and versatile guest.

He appeared in a "Family" sketch as Larry, Eunice's brother, who pays Eunice, Ed, and Mama a visit on Christmas Day. Larry is a successful freelance artist but is considered by Eunice and Ed to be somewhat of a "nance," just because he's artistic and single. They also keep harping on the notion that if Larry doesn't have a steady job, then he must keep getting fired! Every time Larry tries to explain what being a "freelance" artist means, they keep interrupting him with their own petty arguments, ignoring him completely. Things reach a fever pitch when Larry finally explodes, telling them off in no uncertain terms!

Alan exited to thunderous applause from our studio.

In another sketch, he played a nerd, Morton, who could impress his girlfriend, Selma (me), only by pretending to be famous movie stars, such as Humphrey Bogart, Robert Redford, etc. He quotes his favorite lines from classic movies, thereby fooling the adoring Selma, until she finally catches on when she turns on the TV and sees a couple of late-night movies where the exact same lines are being said by the actors on the screen! Angry as hell, she confronts Morton on their next date. He explains that the real Morton is dull as dishwater. After he begins behaving and speaking like the "real" Morton, Selma realizes that she's better off when he's "Robert Redford."

Since this was our Christmas show, Alan and I also played a couple of department store workers on Christmas Eve who have had it with all the late shoppers and their demands. They run into each other after the store closes, and there's immediate chemistry. They sing "Nobody Does It Like Me," and wind up exiting arm in arm.

The show ended with our musical finale featuring Alan and me and our dancers in a salute to Manhattan.

AN INTERESTING SIDE note: in the mid-forties, Alan and I just missed being childhood buddies. When I was growing up on Yucca Street and Wilcox Avenue in Hollywood, Alan's father, Robert Alda, was starring as George Gershwin in the Warner Bros. movie *Rhapsody in Blue* (1945). During the filming, his family rented an apartment across the street from where I lived with my grandmother.

When Alan was seven years old, he contracted polio. To combat the disease he went through a very painful treatment regimen developed by Sister Elizabeth Kenny that consisted of applying hot woolen blankets to his limbs and stretching his muscles, which hurt like hell. He told me he used to look out the window and watch the neighborhood kids roller-skating up and down Wilcox Avenue, between treatments, wishing he could come out and play. He never did . . . and I was one of those kids.

The painful treatments he suffered through did the trick. He recovered beautifully, and to this day, he can kick as high as a Rockette.

Sammy Davis, Jr.

S ammy was a special guy. Not only was he one of the most versatile and talented human beings on the planet, he was one of the easiest people I ever had the pleasure of working with. He threw himself into some of our silliest sketches with abandon, and there were moments when he would lose it and crack up in front of the audience, topping even Harvey when Tim would get to him.

Musically, he was a master. He sang. Oh, how he could sing. He had a God-given voice that (in my opinion) rivaled Sinatra's. We did a medley of Broadway tunes that remains, to this day, one of my very favorite duets.

However, there was one sketch that Sammy and I did that was just this side of being fairly serious. It was called "Backstage." Sammy played a major star entertainer, Johnny, who after twenty years has returned to his hometown in the South to perform. I played a woman, Eleanor, who knew him when they were both kids, his mother being her family's maid.

The setting is the backstage dressing room. Johnny has just entered after a successful performance and is being interviewed by reporters. He's asked about his upcoming show business plans. He's going to do a Broadway show, and then star in a Western movie, etc., etc.

Sammy "backstage" with my Eleanor.

Eleanor, in a pale blue evening gown, sporting a white fur stole and wearing a teased beehive hairdo, has followed the reporters into the room, and even after all these years, Johnny recognizes her. "Eleanor Simpson!" he says, delighted to see her. She corrects him. She's now married and her name is Eleanor Wheatley. He introduces her to the reporters, and after they all leave, he asks Eleanor to sit and visit. She's more than happy to do so. During the sketch, we discover that Eleanor is a passive-aggressive bigot. She asks about his "Mama," and bemoans the fact that they never had such a good maid, adding, "And, Johnny, you were no slouch when it came to shinin' my daddy's boots! He always used to say he thought maybe you had some kind of magic spit!"

Johnny is taking all this in stride and is very polite, even though it's turning into a most uncomfortable visit. After a somewhat barbed exchange, he asks Eleanor if she thinks he's a little out of his "place," and she insists that it's important for people to "stretch!" Oblivious to her insults, she rattles on. "Although people *might* say you're a little out of your place doin' a *Western* . . . I mean you don't see John Wayne goin' off and pushin' himself into a remake of *Porgy and Bess!*"

Johnny asks about Eleanor's husband. She explains, "I'm sorry I didn't bring my Justin back, but he thought he'd be intruding seein' as how you're *my* old acquaintance, so he said he'd wait in the bar." Johnny suggests that they join him for a drink, but Eleanor is uneasy with that thought, telling him that maybe he can meet Justin some other time when her husband's in a better mood. She goes on to say that when the check was presented to them after the show, Justin was livid, saying, "A ten-dollar cover check just to watch a . . . !" Eleanor catches herself just before finishing the sentence. She insists that Justin is very liberal. "We own a cute little restaurant over on Walnut Street, and we hired all black waiters. Naturally, the cashier is white."

Johnny is holding his tongue. Eleanor keeps putting her foot in her mouth. "Remember all the fun we had as kids? We had fun, fun, FUN! But there was one thing I learned from you when we were kids!"

"What's that?"

"Never to play Hide and Go Seek with you at *night*! I mean, you coulda been standin' right in front of me and I never woulda known it . . . unless you smiled!"

Johnny has finally had enough, and politely escorts her to the door. He calls her "Eleanor, honey." Smiling, she sweetly tells him she thinks that's a little overstepping his place. He apologizes and offers her his hand. Still smiling, she avoids taking it, but as she leaves, she says, "Good-bye, Johnny, and . . . God bless." The door closes, and Johnny says to himself, "Good-bye to you, too, Mrs. Wheatley. And God bless . . ."

Sammy loved this sketch. So did I.

That week, after we had our regular Wednesday run-through at 3:00, Sammy surprised everyone by inviting us all down to Studio 33, where he had set up his seventeen-piece band that played for him when he performed in Las Vegas and around the country, and doing his full nightclub act for us and anyone else who worked at CBS who wanted to come. The joint was jumping for an hour and a half.

What a nice thing to do.

Roddy McDowall

I had a crush on Roddy when I was ten years old after seeing him in *Lassie Come Home*.

It was a thrill to meet him years later and have him as a guest on our show, but it was even nicer when he became a very close friend. Without a doubt, Roddy was one of the loveliest people in show business. He was also one of the most loved people in show business. He started out as a child actor in the movies, gaining stardom at age twelve in *How Green Was My Valley* and then going on to make *Lassie Come Home* (where he and Elizabeth Taylor bonded and became life-long friends), *My Friend Flicka*, and others. I say he was loved by the industry because, although he knew just about everyone and was a confidant of many, he never, ever told stories out of school. Roddy McDowall was born free of the "gossip" gene.

He had the distinction of being one of the rare child movie stars who grew up unscathed by the business. When he reached adult-hood, he easily moved into grown-up roles, and became one of film-dom's most admired character actors.

He was also a crack photographer and published several books under the title *Double Exposure*, featuring celebrities writing about celebrities accompanied by the portraits he had taken. I wrote about Jimmy Stewart, and was thrilled when Anthony Hopkins wrote about me.

Roddy guested on our show five times, the first of which was in March 1974. That was the first time we did "The Family" sketch where he played Eunice's brother Phillip. I always loved it when he got in the sandbox with us. He was a wonderful actor who jumped into every sketch with abandon. That first Friday morning, which was our tape day, he spent three and a half hours in the makeup chair getting into his famous *Planet of the Apes* character, Cornelius. He appeared with me during the Q&A, where we sang a very funny duet of love songs. After that, he had to run like hell back to his dressing room and quickly get out of all that ape drag to do the rest of the show! It was above and beyond the call of duty.

Tall, dark, and hairy!

Eunice and her brother Phillip.

His cozy home in the Valley was the setting for countless Wednesday night dinner parties. In the style of eighteenth-century French salons, he would usually invite no more than ten or twelve guests and the evenings were all about conversation. Who would be there? On any given Wednesday, the guest list might include Elizabeth Taylor, Ava Gardner, Alec Guinness, Bette Davis, Laurence Olivier, and Mae West! I was invited often, and those parties—hands down—were the best. We'd start with cocktails in the living room and graduate into the dining room for dinner. After dinner, we'd all go back into the living room for coffee and conversation. I usually sat in a particular antique armchair where I was the most comfortable, in the corner next to the fireplace. The stories would fly and the laughs were plenty. Being the movie fan I had always been, I felt like I had died and gone to heaven.

Roddy was on the Selection Committee for the Kennedy Center Honors, and every year, we would put our heads together and come up with names we thought should be honored. Several made the cut, among them Irene Dunne, Myrna Loy, and Shirley Temple. No doubt, both of us idolized the movie stars we had grown up with. Had he lived, I have no doubt that Roddy would've been an honoree. He left us in 1998. At the Motion Picture Home in Woodland Hills, California, there is the Roddy McDowall Rose Garden, a beautiful tribute to a beautiful soul.

The antique chair I always sat in was left to me in his will. It's in my office. He also wrote a note that came with it:

". . . and my dear, dear CB

we have so far to go

Ever, R."

Vincent Price

Vincent was an absolute hoot. A fabulous character actor in such films as *Laura* and *Leave Her to Heaven*, he went on to make his mark in horror films such as *House of Wax* and *House on Haunted Hill*. As a guest, he threw himself into our brand of wackiness wholeheartedly. He was on our show four times. One time we did a takeoff on a horror movie, which we titled "House of Terror."

Setting: A spooky castle in England in the early 1900s. Vincent played a devious scientist who marries and brings home an unsuspecting Cockney Tart, played by me. He plans to put the brain of his elderly mother (Vicki) into his new bride's younger body. The servant Igor (Harvey) has feelings for the new bride and warns her of his master's dastardly plot. They overcome the evil scientist and zap his body, turning him into the handsome Lyle, much to the Tart's delight.

(Harvey stole the sketch with his hilarious physical interpretation of Igor. Also, the door to the laboratory set accidentally came off its hinges and we had to work around it. Vincent very cleverly ad-libbed: "That's the third broken door this week!"—much to the delight of the studio audience, proving, once again, that we treated each taping as if it were a live show.)

Vincent also wrote several books about his love of food. *A Treasury of Great Recipes* has come to be regarded as "one of the most important culinary events of the 20th century" (*Saveur* magazine) and was named the eighth most popular out-of-print book of any kind by Booklist. It has inspired countless chefs around the world.

Our cue card boys had their table set up right outside my dressing room. On Thursdays, our blocking day, they would bring in a hot plate, various ingredients, and magically cook up a meal for their lunch, worthy of a five-star restaurant! Including the sauces! I don't know how they did it, but they did. One week when Vincent was on the show, they chose to create one of his favorite recipes from his book and invited Vincent and me to join them during our lunch break. It was an amazing spread and Vincent was absolutely overwhelmed. Me, too.

Donald O'Connor

D onald O'Connor was on our show twice. It was a thrill for me in a special way. When I was ten or eleven years old and living in Hollywood with my grandmother, a friend of ours who worked as a stagehand at Universal Studios took me to the set of a movie, *Mister Big*, starring Donald O'Connor, who was around eighteen or nineteen at the time. I was a huge fan.

It was the very first time I was on a movie set, and the very first time I was *up close* to actual movie stars! Enthralled, I watched Donald do a number with his costar Peggy Ryan. They were playing a song with hand bells. After the take, I was over the moon when I got to meet Donald. He signed my autograph book, "To Carol. Love, Donald O'Connor, 'Mr. Big.'" And here we were, working together twenty-six years later! I was still a huge fan! Who can ever forget his star turn in *Singin' in the Rain* when he performed "Make 'Em Laugh"? "Fantastic" isn't a big-enough word.

Lucille Ball

I t was Tuesday night, May 12, 1959. I had just opened the night before in the Off-Broadway musical *Once Upon a Muttress*, playing the role of Princess Winnifred. We had received pretty good reviews and we were settling in for our limited six-week run. I was happy and pretty relaxed that evening, compared to the butterflies in my stomach just twenty-four hours before. Now I could just kick back and have fun without thinking about the critics. I was in my funky dressing room, at the Phoenix Theatre, which was partly furnished with a couch that had seen better days (one of its rusty springs coiled up through the cushion looking like a dangerous Slinky), getting ready for the 8:30 curtain, when I heard a distinctive "buzz" backstage. I opened the door and walked to the wings and saw several cast members excitedly peeking through the house curtain. I asked our stage manager, John Allen, what was going on.

"Lucy's in the audience!"

"What???"

"Lucy! Lucy's in the audience!"

"*THE* Lucy?"

I peeked through the curtain, and spotted her smack-dab in the middle of the second row. You couldn't miss that bright orange hair.

I thought I might faint. The butterflies were back with a vengeance.

Somehow, I got through the show intact. I swear I was more nervous than I was on opening night. While we were taking our bows, Lucy was on her feet clapping away. I was back in my funky dressing room and there was a knock at the door. I opened it, and there was Lucy. I invited her in, and she said, "Kid, you were terrific." I almost fainted again. She approached the couch, and just as I was about to warn her about the offending spring, barely glancing at it, she said, "I see it." She stayed for several minutes and left saying, "Kid, if you ever need me for anything, call me." After she left, I was ten feet off the ground.

I *did* need her five years later, when CBS had offered me an hour special, *if* . . . I could produce a big star as my guest. I got in touch with Lucy, and without hesitating she signed on. We had a wonderful time doing sketches and the finale where we played two cleaning ladies in a talent agency who think they know more about making movie deals than William Morris. We wound up dancing and singing an original song written for us by Ken and Mitzie Welch, called "Chutzpah!" Lucy tore into it and afterward said it was one of her very favorite musical experiences. Mine, too.

In 1966, when I was pregnant with my daughter Jody, Lucy gave me a baby shower. And what a shower! It was a *black-tie affair* at her home, with both women and *men*! Gary Morton, Lucy's second husband, was given the job of opening the gifts, and being a successful comedian in his own right, he kept everyone in stitches with his comments and one-liners about diapers, baby booties, and rattles. Lucy and I became close friends, and she always sent me flowers on my birthday, with the card reading "Happy Birthday, Kid."

When I got my variety show, we traded guest shots. After *I Love Lucy*, she had two other shows, *The Lucy Show* and *Here's Lucy*. I did a few of those, and she was on my show four times.

Lucy had a reputation for being somewhat "tough" when it came to running her show. "Tough" could be a compliment if you were talking about a Milton Berle or a Jackie Gleason, but back in the sixties it was just the opposite if you happened to be talking about a *woman* in the same business. I saw her as simply being *honest*. She didn't mince words when it came to voicing a negative opinion (about the writing, lighting, or whatever), and the funny thing was, none of her coworkers or crew took it personally, because she was just as free with her praise for jobs well done.

One week when she was my guest, we walked across the street to a Chinese restaurant in the farmers market during a dinner break and settled down in a booth. She began to talk about the time she and Desi were doing *I Love Lucy*.

"Y'know, kid, when I was married to the Cuban, I never had to worry about the writing, or any of the inner workings of the show. Desi did all that. He ran the show. He was the boss." She went on to say that all she had to do was come in on Mondays, read the polished script, and simply be "Lucy." Desi took care of all the rest. We talked about how I was lucky to have my husband, Joe, to do the same for me. I was never one to make waves with the writers or the crew. I was totally nonconfrontational. Actually, you could say I was chicken. If a sketch wasn't working, I would often wind up *apologizing* to the writers when asking for a little help.

Lucy understood, exactly. Then she told me about the first day she had to do Desi's job. She and Desi had parted and Lucy was embarking on a new project: "*The Lucy Show*, starring Lucille Ball."

There was a table reading of the show that first Monday, and the script was . . . *no good*. "No good?" she said. "It STANK!" She went on, saying she was at a total loss for words and told everybody to break for lunch. "I went into my office, and just sat there for over an hour, trying to figure out a 'nice' way to handle the whole thing." She came to the conclusion that there really wasn't a *nice* way to do it, and went back to face the writers. She screwed up the courage to tell them exactly what she thought of the script, not mincing her words, but being brutally honest.

"And, kid, that's when they put the 's' on the end of my last name!"

I loved Lucy. She died on my birthday in 1989. Her flowers arrived late that afternoon, "Happy Birthday, Kid."

There was no one like Lucy!

There's a quote of hers that I've always loved: "I guess I would rather regret the things I've done than to regret the things I've never done."

"LOVELY STORY," "THE FUNN FAMILY," AND OTHER GUESTS

"Pillow Squawk"

Another sketch that was fun to do was our takeoff on the Doris Day/Rock Hudson movies of the late fifties and early sixties, such as *Pillow Talk,* produced by Ross Hunter. This particular sketch was a spoof on the genre, not the specific movie. We called our version "Pillow Squawk"!

I was the perennial blond freckle-faced squeaky-clean virginal-type character that Doris played in these films, and Lyle was the handsome playboy bachelor and ladies' man (à la Rock Hudson).

The plot: Doris is fresh off the farm and has traveled, with her teddy bear, to the big city to find fame and fortune. Innocent as the driven snow, she is shown into a penthouse apartment by the snooty manager of the building (Harvey), who explains that she'll be "baby-sitting" the apartment while the playboy owner is out of town. All she has to do is make sure his electric toothbrush is fully charged. Doris is thrilled, and excitedly bounces and twirls around the apartment shouting "Gloriosky Zero!" and "Jumpin' Jehosaphat!" while the manager looks at her with disdain.

> **MANAGER:** (Anxious to get away from this ding-a-ling) "I'll help you with your bags."
> **DORIS:** "Oh, be careful with the big one!"

MANAGER: "What's in it?"
DORIS: "Extra freckles!"

The manager shows her around the apartment and she shyly asks, "Where is the" (Embarrassed to say the "naughty" word, spells it out) "B-E-D?"

The manager points to a button in the wall.

MANAGER: (Sarcastically) "Is it all right to say 'button'?"
DORIS: "'Button' is okay . . . 'zipper' is a no-no."

He pushes the button in the wall and the bed
flies down. He gladly exits while Doris
happily skips over to the phone.

DORIS: (Unbelievably cheerful) "Hello, Operator? I'd like to talk to my mom in Minnie Falls, Iowa." (Immediately) "Hello, Mom? This is Mary Ellen Janie Sue! Golly, it's sure good to hear your voice again! Oh, it's *you*, Dad!" (Giggling) "Oh, Daddy, how are all the chickens and the piggies and the horsies and Mom? Oh good! Well, I'm here in New York and I have an appointment tomorrow morning with H. L. Smith, the King of Advertising, and with any luck, I'll become his secretary or even a vice president! Oh, golly, Dad, it sure was fun talking over the plot with you! Well, now I have to go brush my teeth, up and down and all around, so Mr. Tooth Decay won't come my way. And then I'm gonna recite the Girl Scout rules and sing myself to sleep, and then in the morning . . . hello? Hello?" (To herself) "Golly, that was nice of Dad. Mom usually hangs up much sooner."

Doris, cradling her teddy bear, skips into the bathroom to change into her pajamas. Enter the Handsome Playboy with two ladies in tow. He shoos them off, claiming to be tired and needing some sleep after having flown his private airplane all the way from Rome. The ladies reluctantly leave. Complimenting the departing women for having "such good taste in men," he cockily walks into the kitchen for a drink. Doris reenters wearing only a pajama top (decorated with red hearts). She has blindfolded her teddy bear. "Sorry, Teddy, but Mom forgot to pack my bottoms!" She sits on the edge of the bed, takes out a mirror, and proceeds to draw more freckles on her face. The Playboy, oblivious to Doris's presence, comes out of the kitchen and goes into the bathroom. Not having seen the Playboy, Doris is thirsty and *hopscotches* into the kitchen to get (naturally) a glass of milk. The Playboy reenters wearing only his pajama bottoms (also decorated with red hearts!) and gets into the far side of the bed and covers up. Doris returns with her milk. Not seeing that she has a bed partner, she sits on the side of the bed, focuses the lamp on her face like a spotlight, and belts out: "QUE SERA! SERA! WHATEVER WILL BE! WILL BE!" (a Doris Day hit song).

Suddenly she flings her arm back and feels someone else in the bed!

PLAYBOY: (Smiling) "Hello!"
DORIS: (Horrified! Jumps up screaming and begins running around the room in circles) "Oh! Oh! OHHH! Who are you???"
PLAYBOY: "Who am I? Who are you? What are you doing in my apartment?"
DORIS: "This is *my* apartment! And that's *my*" (Spelling) "B-E-D!"
PLAYBOY: (Amused) "I beg your pardon, but this is my B-E-D."

He approaches her.

DORIS: "OOOH! Don't you come near me! You . . . you . . . MAN!"

She dashes into the bathroom, slamming the door.

PLAYBOY: "What's going on here?" (To the door) "Lady! Will you come out of there?"

DORIS: "NO! I WILL NOT!!"

PLAYBOY: "Come out! I wanna talk to you!"

DORIS: "NO! And if you were any sort of a gentleman, you'd do me a favor!"

PLAYBOY: "What?"

DORIS: "Call the police!"

PLAYBOY: "Stop acting silly and come out!"

DORIS: "I will not!"

PLAYBOY: "Please come out! I LOVE YOU!"

DORIS: "You're just saying that."

PLAYBOY: "No, I'm not just saying that. If you come out, I'll marry you!"

Doris enters, smiling and wearing a wedding gown!
(Quick change!)

PLAYBOY: "Sweetheart, you get more beautiful every day."

DORIS: "Thank you, Mr. . . . . Mr. . . . ."

PLAYBOY: "H. L. Smith."

DORIS: (Delighted) "Not the millionaire advertising executive?! Why, I have an appointment with you tomorrow morning!"

PLAYBOY: "I won't be there, I'll be on my honeymoon."

DORIS: "Watch your language!"

PLAYBOY: "Sorry. Now, this is the plan. It's late, so we'll get a good night's sleep, and then the first thing in the morning, we'll go down to City Hall and get married!"

DORIS: "That's lovely, dear, but wherever will we stay tonight?"

PLAYBOY: (Eagerly getting into the B-E-D) "Well, right here! You don't mind, do you?"
DORIS: "Why no, not at all. I know I'll be perfectly safe. Nighty-night!"

She pushes the button and the bed and the Playboy fly up into the wall! Doris sits on the sofa, puts her feet up on the coffee table, and sings, "QUE SERA, SERA!"

THE END

*I get to become a Little Miss
Goody Two-Shoes.*

I GOT A phone call from Rock Hudson, who told me he got a big kick out of our takeoff.

I was told that Doris Day *didn't* get a big kick out of it. In watching it after all these years, I can understand why she didn't like it. I was pretty much over the top in my portrayal of her goody-two-shoes persona. But again, we were really spoofing the typical romantic comedies she made with Rock Hudson (as well as Cary Grant and others).

As a matter of fact, Ross Hunter himself was in the audience the night we taped this show, and he laughed like crazy. During our bows, he came on stage, surprising me by saying he always presented his stars with their "million-dollar wardrobes" and, as a gag, presented me with the wardrobe worn by Debbie Reynolds in *Tammy and the Bachelor* . . . a pair of old worn-out jeans.

As for Doris Day, I loved all her movies. My particular favorite was *Love Me or Leave Me*, the Ruth Etting story, which she made with James Cagney in 1955. It was a highly dramatic role, and I always thought she should have been nominated for an Academy Award for that performance.

"Oh! Oh! OHHH! A man!"

Rock Hudson

I n 1966, I signed to do a CBS special, *Carol and Company*. I decided, right away, to ask Ken Berry and impressionist Frank Gorshin to be my guests. Then I remembered seeing Rock Hudson and Mae West at the Academy Awards in 1957, where they sang a very funny rendition of "Baby, It's Cold Outside," and brought down the house.

I didn't know Rock, but I knew he'd be a great addition to the special. He was a major movie star who was a great comedic actor and was definitely musical! Bob Banner was producing and called Rock's agent to set up a meeting.

We met for lunch in the famous Polo Lounge at the Beverly Hills Hotel. Even handsomer in person, he couldn't have been more down-to-earth or nice. He accepted my invitation to do the special and we were off and running. In the special, written by Buz Kohan and Bill Angelos, Ken, Frank, Rock, and I did several musical sketches and we had a great time. Our favorite number was when all of us played six-year-olds and sang an original song, "It's Our First Day of School."

Rock and I kept in touch after that.

Early in 1973, Gower Champion, the great director/choreographer, called on me at my house saying he would like to direct me in the two-person musical, *I Do! I Do!*, which had been done on Broadway starring Mary Martin as The Wife and Robert Preston as The Husband. We would do it at the Huntington Hartford Theater in Hollywood, during my summer hiatus. I jumped at the idea and suggested Rock as The Husband.

"He sings?" Gower asked.

"Yep," I replied.

Gower loved the idea, so I picked up the phone and dialed Rock's number. I told him Gower and I would like to meet with him about something, and he said, "Come on up!" He lived just up the hill from my home and we were there in five minutes.

Rock had never performed on stage as an actor, much less as a musical comedy performer. Gower assured him that he would be in good hands and be well taken care of. I just kept saying how much fun we'd have!

An hour later, it was all settled. Rock was all for it.

I wasn't wrong about the fun!

After the successful run at the Hartford, Rock and I decided to take *I Do! I Do!* on the road the following summer. We played major venues in Dallas, Indianapolis, and St. Louis and wound up at the

Kennedy Center in Washington, D.C. It was a great success, selling out in every venue.

Rock and me in "When My Baby Laughs at Me."

Washington Star-News critic David Richards wrote: "If they had chosen the Yellow Pages or the Amana Home Freezer manual as a vehicle, I doubt it would have made one iota of difference."

Rock was a guest on my variety show three times. On one show, we did another one of our backstage movie musical parodies. This time, it was a tribute to the Betty Grable/Dan Dailey movie *When My Baby Smiles at Me.* We called ours "When My Baby Laughs at Me." Rock threw himself into it wholeheartedly.

Our paths didn't cross much after that, but we kept in touch.

I visited him in the hospital shortly before he died.

"*Double Calamity*"

The classic 1944 film noir *Double Indemnity* starred Barbara Stanwyck and Fred MacMurray and was directed by Billy Wilder.

We called our version "Double Calamity," and we pretty much

stayed faithful to the original story. Steve Lawrence was Walter Leff, and I played Phyllis. It opens with Leff entering his office late at night. He's riddled with bullet holes, and staggers to his desk to talk into his Dictaphone and confess to a murder. "It all started . . ."

While he's dictating a confession, the night janitor enters and strikes up a conversation with Leff, who tells him to get lost because "I've got a score to settle, a roller coaster to get off of, and a movie to narrate!" The old janitor leaves, and Leff continues his confession, saying, "I killed him for money and a dame. I didn't get the money and I didn't get the dame . . . easy come, easy go."

Leff continues to narrate, and we flash back to his coming into the Dietrichson home to renew an insurance policy. The maid lets him in, and Phyllis, dressed only in a towel, appears at the top of the stairs. Romantic music plays. She and Leff are immediately attracted to each other.

They engage in a typical film noir conversation, which, of course, we exaggerated.

LEFF: "I'm here to see Mr. Dietrichson."
PHYLLIS: (Seductively) "I'm *Mrs.* Dietrichson." (Flashing a leg, wearing an ankle bracelet) "Could I be of some help?"
LEFF: (Eyeing her up and down) "Yeah. Sure, sure. You can be of some help . . . baby."
PHYLLIS: "Excuse the way I look, but I've been sunbathing."
LEFF: "At night?"
PHYLLIS: (Teasingly) "I *burn* easily."
LEFF: "You always wear that anklet when you moon-bathe, baby?"
PHYLLIS: "Don't race your motor, Mister . . ."
LEFF: "Leff."
PHYLLIS: "Leff."
LEFF: "Right."
PHYLLIS: "Right . . . say, if you promise to keep your hands

off me, I'll slip into somethin' more comfortable and be right down."

LEFF: "I'll slip into neutral, and keep my motor running."

She leaves and returns in a sexy gown.
Leff has put his foot up on the coffee table,
and we see he's wearing an ankle bracelet, too.

PHYLLIS: "Say, you've got a pretty swell anklet yourself."

LEFF: "Yeah, well, uh . . . maybe they should get together."

PHYLLIS: "Look, Mr. Leff . . ."

LEFF: "Right."

PHYLLIS: "Right. There's a speed limit in this town."

LEFF: "Yeah, well, I'm allowed forty-five in this area."

PHYLLIS: "Yeah, well, I'd say maybe you're going more than ninety."

LEFF: "Yeah, well, suppose I am."

PHYLLIS: "Well, suppose you slow down."

LEFF: "Suppose I don't, baby."

PHYLLIS: "Suppose you get a ticket." (He starts to kiss her) "Suppose you don't . . ." (He's really coming on to her) "Suppose I call my husband."

LEFF: "Yeah, why don't you do that, baby. See I gotta get his signature on this auto insurance renewal."

PHYLLIS: "Insurance?"

LEFF: "Yeah, y'know, 'auto,' 'life,' 'accident . . .'"

PHYLLIS: "Accident?" (Sinister music) "Suppose you do me a favor. Suppose you get my husband to sign an accident insurance policy, but don't let him know he's signing it, and then suppose you kill him for me."

LEFF: "You think I'm some kind of chump?" (She kisses him passionately) "All right, where is he? I'll kill him!"

Phyllis's dim-witted husband, Carl (Harvey), enters, oblivious to the fact that his wife is kissing another man. He's so smitten with Phyllis that he ignores the obvious. "Isn't she precious?" They get him to sign the policy without knowing what he's signing. His highly overwrought daughter, Lola (a very funny Vicki), is the witness. Lola hates her stepmother and has a beauty of a temper tantrum before she exits.

Steve as Leff and I'm Phyllis in my
"Barbara Stanwyck" wig.

Phyllis and Leff agree to meet somewhere that's inconspicuous, a small grocery store, to hatch their murderous plan. Wearing dark glasses and standing back to back, they both start whispering, then kiss furtively.

LEFF: "Listen baby, I've been thinking, would you rather get $50,000? Or would you like to get twice that much?"
PHYLLIS: (Thinking it over) "Twice that much would be double!"
LEFF: "Right, we could take advantage of the 'Double Calamity Clause.'"
PHYLLIS: "What's that?"

A very old lady walks between them,
heading down the aisle.

THE OLD LADY: "EXCUSE ME, PLEASE!"

LEFF: (Continuing) "That means we collect the Double Calamity if he dies in one of three ways . . . He has to crash in a
train, drown in a submarine, or fall from a blimp. Will he be
traveling in any one of those ways soon?"

PHYLLIS: "He's taking a blimp to San Francisco tomorrow
night."

Leff begins to softly whisper his plan to Phyllis.

PHYLLIS: (Not hearing him) "What? What? I didn't catch
that!"

THE OLD LADY: (Loudly) "HE SAID HE'D COME OVER
TO YOUR PLACE TOMORROW, STRANGLE YOUR
HUSBAND, AND THROW HIS BODY OUT OF A
BLIMP!"

The next night, Phyllis is keeping Carl busy in a game of Chinese
checkers when Leff shoots him and he collapses facedown into the
game board, scattering all the marbles.

Leff's narration tells us he was successful in throwing Carl's body
off the blimp, even though it landed smack in the middle of a football
game at the Rose Bowl. He thought he was in the clear when his
boss, Keyes (Lyle), calls him into the office.

KEYES: "Come in, Leff, I wanna talk to you. I've got one of
my stinkin' hunches about this Dietrichson thing."

LEFF: (Wary) "Oh?"

KEYES: "Yeah, it just doesn't add up. Here's a man with a bullet in his back, his mouth full of marbles, he's fallen out of a
blimp, and he ends up in the Rose Bowl stuffed in a tuba!"

LEFF: "It sounds like suicide to me."

The rest of the plot has Leff learning that Phyllis is cheating on him and that she plans to knock off "a dumb insurance agent." Leff confronts Phyllis at her home, and they wind up in an epic gun battle, shooting each other over and over. Leff leaves Phyllis, lifeless, on the living room floor.

We return to the beginning of the movie with Leff speaking into the Dictaphone.

LEFF: "Well, that's my story, Keyes. I'm signing off now." (Looking at the Dictaphone) "Aw nuts, I forgot to turn this thing on." (Turns it on and begins all over again) "Oh, well, it all started . . ."

KEYES: (Enters) "Never mind, Leff, I heard the whole thing."

LEFF: "Keyes. I hope you're not too disappointed in me."

KEYES: "Well, you're all washed up in the insurance game, I'll tell ya that much."

LEFF: "Please, Keyes, gimme another chance, will ya?"

KEYES: "Okay. Oh, by the way, somebody's out here to see you."

Phyllis crawls in on her belly, and fires one last
shot at Leff. Leff picks up the Dictaphone,
aims it at Phyllis and fires. They both die.

THE END

THIS WAS A hoot to do! In the original movie, the director Billy Wilder made the mistake of having Barbara Stanwyck wear a very unattractive blond wig, which was unflattering and looked totally false, so naturally I wore a wig just like it. Steve, as always, would come up with funny shtick that hadn't been in the script. For instance, I wore large pearl earrings, which Steve decided would be fun to toy with, as he was kissing my neck. When we broke away from each other, he had the earring in his mouth, and spit it out clear across the room! One other interesting tidbit happened during the scene when Steve and I are plotting my husband's demise. Over our shoulders, you can see a prop man's hand surreptitiously slip into the picture, placing a small objet d'art on the table behind us! This is just more proof that we did our show like a live show and never stopped to do a retake.

"Caged Dames"

This was great fun. It was our tribute to those movies featuring women in prison, usually from Warner Bros.

I play a tough convict, Spike DeBouvier. The wonderful Lily Tomlin is the sadistic matron, Munsie Riffka. Vicki is a dim-witted, wet-behind-the-ears prisoner and steals every scene she is in with her dumbbell persona.

We open with the sadistic matron, Munsie, who has lined up her jailbirds and is reading them the riot act, telling them that she treats everyone the same. A very old woman convict tries to speak up and Munsie slaps her silly, saying that she doesn't play favorites even though the old lady happens to be her own mother!

At this point, a tough-cookie convict, Spike, is brought in. Munsie's face lights up at the sight of her. They are old arch-enemies and Munsie is delighted to welcome her into "our little sorority house."

Spike laughs in Munsie's face and in no uncertain terms tells her that she's going to bust out of this prison, just like she has out of every prison in the country! Munsie laughs right back and tells Spike she's going to break her.

Spike is thrown into a jail cell with Vicki's character. She's determined to break out, but gets a little sentimental when she hears the lonely strains of "Goin' Home" being played on a harmonica by the young dimwit. Sitting down next to her on the cot, Spike says wistfully, "Y'know, kid, that sounds pretty good." The dimwit takes her empty hands away from her mouth and gleefully says, "Yeah, I can hardly wait till I get a harmonica!"

Spike asks the dimwit how long has she been in here and the dimwit replies, "Twenty-three," saying that in another hour it would be a whole day.

Spike says she plans to escape by confiscating spoons from the mess hall and digging her way out . . . *through the ceiling!* She's oblivious to the fact that the dimwit is writing down everything she's saying and passing the information through the cell bars to Munsie.

Munsie enters the cell and confronts Spike with the knowledge that she's onto Spike's plan to dig her way out through the ceiling! She then tells Spike that she's going to torture her.

Spike scoffs at the idea, telling Munsie that she has been in the hole, been in the sweat box, and been stretched on the rack!

Smiling, Munsie pulls out a small portable blackboard and shoves it in Spike's face.

She scrapes her fingernails down the blackboard, making a horrible screeching sound, causing Spike to collapse to the floor holding her ears and screaming for Munsie to stop, and swearing to behave. Munsie exits laughing and says that when she comes back, she's going to crack her knuckles. Spike thinks there's a stoolie in the cell, but is still in the dark as to who it might be.

Lily as Munsie, torturing me with her nails!

Spike picks the lock with a file and when Munsie returns to crack her knuckles, Spike overpowers her and grabs her gun, taking Munsie as a hostage.

Spike says she's getting out and taking Munsie as a hostage. The dimwit gets hysterical, and begs to go along. Spike hits her and she falls to the floor and sings in a bass voice, "Swing Low, Sweet Chariot." Spike asks her if she knows any "up tunes"!

As she exits with Munsie in tow, a priest enters (Steve Lawrence). It turns out he's Spike's brother! Munsie takes this opportunity to grab her gun and she and Spike wrestle for it. The gun goes off and Munsie is fatally wounded! Spike tells Munsie she's sorry and asks her forgiveness.

MUNSIE: (Beckoning) "Come closer . . . come a little closer . . ."

Spike bends closer, and Munsie gives the blackboard one final scrape with her fingernails, and dies.

SPIKE: "Rotten to the end."

Spike and her brother, the father, begin the long walk to the electric chair. Spike asks him to give their mother a message, and suddenly Harvey, in drag, as Mother Marcus enters. Mother Marcus has convinced the warden to pardon her daughter, and grabbing both Spike and her son, the father, she rants and raves about having them live with her again, smothering them into her ample bosom. Spike has had enough.

SPIKE: "I'd rather go to the chair!"

THE END

. . .

I HAD BEEN a fan of Lily's since I first saw her do her hilarious characters on *Laugh-In*, so I was thrilled when she agreed to get in the sandbox with us. A consummate actress, she brilliantly chose to play Munsie as a syrupy sweet sadist with a soft voice and a constant smile, making her all the more evil, instead of doing the character as the obvious tough and hard-as-nails prison matron.

I have to add here that when this was taped, I had a frozen shoulder, a "rotator-cuff" thing, and I had a rough time doing some of the physical stuff as this "tough cookie." I got through it okay, and nobody caught on. After several months of physical therapy, I was able to jump back into doing the stunts that I loved doing!

Shirley MacLaine

I first met Shirley when I was just starting out and was asked to do a guest shot on *The Dinah Shore Show* in 1958 (which was produced by Bob Banner). Dinah's show was very popular, and I was thrilled to be asked. Shirley, along with Pat Boone and Robert Cummings, were the other guests. I did a bit from my Blue Angel nightclub act. Shirley had just done a triumphant turn in the movie *Some Came Running*, receiving an Academy Award nomination for Best Actress. She was twenty-four. I was staying in the Hollywood Hawaiian Motel, which was just two blocks from where Nanny, Mama, and I had lived. In fact, it had been built on the site of my childhood playground where my friends and I played Tarzan and flew kites. Shirley sweetly offered me a chance to stay in a guest room in her home, but I shyly declined. Our paths crossed off and on during the next few years. She was terrific to work with. She was a guest on my show in 1975, and one of the bits we did was a number about the kinds of fan mail we get. In the middle of the song, we read some of the letters we had received. They weren't made up. They were real. For instance:

CAROL: (Reading) "Dear Carol Burnett, I have never missed one of your shows. I love everything you do. You're the funniest person alive and your show is the greatest. I have pictures of you all over my room. Every night before going to bed, I say 'Goodnight Carol, I love you.' And when I wake up, you're the first one I say good morning to. I thought it would be nice if you had a picture of me, too, so I'm enclosing a snapshot of myself." (Showing it to Shirley) "Here's her snapshot and on the back she writes, 'To my very favorite in the whole wide world, Lucille Ball!'"

SHIRLEY: (Reading) "Whenever my friends are talking about actresses they can't stand, I always stick up for you!"

CAROL: (Reading) "I don't know if I should tell you this or not, but every time you sing, my cat goes over to the TV set and puts his paws over your mouth!"

SHIRLEY: (Reading) "Dear Shirley, you're tops in my book. In fact, you're my idol. I think it's because we're so much alike. You see, my brother got all the looks in the family, too!" *(Shirley's brother, of course, is Warren Beatty.)*

CAROL: (Reading) "Dear Carol Burnett. My daughter looks exactly like you. Please write, and tell her there's hope."

Shirley and me singing about our fan mail.

We sing:

Are those your real teeth?
Is that your real hair?
Please could you send me a picture of Cher?
But please keep 'em comin'
It shows that you care
It's you who keeps screwballs like us
On the air
With your FAN MAIL, FAN MAIL, FAN MAIL!

The number ends with tons of letters dropping from the ceiling on top of us.

After the show Shirley gave me a beautiful silk sari that had been given to her by one of her Yoga teachers in India. It was such a thoughtful gesture. I still have it.

"Lovely Story"

Then along came our spoof of the 1970 tearjerker of a movie *Love Story*, which we called "Lovely Story." The film was a megahit starring Ali MacGraw as Jenny and Ryan O'Neal as Oliver, two star-crossed lovers from two different worlds who meet with a tragic end.

Harvey and I had a lot of fun doing this one.

"Tear Jerker Theater" features Vicki tearfully introducing the movie "Lovely Story." Harvey, as Oliver, a very wealthy heir to a vast fortune, enters the college library and falls in love with me as Jenny, working behind the desk. He is smitten, but she's not impressed with him at first. Eventually, after two minutes, they are head over heels in love and romp through the library *in slow motion* while fellow students enter playing violins.

Oliver takes her to meet his overbearing father, who, seeing that

Jenny is from the wrong side of the tracks, cuts Oliver off without a penny. Penniless, Oliver and Jenny live in a one-room apartment and are deliriously happy. Barely letting each other out of sight, they are constantly kissing and hugging and hugging and kissing, ad nauseam.

Maybe Ryan O'Neal didn't like Harvey's hair.

Oliver has been away and returns. Having missed him terribly, Jenny rushes into his arms, they kiss and kiss and kiss, and he finally suggests that next time, they both should take out the garbage.

There's a knock on the door, and Oliver gets a telegram with the good news that his law studies have paid off, and he has suddenly been appointed chief justice of the Supreme Court! They are over the moon, until Jenny *coughs* . . . Uh-oh.

She assures Oliver that it's nothing! And then faints dead away in Oliver's arms. He carries her to their bed, promising her the "best doctor money can buy!" As the sappy music swells in the background, Lyle enters.

Oliver wants to know who he is, and Lyle tells him that he is the best doctor money can buy. Oliver wants to know how the doctor knew Jenny was sick, and he replies that he heard the sappy music.

He examines Jenny and quietly informs Oliver that she has only five minutes to live. Devastated, Oliver puts on a happy face and skips over to Jenny, and lies to her, saying that the doctor says she's going to be fine. She's thrilled to hear the news and when Oliver asks her if she'd like something to eat *(What she says next is one of my very favorite lines in all the sketches we did)*, she replies, "I'd love a four-minute egg."

The sketch ends when Lyle informs Oliver that whatever disease Jenny had . . . "is very contagious" and Oliver coughs and collapses on the bed next to Jenny, while the doctor pulls out a tiny violin and plays sad music.

THE END

I HEARD FROM Ali MacGraw that she loved our spoof. At a party, not too long after the show aired, Ryan O'Neal, who played Oliver in the movie, cornered me and told me in no uncertain terms that he hated it, and "that guy who played me was awful!"

Huh?

"The Funn Family"

Our salute to the backstage musical:
Vicki, John Davidson, me, and Mickey Rooney.

In December 1967, our first season, we did the first of our many takeoffs on a *type* of movie, the backstage musical made popular in the forties and fifties. These were basically soap operas with music, especially those put out by 20th Century Fox. Our plots didn't satirize a specific film, but incorporated several movies. They were written completely from scratch, with the original songs and book by our writers. This particular send-up holds a special place in my heart. It was the first of many to come over the next eleven years.

Our movie musical salute was called "The Funn Family," written by a talented writing team who wrote both the book and the songs. It was the story of a vaudeville family in the early 1900s featuring Papa (Mickey) Funn, Mama (Fanny) Funn, and their children, Sonny Funn and Sissy Funn. Their act was terrible, and they were booed off the stage wherever they performed . . . however, they were grateful to have the fruits and vegetables that were thrown at them every so often.

Our guests that week were John Davidson, who played Sonny Funn, and Mickey Rooney, who was Papa Funn. I played Mama Funn and Vicki was Sissy Funn.

ACT I

The early 1900s. A vaudeville stage.
The Four Funns are singing their signature song:

There's no family like a show family
Like no family I know
Each of us is working for a common cause
And all we want for pay is your applause, applause, applause,
Because you've no business here in show business
If you're only in the business for the dough
Oh! There's no family like a show family
Like no family I know!

> *They finish the number to the sound*
> *of only one person clapping.*

In their backstage dressing room Sonny apologizes to Papa for messing up part of his performance.

SONNY: "I'm sorry, Dad, but there was a guy in the second row who was making strange noises with his hands!"
PAPA: "Sonny, that man was *applauding*!"
SONNY: "Well, it was very rude of him, Dad. The only time he stopped was when you came on!"

> *Papa shoots him a dirty look. Mama pulls Papa aside.*

MAMA: "Father, was that really applause?"
PAPA: "I wouldn't swear to it, Mother. It's been a while . . . I think so."
MAMA: "That must be what it's like to be in the big time!"
PAPA: "All we need to break into the big time is to get a new image! A new number!"

At this point, Papa comes up with the idea of writing a "Patriotic Song!" Encouraged by Mama, Sonny, and Sissy, he writes the song for a "Patriotic Trio." Papa (at the piano), Mama (wielding the American flag), Sonny (playing a drum), and Sissy (with a fife) sing the new number, ending with:

Yes, everyone knows
America's foes
Are gonna get their licks
We're the Spirit of . . . Seventy-Six!

As they finish, Ziggy Flofeld (Harvey)
enters the dressing room. He's applauding.

SONNY: (Alarmed) "Dad! Dad! There's that man doing that terrible thing again! Make him stop, Dad! Sing something!"
ZIGGY: "Forgive me for barging in. I'm Ziggy Flofeld."
ALL: "Ziggy Flofeld!!! The world-famous producer???"
ZIGGY: "The one and only. I happened to be passing by your dressing room on my way to Rangoon, and I heard that song you were singing. You may not believe this, but there's a spot in my next 'Flofeld Follies' for a Patriotic Trio."
PAPA: "Patriotic Trio! That's great! How many in a trio?"
MAMA: "Three, Father."

The penny drops (!) and Papa, realizing that there are four of them, begins to unsuccessfully grapple with Sonny for his drum! When Sissy won't relinquish her fife, Papa and Mama struggle over the flag she's holding!

MAMA: (Finally, tearfully crying out) "STOP IT! STOP IT! STOP IT! Is this what show business does to people? Turns father against son? Daughter against father? Wife against husband?" (Pause) "Patriotic Trio . . . against father? I'm sorry,

Mr. Flofeld, but if that's what success in show business does to people, we want no part of it. Do we, kids?"

They don't answer.

MAMA: (Annoyed) "Do we, kids? . . . Kids?"
SONNY AND SISSY: (Reluctantly) "Mom's right."

Papa is touched by Mama's speech, and bravely gives in.

PAPA: (Tearfully) "Here, Fanny, you keep your flag. I don't want it said that I'd stand in the way of my family's happiness. Don't worry, Mr. Flofeld, you'll get your Patriotic Trio." (False bravado) "Yes, I've been thinking of going out on my own! And now I can do it without hurting anybody! Yes, I'm gonna leave. Mother, don't cry." (Kisses her) "This is no time for tears. I'll be back, my darling. I'll be back when I'm a success."

He sadly leaves the dressing room.

SISSY: "I guess we'll never see him again."

ACT II

Four years have passed, and the Patriotic Trio has been a big hit in the "Flofeld Follies." Ziggy is now featuring them in a brand-new "Heavenly Production Number."

The curtain opens and we see angels dancing around. There are clouds high upstage. Sonny and Sissy are sitting together with a gold telephone between them. They sing:

Mother, Dear Mother, Dear Mother's gone away
She's gone away before
But now she's gone away to stay

The angels carried Mother
Way up in the sky
Before she had a chance to say good-bye
We miss the mother we once knew
As orphaned orphans often do
We know that you must miss us, too
And so we've placed this call to you

> *The upstage clouds part and we see Mother up in*
> *heaven. She's wearing wings and sporting a halo. Her*
> *gold telephone rings and she picks it up. They all sing:*

SONNY: *"Hello, heaven, let me speak to Mother."*
MOTHER: *"Hello, son, this is your mother dear. How are you*
and how's your little sister?"
SONNY: *"Sis is fine, and standing over here."* (Hands Sissy the
phone) *"Here."*
SISSY: *"Hello, Mother, how are things in heaven?"*
MOTHER: *"Heaven's heaven, but I miss you all."*
SONNY AND SISSY: *"We miss you, too, let's keep in touch."*
MOTHER: *"But telephoning costs so much. Next time, reverse*
the charges when you call."

Mama, Sonny, and Sissy are now major stars. Unknown to them,
all these years, Papa has been with them, posing as a stagehand, dis-
guised as Old Charlie, watching from the wings!

ACT III

> *Old Charlie is in the dressing room when Mama, Sonny,*
> *Sissy, and Ziggy enter, flush with their latest success. Ziggy*
> *is smitten with Fanny, and when he goes to hug her,*
> *Old Charlie physically puts himself between them. Ziggy*
> *complains, and Mama explains.*

MAMA: "This is Old Charlie, Ziggy, he's one of your stage-hands. You know, he's been hanging around Sonny and Sissy and me ever since Father left years ago. We feel like he's almost one of the family." (Pushing him out of the way, dismissively) "Go over there, Old Charlie."

ZIGGY: "Fanny, I can't wait to tell you about my new idea for the Three Funns!"

SONNY: "Ziggy, Mom, I've got to tell you something."

MAMA: "What is it, Sonny?"

SONNY: "I'm quitting show business. I've been in it long enough and I'm ready to take the next step!"

MAMA: "What next step, Sonny?"

SONNY: "Politics, Mom . . . I wanna be president of the United States!"

There is a pause, and then Mama hauls off and decks Sonny in the breadbasket!

MAMA: "Where did I go wrong???" (She apologizes to Sonny for knocking him down) "I guess from now on it'll just be Sissy and me."

SISSY: "Mom, there's something I've been meaning to tell you, and now's as good a time as any."

ZIGGY: (To Sissy) "Shhhush . . . !"

SISSY: "Not *that*, Uncle Ziggy! Mom, you know I've always had a deep interest in medicine."

MAMA: "But show business is in your blood!"

SISSY: "And I want to get out of it."

Mama relents. Sonny and Sissy leave to celebrate. Ziggy confesses his love to Fanny with Old Charlie still in the room looking on. Fanny tells Ziggy how she feels about love:

FANNY: "I'm a one-man woman, and I'm one woman whose man is a one-woman man, and when a one-man woman has won a one-woman man, the one man that that one woman won . . . is the one."

Old Charlie nods.

ZIGGY: "I knew you were gonna say that."
Ziggy convinces Fanny that he can make her the biggest star ever!
ZIGGY: "What do you say to that?"
OLD CHARLIE: (Piping up) "It's a deal!"

ACT IV

The years fly by, and now we find Fanny, as a very old lady, receiving a big show business honor for all the decades she has been a star: "A TRIBUTE TO THE GREATEST FANNY OF THEM ALL!"

After a huge production number, Fanny enters leaning on a cane and dressed to the nines. She speaks:

FANNY: "Ladies and gentleman, I am told that you have all come tonight to pay tribute to me. If this is so, you are paying tribute to the wrong person . . . True, I have won fame and fortune, but I owe it all to one person." (A very old Ziggy enters from the wings) "I'm speaking of my husband . . ." (Ziggy makes a hasty exit, and Fanny looks after him) "You old fool!" (Returning to her speech) "Mickey's not here. He left me many, many years ago, but he left me with two wonderful children . . ." (She nods off for a minute, then wakes up) ". . . two wonderful children who have gone on to great heights and have made this old woman very proud, indeed. I'm speaking of my son, Sonny Funn, whom some of you might know is president of the United States . . . and my daughter, Sissy Funn, five-time Nobel Prize winner and discoverer of a positive cure for hickeys. And now I would like to ring down the curtain on my fabulous career by singing the first song the Four Funns ever sang together." (Tearfully, looking up to heaven) "Mickey, my dear departed husband . . . wherever you are, darlin', this is for you . . ." (To the band) "HIT IT!"

She begins to sing:

"There's no family like a show family
Like . . . no . . . family I . . ."

She falters, and lo and behold, Sonny Funn, the president of the United States, stands up in the audience and begins to sing! He is followed by Sissy Funn, who joins in the song! They run up on stage and join their overwhelmed mother. They are happily singing away, when Old Charlie enters and, out of the blue, starts singing Papa Funn's part!

FANNY: (Screaming at Old Charlie) "You can't sing that! Papa always sang that!"

Old Charlie rips off his disguise to
reveal his true identity!

FANNY: (Furious) "You mean it's been YOU all this time? You were Old Charlie??? Why didn't you tell me??? You know how many men I turned down???"

They have a very loud argument while Sonny keeps singing away, with Sissy doing a tap dance that ends with her kicking Fanny's cane, causing her mother to collapse as the number comes to a close!

THE END

. . .

THIS TAKEOFF WAS twenty-five minutes long! In future shows we would continue to take our own sweet time with parodies. This wouldn't happen in today's television climate. The networks don't believe that an audience would have the necessary attention span. I disagree. I think it all depends on the quality of the writing.

Mickey Rooney

Mickey was absolutely amazing as Papa Funn, in "The Funn Family." The entire week was a joyful romp. He was fun to be with, and I loved watching him come up with one wonderful bit of business after another during rehearsals.

He brought his original shtick to every scene and enhanced an already hysterically funny script. I had been a huge fan of Mickey's ever since I saw my first "Mickey and Judy" movie. There was nothing he couldn't do as a performer. He sang, danced, played many musical instruments, and was a great comedian. He could also make you cry because he was a fine dramatic actor. He was, without a doubt, one of *THE* most talented people in show business, *ever*. I don't think anyone could argue with that.

So I was thrilled when he accepted our invitation to get in the sandbox with us, and after his performance in "The Funn Family," I couldn't wait to have him back for another "funn"-filled week when we were picked up for our second season.

The second season rolled around, and the script for Mickey's appearance that week didn't measure up to "The Funn Family" episode the previous season. I hoped he wouldn't be too disappointed when he came to the first table reading on Monday. He was right on time and bounded into the rehearsal hall, smiling and waving and even slapping a lot of us on the back. He reminded me of the Road Runner on a pogo stick. He laughed heartily at the (I thought) mediocre jokes in the main sketch. I was relieved that he liked what he read, but he was bubbling over *so* much that it was slightly unnerving. It was as if he had an IV of caffeine constantly pumping throughout his veins. He talked a mile a minute and never sat down for a single second all week. Think of a Ping-Pong ball constantly bouncing off the walls. I worried about him throughout the week, and when our Friday taping day rolled around *I* was exhausted! However, when we taped the show that night, the trouper in him came through. He was as wonderful and professional as ever. He gave the sketch his all, and the audience loved him.

And I was ready to go home and get into bed!

After the show, I knocked on his dressing room door to thank him for being with us again. He took my hands in his and said, "I gotta apologize to you, Carol."

"For what, Mickey?"

He squeezed my hand. "For how I was that whole week last year when I was on your show the first time."

"I don't understand, you were fabulous."

"No. I was *depressed*, but I'm glad I was back to being my regular self this week."

Nanette Fabray

N an was a guest on our show thirteen times. I loved working with her. She could do it all: act, sing, and dance. Plus, she had a great set of comedy chops. I fell in love with her work when she was Sid Caesar's costar on *Caesar's Hour*, for which she won three Emmy Awards. She began her career performing in vaudeville as a child and became a musical theater actress during the 1940s and 1950s, winning a Tony Award in 1949 for her performance in *Love Life*.

We did several sketches together. One of my favorites was our takeoff on *42nd Street*, which we called "43rd Street." She played a musical comedy diva, starring in a Broadway show, who is thwarted at every turn by my character, a dumb, klutzy chorus girl. As her clumsy understudy I accidentally cause *her* to wind up in a wheelchair sporting a leg cast and two arm casts plus a neck brace. At one point, she spits out a mouthful of teeth, while I go on to replace her in the show!

In another sketch, I was the plain, efficient secretary to Harvey's boss, while Nan was the other (very sexy) secretary in the same office, who has trouble sharpening a pencil but no trouble in making the boss hot to trot! She was hysterical.

Nanette singing and signing to
"Over the Rainbow."

Nan had overcome a hearing impairment, and she became an advocate for the rights of the deaf and hard of hearing. Her honors representing the handicapped include the President's Distinguished Service Award and the Eleanor Roosevelt Humanitarian Award.

I'll never forget the number she did on our show when she sang a powerful, poignant sign-language version of "Over the Rainbow," a cappella. As she was singing and signing, our cameras panned the studio audience, and rested on the faces of a couple of children . . . a young boy and a young girl. They sat there, completely still (almost not blinking), looking at and listening to Nan's extraordinary rendition, completely mesmerized.

Beautiful. Simply beautiful.

EMBARRASSING MOMENTS

*B*abes in Arms was the iconic Mickey Rooney and Judy Garland movie made in 1939. Our tribute was called "Babes in Barns," and featured Ken Berry and me as the fresh-off-the-farm teenagers (Mickey and Judy) with stars in their eyes, who decide to put on a show hoping it will wind up on Broadway. With the encouragement of Harvey and Vicki as an old vaudevillian couple and with the help of their local teenage pals, Mickey and Judy write the music and lyrics, build the scenery, sew the costumes, and mount an elaborate musical in a barn in a matter of minutes, hoping to attract a big New York producer.

As Judy, I was singing a song about my love for Mickey. I'm in an outdoor setting, and we have a live horse in the background to complete the bucolic atmosphere. As I'm wailing away doing an over-the-top "Judy," unbeknownst to me, but in full view of the studio audience, the horse decides to answer the call of nature. His handler rushes out to catch it all in a bucket, and hearing the audience howling, I turned around in time to see the handler remove his cowboy hat and take a deep bow. I was hysterical right along with the audience and our crew. When the laughter subsided to a quiet roar, I looked toward our conductor Pete Matz in the band shell and said, "You wanna pick it up from number one or number two?"

Tim later said, "I have a confession to make. I also was peeing while you were singing."

Nature calls.

HARVEY'S MOST EMBARRASSING moment came one night in 1975 when his idol, the brilliant actor Laurence Olivier, was in the audience. Sir Laurence was there because he was renting our beach house while he was in California filming *Marathon Man*, and he asked if he could attend one of our tapings. Harvey was a basket case. He and Tim were doing a sketch where Tim was the inept Old Man who was waiting on Harvey in a deli. The sketch winds up with Tim's character accidentally ripping off Harvey's (breakaway) pants, leaving Harvey standing there in his boxer shorts. Except . . . when he was making his quick change, Harvey forgot to put on the boxer shorts and when his pants fell down at the end of the sketch he stood there, frozen, in his Jockey shorts.

Yes, he flashed Sir Laurence Olivier.

EARLIER THAT SAME year, Peggy, the real estate agent who sold us our beach house, asked us if we'd be interested in renting it out for the summer. This wasn't the first time she had brought up the subject. She had asked us several times before, and I always told her that we had no interest in having other people live in our house for three months. Peggy was like a dog with a bone, and wouldn't give up. Exasperated, this time I said, "Peggy, I'll never rent out our beach house unless it's to Sir Laurence Olivier!" thinking that would forever end the discussion.

Sir Lawrence ogles Harvey.

The following week, I got a call from her: "It seems the film *Marathon Man* is being shot in California, and guess who wants to rent a beach house?"

So that's how it came to be that Sir Laurence was responsible for Harvey's most embarrassing moment.

"ARE THOSE YOUR OWN TEETH?" AND OTHER QUESTIONS I'VE ANSWERED

I bring out Tim, who is asked by an audience member, "How long are you gonna wait before you get a toupee?" Before he can answer, I ask Tim, "I've heard balding men are quite sexy, is that true?" Tim replies, "I don't know, I've never been out with one."

AUDIENCE MEMBER ASKS me, "Have you always been as beautiful as you are now?"

"No, you won't believe this, but at one time I was very plain."

Another question: "Who's your plastic surgeon?"

"Phyllis Diller."

I'M ASKED IF I've always had red hair. "To be honest, no. I was born bald."

ANOTHER TIME A young boy with bright red hair asks, "Were you ever teased about your red hair when you were in school?"

"No . . . I didn't *have* red hair!"

A MAN IN the audience wants to know if the show can be on earlier. "Sometimes I fall asleep during your show."

"DO YOU REMEMBER your first kiss?"

"Yes . . . it was from a dog."

. . .

A LITTLE BOY in the audience asks, "What are your measurements?"
"What do you think they are?"
He says, "46, 24, and 108."

THERE WAS A week in January where we had a lot of rain in Los Angeles. I'm asked about it, and I go on and on about how much I love rain, finally winding up with "To me a day without rain is like a day without sunshine." The audience howls.

I'M ASKED ABOUT the Mickey Mouse watch I'm wearing. "It's so easy to tell time with the little hand and the big hand. He's really cute when it's 6:30."

ANOTHER AUDIENCE MEMBER wants to know, "How'd you get such white teeth?" I brag about how I brush them six or seven times a day, which prompts cameraman Pat Kenny to applaud sarcastically. I look straight into his camera and say, "Why don't you run home and pick yours up off the bedside table?"

SEVERAL AUDIENCE MEMBERS ask me to say hello to relatives or friends who are not present. It gets to be a running gag, and then Pat Kenny pipes up, "Would you say hello to my wife?"
"I would, Pat, but I don't know *which* one of them *is* your wife!"

I'M ASKED, "ARE those your own teeth?"
"Do you think I'd *buy* these?"

A LITTLE BOY asks, "How does a boy get to be an actress?" The audience cracks up. I tell him, "That's not too hard nowadays."

. . .

A MAN IN the audience: "Is it true to get on TV all you need is a pretty face?"

"Yes."

I'M ASKED ABOUT violence on television. "I can't watch it. I know we do a lot of it in our show, getting shot, pushed out of windows, having fistfights, getting blown up, etc., etc., but it's all *cartoon* violence. Think Bugs Bunny."

I TELL THE audience about a woman who raised her hand during the Q&A three weeks ago and said she had written a song for me to sing. We then showed the three-week-old tape to the audience, where I called her up on stage and asked the woman her name: "Sue Vogelsanger." I promised to sing the song on a future show.

"That was three weeks ago, and tonight I'm going to sing Sue's Song." I introduce Sue and her husband, who are in the audience to hear my rendition of her song.

Naturally, it was thought that I would simply stand there and sing Sue's song in front of a curtain, but . . . the curtain rises, and we're into a full-blown major production number staged by Ernie Flatt, with all the dancers and me in formal attire. There are humongous (over six feet tall) white letters on wheels spelling out S-U-E V-O-G-E-L-S-A-N-G-E-R, which the dancers push around, while I'm singing, to spell out, among other things, "SUE'S SONG SAVES LOVERS."

After the number, I go into the audience and hug a very surprised Sue Vogelsanger. *(One of our musical writers took Sue's song and arranged it into a jazz waltz, which was a hoot! Needless to say, after that aired we were inundated with tons of songs sent by would-be composers and lyricists!)*

A SURPRISE "GUEST" is introduced. The governor of California, Ronald Reagan, enters to much applause. He is asked if he would ever

With Governor Reagan.

like to live in Washington, D.C. His reply: "I don't understand why anyone would want to live anyplace else but California!"

ONE WEEK A woman waved her hand eagerly, I called on her and she stood up and said, in no uncertain terms, "I wanna come up and sing a song!" She looked like Bea Arthur and was even dressed in a Maude-like outfit. I said, "C'mon up." Well, she immediately shot up onto the stage and before I could ask her what she wanted to sing, she turned to the band shell, pointed her finger, and hollered to Pete Matz and the orchestra, "'YOU MADE ME LOVE YOU' IN THE KEY OF G!"

The audience screamed with laughter, but she just shushed them and began belting it out—and I do mean belting it! She was fearless and she was pretty good, too. After she got through the first couple of bars, I thought it would be fun to join her, and the solo became a duet. We were both wailing away in harmony and the audience was clapping to the rhythm. We were having a ball. Until, that is, we began to have different ideas as to how the number should wind up. I had one idea for ending it vocally and she had a completely different one. The number was petering out, and we were just kind of hanging there looking at each other, not knowing how to finish when, obviously pissed off, she shot me a look and said, "YOU SCREWED IT UP!" The audience ate it up and I thought she was pure gold.

AN AUDIENCE MEMBER asks if there are "planned questions."
   "NO."

THE NIGHT I GOT EVEN

On several occasions I noticed that I would get a question, and before I could answer, the entire crew, including the cameramen, would burst into laughter. Why? Because someone in the director's booth had made a wisecrack that elicited guffaws from everyone in the crew, who wore earpieces and therefore could hear what was being said in the booth. It irritated me to be in the dark about what they were laughing at, sooo . . . one week, I decided to get back at the culprits in the booth, i.e., our director, our associate director, our script supervisor, our head writer, and, of course, our producer, Joe. I asked Bob Mackie to make me an opening dress that sported a turtleneck. I confiscated one of the earpieces that connected to the booth and hid it in my ear, camouflaging it with my hair. The wire was tucked down and hidden by the turtleneck on my gown and you'd never have known I was "wired for action." The only ones in on the gag were Bob and my dresser, Annette Gagnon. The overture to our theme began, and I heard our director, Dave Powers, from the booth say, "Okay, cue Carol!" It was working! I could hear every word they were saying in the booth. Our stage manager, Willie Dahl, waved me on and I walked out on stage waving to our audience. As usual, I announced who our guests were for that evening and then asked for the lights to be bumped up so I could kid around with the audience.

QUESTION: "Will you ever make another movie?"

(I hear Dave in the booth quip, "Who the hell cares?")

CAROL: (Paraphrasing) "I don't know, but who the heck would care?"

(Surprised laughter in the booth, thinking my answer is a coincidence.)

QUESTION: "How do you keep your figure?"

(Quip from the booth: "No one else wants it!")

CAROL: (Paraphrasing) "Who else would want it?"

(The booth: "What's going on?")

QUESTION: "Would you do the Tarzan yell?"

(Quip from the booth, "Yeah, we can't wait to hear that for the thousandth time!")

CAROL: (Paraphrasing) "You know, I bet I've done the yell over a thousand times, but here goes!"

Now the booth is catching on, and I hear them all screaming, "She's wearing an earpiece! She's got an earpiece on!" I hear them tell Pat Kenny, who's on Camera 4, to swing around behind me and look for the wire. He does, and there's nothing to see because my hair and turtleneck costume are fulfilling their mission. I completely ignore Pat's camera maneuver and the very loud hoots coming from the booth of "We know you can hear us!" I continue to take questions from the audience, and all the while, at the same time, the booth is yelling in my ear (including a few obscenities) to get a rise out of me. Some Girl Scouts come up on stage, and as I'm buying cookies from them, the booth is screaming, "Look out! They're really enemy midgets in drag! The cookies are going to explode!"

Even though it was hard, I never let on that I could hear them screaming at me throughout the rest of the Q&A bit. After the show, as we were driving home, Joe asked me about it.

"C'mon, you were wearing an earpiece during Q&A, right?"

"What are you talking about?" I asked innocently.

Ken and Mitzie Welch

Even though Ken and Mitzie didn't come on our show until the fifth year as special musical material writers, our relationship dates back to 1955. I met Ken when I was auditioning for summer stock that year and he was the piano player. He was also a vocal coach and special material writer. He gave me his name and phone number, saying he'd like to work with me someday. In the fall, after I returned from doing summer stock at Green Mansions in the Adirondacks, I called Ken and we began to work on material for future auditions. At the time, I was living at the Rehearsal Club in New York City, which was a boardinghouse for young women hoping to be in the theater. The rent was eighteen dollars a week, room and board! This was when I had a part time job as a hat-check girl, so I paid Ken ten dollars a session in dimes and quarters. In 1957, he and I auditioned our special musical-comedic material at the Blue Angel nightclub. The Angel was the "in" cabaret, over on the East Side of Manhattan. I was hired!

As my opening number, Ken wrote a very funny song, "I Made a Fool of Myself Over John Foster Dulles." This was during the height of the Elvis craze, and the song was about a young girl going ape, not over a rock star but over our then Secretary of State, Mr. Dulles. As far as his public image was concerned, he was aptly named. He wore glasses, a fedora, a heavy coat, and, usually, a very dour expression. He was the least likely candidate for anyone to swoon over, which is what made the number so funny. The song caught on, and I performed it three times in one week on television, twice on *The Jack Paar Show,* and once on *The Ed Sullivan Show.*

A week later, I was watching *Meet the Press,* and Mr. Dulles was the guest. The hour was almost over and there was one final question: "Mr. Secretary, what's going on between you and the young lady who sings that love song about you?" I was glued to the set. He kind of smiled—an actual smile!—I swear I could see a twinkle in his eye, and he said, "I make it a policy never to discuss matters of the heart in public." After that, nobody could tell me he didn't have a sense of humor.

After I got on *The Garry Moore Show,* Ken was hired to write the musical material. That's when Julie Andrews and I first performed together. Ken wrote a special treatment of the song "Big D," from the musical *The Most Happy Fella,* which featured Julie and me as cowgirls. The chemistry between the two of us clicked so much that the studio audience that night gave us a standing ovation. It led to *Julie and Carol at Carnegie Hall,* in 1962, which won all sorts of awards.

The writing credits read Ken Welch and Igor Peschkowsky (Mike Nichols), who worked with Ken on the special material and chose to have his real name listed in the credits.

After that, Ken teamed up with his talented wife, Mitzie, and they wound up writing all the musical material for several specials I did: *Carol + 2* with Lucy and Zero Mostel, in 1966; *Julie and Carol at Lincoln Center,* in 1971; *Sills (Beverly) and Burnett at the Met,* in 1972; (and later on) *Burnett Discovers Domingo (Placido),* in 1984; and *Julie and Carol Together Again,* in 1989.

THE MINI-MUSICALS

The medleys weren't the only times we sang. Our wonderful writers came up with the brilliant idea of putting together "mini-musicals," which were "salutes" to various composers and lyricists, weaving stories around their songs, creating an original story line with a beginning, a middle, and an end.

One of my favorites was a salute to Richard Rodgers. Our guest that week was Eydie Gormé, who was perfect for this material. In introducing the musical sketch, I told the audience that Richard Rodgers wrote over 750 songs, and we apologized for leaving out 730! The plot was based on *The Captain's Paradise.* I loved it, because it was not only brilliant musically, it was funny. This is how it was done. (The songs we used are in *italics.*)

The setting is the early 1900s. We're in a hospital room where Judd (Harvey) is a pilot who flew a mail route for the U.S. Postal Service. He's hovering between life and death after having crashed his plane. His faithful mechanic, Eddie (Tim), asks the nurse (Vicki) if Judd's going to make it. It's "iffy," he's told. They sit vigil at the foot of Judd's bed, and Eddie begins to tell the saga of Judd, as *"Climb Ev'ry Mountain"* plays in the background.

EDDIE: "Why he's the best darn pilot in the whole sky! He was the first guy to carry the U.S. mail from Tulsa to Kansas City. Boy, *'If They Asked Me, I Could Write a Book'*! I remember the first flight he made from Kansas City all the way to Tulsa! Two hundred miles, nonstop!"

FLASHBACK: We see Judd in his plane, happily singing "Oklahoma!"

Eddie (voice-over) tells the nurse that Judd had fallen for a clean-cut cheerleader. We see Maria (Carol) waiting for Judd at the airport with flowers. They sing:

JUDD: *"Don't throw bouquets at me."*
MARIA: *"Don't please my folks too much."*
JUDD: *"Don't laugh at my jokes too much."*
BOTH: *"People will say we're in love."*
EDDIE: (Voice-over) "Yeah, and they were, too. Course, he had to deliver the mail."

Judd lands in Kansas City and goes to "Mimi's Club," where he meets the sexy nightclub singer Mimi (Eydie Gormé).

MIMI: (Singing slowly and provocatively)
*"Everything's up to date in Kansas City
They've gone about as far as they can go!"*

*Judd is immediately smitten!
Mimi reciprocates! They sing:*

JUDD:
*"Some enchanted evening
You may see a stranger
You may see a stranger"*

BOTH: *"Across a crowded room!"*

MIMI:
"I took one look at you
It's all I meant to do
And then my heart stood still"

EDDIE: (Voice-over) "Yeah, and it did, too. It was love at first sight for Mimi and Judd . . . *and Maria!*"

> *Judd exits and is in his plane, on the way back to Maria.*

JUDD: (Singing)
"How do you solve a problem like Maria?
How do you catch a cloud and pin it down?"

> *The plane turns around and he's flying back to Mimi.*

JUDD: (Singing)
"Mimi, you funny little good for-nothing Mimi
Am I the guy?"

> *He turns around again, flying back to Maria.*
> *He's courting both of them!*

> *We see Maria and Mimi (split screen),*
> *each holding the same photo of Judd, singing:*

MARIA AND MIMI:
"Lover, please be tender
When you're tender
Fears depart
Lover, I surrender to my heart!"

EDDIE: (Voice-over) "He got married . . . to both of 'em!"

> *Judd is marrying Maria. They sing:*

Judd marries Maria.

JUDD: *"Thou swell"*
MARIA: *"Thou witty"*
JUDD: *"Thou sweet"*
MARIA: *"Thou grand! Wouldst kiss me pretty?"*

They exchange rings and kiss.

Next, we see Judd marrying Mimi! They sing:

Judd marries Mimi.

JUDD: *"Thou swell"*
MIMI: *"Thou witty"*
BOTH: *"Thou grand!"*

They exchange rings and kiss.

EDDIE: (Voice-over) "Yes, for four years he lived two lives, just hoppin' back and forth like a sparrow in heat!"

*Maria and Judd are in their cozy home
snuggling happily. They sing:*

MARIA:
*"In our mountain greenery
Where God paints the scenery
Just two crazy people together!"*

JUDD:
*"This can't be love
Because I feel so well
No sobs, no sorrows, no sighs . . ."*

He checks his watch. Time for Mimi!

JUDD: (Singing)
*"So long, farewell
Auf Wiedersehen
Good-bye!
I leave and heave a sigh
I have to fly!"*

EDDIE: (Voice-over) "Yeah, and he flew to Mimi! She was ready for him, the lucky devil! Boy was she ready!"

MIMI: (Singing, hot to trot)
"I couldn't sleep
And wouldn't sleep
Bewitched, bothered, and bewildered
Am I"

JUDD: (Singing apologetically)
"I didn't know what time it was!
Life was no prize
I wanted love
And here it was
Shining out of your eyes!"

They embrace passionately. He glances at his watch.
Oops, time to get back to Maria!

JUDD: (Singing)
"I'm wise and I know what time it is now!
So long, farewell
Auf Wiedersehen
Good-bye!
I leave and heave a sigh
I have to fly!"

EDDIE: (Voice-over) "He sure had the best of both worlds.
Let's see now, whose turn was it next? Oh yeah, Maria."

Judd is hugging Maria.

JUDD: (Singing)
"A hundred and one
Pounds of fun

That's my little Honey Bun
Get a load of Honey Bun tonight!"

> *Maria turns around and we see she is very pregnant!*

MARIA: (Singing, patting her stomach)
"June is bustin' out all over!
All over the meadow and the hill!"

JUDD: (Singing)
"So long, farewell
Auf Wiedersehen, good-bye!"

> *Judd is back with Mimi, who pleads with him.*

MIMI: (Singing)
"Don't change a hair for me
Not if you care for me
Stay, little Valentine, STAY!"

EDDIE: (Voice-over) "And he did. But only long enough to deliver his mail!"

> *Judd passionately kisses Mimi. We see*
> *Maria at home feeding the baby.*

MARIA: (Singing)
"I'm just a girl who can't say no!
I can't be prissy and quaint
I ain't the type that can faint
How can I be what I ain't?
I can't say NO!"

Judd is flying back to Maria.

JUDD: (Singing)
"The hills are alive
With the sound of music
With songs they have sung
For a thousand years . . ."

UH-OH! Engine trouble!

JUDD: (Singing, nervously)
"Whenever I feel afraid,
I hold my head erect
And whistle a happy tune (He tries, but nothing comes out!)
So no one will suspect . . .
I'M AFRAID!!!"

The plane crashes! We're back in the hospital room, where
Eddie is telling Judd's story to the nurse, who has fallen
asleep from boredom.

EDDIE: "I always said I was the world's best mechanic. I took
care of that plane as if she were mine. Greased her wingtips,
flipped her flaps . . . yeah, the only thing I forgot to do was
put enough gas in her. She sure was a special plane, the old
Maria-Mimi, she had everything!"

We hear Judd waking out of his coma.

JUDD: (Weakly singing about his beloved airplane)

"The wheels are yellow
The upholstery's brown
The dashboard's genuine leather . . ."

Eddie and the nurse rush to his side. Eddie confesses
that his goof made the plane crash and begins to cry.
Judd forgives him and they hug.

JUDD: (Singing)
"Climb ev'ry mountain
Ford every stream
Follow every rainbow
Till . . . you . . . find . . . your dream . . ."

He relapses. Eddie is bereft.
The nurse puts her arm around Eddie.

NURSE: (Singing)
"Happy talk
Keep talkin'
Happy talk
Talk about things you like to do
You've got to have a dream
If you don't have a dream
How you gonna have a dream come true?"

Suddenly both Maria and Mimi show up! They stare at
each other suspiciously and then, uh-oh, Mimi spots Maria's
picture on one side of Judd's bed . . . and Maria spots Mimi's
picture on the other side! The strains of "Getting to Know
You, Getting to Know All About You!" are heard! Judd
comes to again and sees his wives together. He's caught!

JUDD: (Singing) *"One girl for my dreams"*

Maria and Mimi are livid. They remove their
wedding rings and throw them on the bed.

JUDD: (Continuing)
"One partner in Paradise
This promise of Paradise
This nearly was mine!"

MARIA AND MIMI: (Singing)
"I'm gonna wash that man
Right outta my hair!
And send him on his way!"

JUDD: (Singing, and dying)
"Adieu, adieu,
To you, and you and you . . ."

　　　He's gone. Eddie wails, "Poor Judd is dead!"

　　　Maria and Mimi cry. They're now widows.
　　　　They sing about their predicament.

MARIA AND MIMI:
"The broken dates
The endless waits
The lovely lovin'
And the hateful hates
The conversation with the flying plates!
I wish I was in love again."

　　They keep singing, and Eddie and the nurse join them.
　　Maria and Mimi come on to Eddie, much to the annoyance
　　of the nurse. They finish with a rousing "I WISH I WAS
　　　　　　IN LOVE AGAIN!"

　　Who should appear as a vision in the sky but Judd! He's
　　　sporting wings and benevolently sings:

Judd goes to Heaven.

JUDD:
"Hello, young lovers
Whoever you are
I hope your troubles are few
All my good wishes go with you tonight
I've been in love like you
I've had a love of my own like yours
I've had a LOVE OF MY OWN!"

Judd floats away into the clouds and the nurse grabs
Eddie for herself, leaving Maria and Mimi in the dust.

THE END

THE WRITERS CAME up with several more of these mini-musicals, featuring salutes to Irving Berlin, Cole Porter, the Gershwins, Frank Loesser, Lerner and Loewe, Harold Arlen, Stephen Sondheim, Harnick and Bock, Rodgers and Hammerstein, Jerome Kern, Jule Styne, and on and on. Sometimes running as long as fifteen minutes, each one was amazingly conceived and produced as our finale. The sets, the costumes, the orchestrations, and the execution were worthy of a Broadway show.

We sang live, the orchestra was live, and we did all of these in one take. The only time we had to prerecord and lip-synch part of a number was when the camera was in a wide shot and we couldn't have a microphone showing! However, when we did prerecord, we still sang with the orchestra, which made it sound more "live."

Today there are filmed shows where the music comes from someone sitting at a computer using something called Pro Tools, which is a computer editing program that puts together all the various components of a recording—singers, orchestra, etc. An orchestration is sent overseas to be prerecorded by musicians in a foreign country. The performer then records the song to that orchestration in a sound studio, and will lip-synch the entire number when it's shot. Also, if there is more than one person in the number, they are often recorded separately, and their voices are put together later in the studio. Pro Tools also has the capability of correcting the pitch of a sour note or changing entire keys without affecting the tempo.

Naturally, when it comes time to shoot the number, there are many takes because of the several camera angles needed.

I realize that I'm comparing film with the live feeling of taping in front of an audience. I know it's apples and oranges. I understand that this is pretty much the way it's done today, and I can appreciate that fact. I'm sure cost figures in, but sometimes after all the prerecording and tweaking, when it's all over, everything is so darned perfect it sounds fake. When I did the movie *Annie*, we recorded all the songs with the orchestra right there—in the same room—just like when they record a Broadway original cast album.

Frank Sinatra and many other singers of his era also insisted on recording their albums in the same room with the orchestra. To me, this sounds a hundred times better than these manufactured recordings. Tony Bennett still does it that way.

If these mini-musicals were to be taped today, it would be an entirely different ball game because not too many folks in front of, or behind, the camera were raised on live television. Also, many of us were coming from theater back then, which gave us a leg up. Added to that, we mounted our entire one-hour show, often featuring these elaborate fifteen- to twenty-minute finales, in five days, taping the entire thing in front of a live studio audience in less than two hours! I was spoiled. I admit it.

We had brilliant writing, music, costumes, choreography, direction, camerawork, and a crew that became family from the get-go.

And boy, did we have fun.

AUSTRALIA

We got some great news in the fall of 1973: an invitation to be the first television show to premiere at the new Sydney Opera House! We were pretty excited. Joe would produce, of course. Our director, Dave Powers, would be on board, as well as our associate producer, Bob Wright; our associate director, Roger Beatty; our choreographer, Ernie Flatt; our lead dancer, Don Crichton; a couple of our writers; and Vicki, Tim, Harvey, Lyle, and I. We booked the brilliant ballet artist Edward Villella to be our guest star.

But first, we had to get there. Joe and I, along with Harvey, Tim, Lyle, and Vicki, decided to break up the long trip by stopping off in Honolulu at the Kahala Hilton Hotel for a couple of days, so we wouldn't be laid low by jet lag.

Bob Wright, Dave Powers, and Roger Beatty were going to fly to Sydney nonstop, but something went wrong with their plane, and after the six-hour flight from Los Angeles, they wound up having to stop in Honolulu so that whatever the problem was could be fixed. An hour or two went by while they were waiting by the hotel pool. Unfortunately, they were dressed in warm clothes . . . sweaters, heavy jackets, etc., which were becoming pretty uncomfortable under the hot Hawaiian sun. Since they weren't registered at the hotel, as the afternoon wore on without any update on the plane repairs, they decided to buy some cooler Hawaiian shirts from the gift shop and sit outside on the hotel's beachfront and partake of several mai tais. With the sun shining down on them ever so brightly, Bob, Dave, and Roger . . . got drunk. Bob was still able to keep it together enough to continue calling the airport, hoping for any news about when the plane was going to resume its flight to Sydney. Still no luck.

It was decided that we should all go out to dinner and get some food into our tipsy trio. The food didn't help much. The guys were still pretty "jolly," so Joe said he would take over and keep calling about the flight. However, Bob *insisted* that he was on top of things (thank you very much) and was perfectly capable of calling the airport from the restaurant to find out if they should go straight out there or needed to return to the hotel.

There is something very funny about a person who has had one too many and tries his best to look, act, and speak as if he's sober. He speaks and walks *very* carefully. That was Bob that evening in the restaurant. When we were finished with the meal, he pushed back his chair, *very slowly* got up, and looking down at the floor, very deliberately put one foot in front of the other as he headed for the telephone, slightly swaying from side to side. After a few minutes, he (again) *very slowly* made his way back to our table. After some effort to sit down again, he paused, trying to collect his thoughts, and finally he looked at all of us (breathlessly waiting for him to say *something!*).

"Go. . . . . , hotel."

We teased Bob about that night forevermore. "Go hotel" became our nickname for him.

Bob, Dave, and Roger finally took off safely, and the rest of us had another two days in paradise before we were to follow. The last night in Honolulu, we were all sitting around a little outside bar on the beach that had a thatched roof with a palm tree growing straight up through an opening in its ceiling, stretching out over the roof. It was getting late, and we were having a final nightcap before turning in. As we were getting ready to leave, Tim got off his stool, said "Night all!" and, jumping over the bar, proceeded to *climb up the palm tree* like a monkey and disappear through the opening. Laughing hysterically, we waited and waited, and he never came down. He was determined to stay up there on the roof and wait for all of us to give up and go to our rooms. We finally did. I'll bet he practiced climbing on that palm tree earlier in the day, knowing exactly what he was going to do that night.

We all got to Sydney in one piece and started to rehearse. After a few days we got a call from the prime minister's office. The prime minister, Gough Whitlam, was in Japan, but his wife, Margaret, invited the cast and crew to their residence for a lovely lunch. She was a very tall, cheerful woman and a great hostess. At one point during the lunch, the doorbell rang and Mrs. Whitlam answered it. When she returned to the dining room, she informed me, "There are several newspaper reporters outside and they'd like you and me to come out on the balcony and pose for pictures. Do you mind?" Not at all. We went outside and posed for a few minutes while the cameras clicked away. The next day, a huge picture of Mrs. Whitlam and me was on the front page of Australia's main newspaper. The caption was "The First Lady of Australia Hosts the First Lady of Comedy." Very nice . . . but then . . . the article went on to talk about how Mrs. Whitlam had invited us to lunch and how we were all having such an "amusing" time except that "Mrs. Whitlam was *not* so amused when Miss Burnett showed up for lunch bringing with her a gaggle of reporters."

I couldn't believe it. I called Mrs. Whitlam, practically crying, and she told me not to pay any attention to the article, because their newspapers liked to make things up.

So much for the Fourth Estate in Australia.

Back to rehearsals: We decided on a musical opening that would have the dancers outside on the steps of the beautiful Sydney Opera House performing to the tune of "Waltzing Matilda." After that number, we would be inside on the stage, and I would open the show singing "It's Today!" from the Broadway musical *Mame*. Harvey, Vicki, and I would do sketches, and Tim would appear as the world's oldest maestro and conduct the symphony orchestra to the tune of "Flight of the Bumblebee." Edward Villella had a solo turn, and then our finale would be a fractured version of *Swan Lake* featuring Edward as the hero and me as the Charwoman, who gets to dance with him.

Fracturing Swan Lake with Edward Villella
(if you think this action shot is blurry, you
should have been in my shoes!).

We were all staying at the same hotel, which had gorgeous views of the harbor and the opera house, and we would get together in the evenings after rehearsals to try the various wonderful restaurants around town. I noticed that our group began to shrink after a few days, which can happen when you are on location. People split off and form liaisons—major and mini love affairs were blooming like daffodils in spring! I think being halfway around the world must have allowed some folks to throw caution to the wind. Anyway, they all thought their trysts were a big secret. They weren't, but we all did our best to keep mum. Joe and I felt a bit uncomfortable about all the shenanigans, but these were adults and we weren't hired on as chaperones!

One night, a few days before the show was to air, Joe and I made a dinner date with Tim, who was traveling solo. We called his suite, and he asked us to come by and pick him up. When we got there and knocked, he yelled, "Come on in." We opened the door and walked into the living room. No Tim.

"I'm in here. C'mon back," he called from the bedroom.

We looked at each other, shrugged, and hesitantly approached the open door of the dimly lit room.

Tim was bare-chested, covers to his waist, smoking a cigarette, while cuddling with a sheep whose head was peeking out from under the comforter.

"Hi, guys. Be right with you." He got up, kissed his bed partner, patted her on the head, and said, "Don't wait up, Barbara. I'll see you in the morning."

He looked at us and winked. "I know you'll keep this to yourselves."

Joe and I collapsed with laughter. "Barbara" was an unbelievably realistic life-size sheep Tim had bought at the gift shop.

No lamb chops for any of us that night.

LIGHTS, CAMERA, ACTION:
MORE MOVIE PARODIES I LOVED

"Sunset Boulevard"

W ho can ever forget "I'm ready for my close-up, Mr. DeMille,"
spoken by the brilliant Gloria Swanson as the fading actress
Norma Desmond, in Billy Wilder's classic *Sunset Boulevard*?

The movie was a natural for us to parody. Actually, we didn't stick
to the original story, the way we did with *Double Indemnity,* for instance. We just put the characters in different comedic situations.
Harvey was spot on as Max, Miss Desmond's loyal servant (bald pate,
German accent, and all). Bob Mackie outdid himself outfitting me,
as *"Nora* Desmond." I wore a black wig with waxy spit curls on my
cheeks and forehead, a gown (vintage silk and velvet) that could best
be described as something that had been packed away in a trunk in
the attic for fifty years, torn fishnet stockings, and silver shoes with
buckles. My makeup, which I had a happy hand in helping to create,
was smeared fire-engine-red lipstick, smeared "beauty marks," etc. I
looked like someone straight out of a Gothic novel, with boobs down
to my belly button. Instead of padding, Bob filled the boobs with *rice,*
which made them move like real ones whenever I twirled around. (*I
should add that the rice was uncooked!*)

We had done a few of these sketches when one day, in 1973, I got
a note from . . . well, I'll let her tell it.

My Nora to Harvey's Max.

Gloria in all her glory.

Below is an excerpt from Gloria's book, *Swanson on Swanson*.

I've played a wide variety of roles on many of the big TV dramas and comedy series—Dr. Kildare, Burke's Law, and The Beverly Hillbillies, to mention a few. My greatest television experience was appearing with Carol Burnett. I watched her show for eleven years, and I still collapse with laughter every time I see a rerun of her Norma Desmond takeoff. It's even better than her Mildred Pierce takeoff. When I wrote to tell her so, in 1972, she wrote back and asked if I would be her guest star on a show during the coming season. I said I would be thrilled, and soon she called back to ask if I could tango and if I would do a Charlie Chaplin impersonation and sing a song. I said I could and would. We rehearsed and taped the show in five days. I danced the tango with six gorgeous Valentinos, I sang a song, and Carol and I, as a charwoman and Charlie Chaplin, did a Sennett-type skit complete with a Keystone Kops chase. It all came out predictably wonderful.

It *was* wonderful. She was seventy-five at the time and looked years younger. Her skin was flawless. Also, she had the energy of a twenty-year-old. When we were working on the finale where she played Chaplin, she never took a break. She was constantly working on bits of comic business to make it perfect. And she did just that!

A Woman's Picture

There were a lot of movies in the forties where a young woman falls in love, but her happiness is short-lived. Either her lover dies or is married or comes down with amnesia. Sometimes she sacrifices her life to save her child, who has no idea she is his biological mother.

I mean how ripe are those for satire?

Bette Davis, Olivia de Havilland, Lana Turner, and Greer Garson were some of the actresses who tore up the scenery in these "three-handkerchief" stories, as they were known for obvious reasons.

Nanny adored these "women's pictures." Even at a very young age, I was caught up in them, too, so when we started doing takeoffs on the movies, they were at the top of my list. One of my favorite sketches we did was a combination of *Now, Voyager*; *To Each His Own*; and *Back Street*.

"To Each Her Own Tears"

O ur guest stars that week were Chita Rivera and Vince Edwards. Emily (me) is a very rich old woman who forces her nurse to listen to her life story day after day after day after day. We are taken back in time to learn that Emily is the very plain daughter of her rich mean mother (Chita), and the sister of her equally mean sibling, Lydia (Vicki). Old Dr. Wilcox (Harvey) looks at Emily's tongue and recommends an ocean voyage to help prevent her from having a nervous breakdown. During the voyage (on the SS *Mildred Pierce*) Emily is approached by dashing Robert Barrington (Vince). He sits on the deck chair next to Emily, lights two cigarettes (à la Paul Henreid in *Now, Voyager*), and proceeds to smoke *both* of them! Emily and Robert fall in love on the spot and ask the ship's captain (Lyle) to marry them. As soon as they are pronounced "man and wife," the ship lurches and Robert is thrown overboard. Emily is handed a telegram, which announces Robert's demise, and she immediately says, "At least I'm carrying his child." Months pass and we find Emily, with her baby in her arms, being met at the dock by her mother and her sister, Lydia.

> **EMILY:** "Hello, mother. Hello, Lydia." (They're unresponsive) "How are you?"
>
> **LYDIA:** "I'm fine. I married a wealthy millionaire."
>
> **MEAN MOTHER:** "I lost everything in the stock market and they won't give me a dime."
>
> **EMILY:** "Oh, Lydia, how could you be so cruel?"
>
> **MEAN MOTHER:** "Don't yell at your sister! I still like her better than I like you."
>
> **LYDIA:** "I have everything in the world now, except a child."
>
> **EMILY:** (Cradling her baby) "I have nothing in the world now . . . *except* a child."
>
> **MEAN MOTHER:** "What are you talking about, Emily?"

EMILY: "Oh, Mother, didn't I tell you? I got married and my husband drowned at sea, I lost my sight in Italy, and regained it in Switzerland, I had amnesia . . . and then I caught a really bad cold on the Riviera."

MEAN MOTHER: "And all we got was a postcard saying, 'Having a wonderful time.'"

With Chita Rivera as my mean mother.

EMILY: "Mother, this is my baby, the most precious thing in the world to me. My only reason for living, my love, my life, my magnificent obsession!"

MEAN MOTHER: "Isn't it sweet? May I hold the baby?"

EMILY: (Delighted and touched) "Oh, Mother, of course . . . Here, darling, go to Grandma!"

MEAN MOTHER: (Handing Emily's baby over to the sister) "Here you are, Lydia, now you have everything!"

Emily protests, and grabs the baby back.

LYDIA: "I want this child. It'll have everything, a rich father and an ambitious social-climbing mother."

MEAN MOTHER: "And Lydia will cough up a lot of cash for the kid, won't you, Lydia?"

EMILY: "Mother, how could you? Are you asking me to *sell* my child??"

LYDIA: "How does fifty thousand dollars sound to you?"

EMILY: (Holding the baby close) "There's more to life than *money*. A child needs love, protection, the emotional security that he can only get from his *natural* mother!"

LYDIA: "One hundred thousand?"

There is a LONG pause.

EMILY: (Whispers to the baby) "Take good care of yourself." (She hands the baby over to Lydia.)

Left all alone, a distraught Emily is approached by the captain, who propositions her by saying he'll set her up in a "cheap back-street apartment" even though he's married with children. She says, "Swell." He gives Emily a handsome photo of himself and charges her two dollars.

After the next ten years have passed, Emily has gone into business and created a little company called "IBM." She's now very rich and living in her mother's house, which she bought. There are photos of the captain all around the drawing room. She decides to call her son on the telephone to try to get him back. Little Tommy, now ten, answers the phone, and Emily has a teary ("Oscar-winning speech") one-way conversation with him.

EMILY: "Tommy sweetheart, I just called to wish you a Merry Christmas, darling. This is your aunt Emily . . ." (Spells) "E-M-I-L-Y. You remember me, Tommy, the nice lady who sends you expensive presents? How was your Christmas? Was Santa Claus good to you? Did you like the long pants I sent

you? And the pony? And all the real estate? Of course you
can take them back, Tommy, it won't hurt my feelings." (Fighting back tears) "How's school? That's wonderful, darling . . .
Tommy, would you . . ." (Haltingly) "would you . . . like to
come and live with me?" (Pause) "Hello?"

He has hung up on her. She cries, "Oh, if only my dear dead husband were here!" The doorbell rings and it's Robert, her dear dead
husband, in a soldier's uniform! Emily quickly hides the captain's
photographs. Robert explains that after he fell overboard, he swam
ashore and stopped by for World War II.

EMILY: "Oh, Robert! Now that you're here, we can get our son
back!"

Robert says he came by taxi and goes out to pay the driver. Emily
watches him through the window, and we hear the screeching of
brakes and a body fall. Emily sadly reinstates the captain's photos.

We return to the present time and old Emily (whose nurse has
fallen fast asleep from boredom), who says, "Soon I shall die and
my son will never know his real mother." The mean mother and sister Lydia enter, followed by Tommy now grown (Vince Edwards),
who kindly tells Emily there's a "Mother-Son Dance" at his school.
Thrilled, Emily thinks he means to ask her, but instead he goes over
to Lydia and asks *her* to the dance, while poor old Emily clutches her
heart.

THE END

CHITA RIVERA WAS absolutely hilarious wearing a gray wig and playing my nasty mother. Bob Mackie covered her fabulous figure by putting her in a fat suit. There aren't too many actresses who would agree
to appear in such an unattractive getup, but Chita was gung ho.

This was one of the reasons I liked using many of our musical guest stars throughout the entire show, such as in a sketch, as opposed to having them just do their thing and not be part of the whole shebang. They were always more than happy to join in the fun.

Lana Turner

One of the most beautiful movie stars ever, Lana was another one of my favorites when I was growing up in the forties. During the week she was with us, she couldn't have been nicer . . . or more nervous. We featured her in a musical number, "Heavenly Music," with our dancers and Don Crichton, who partnered her during the taping. He would whisper in her ear throughout the dance, telling her what steps were coming next. Bob Mackie dressed her in a gorgeous flowing white gown and she lip-synched to the playback. As scared as she was, the number came off without a hitch.

She was more secure in the sketch with our other guest, Frank Gorshin, and me where she was playing Frank's devious lover in "The

The beautiful Lana singing
"Heavenly Music."

Sound of Murder," set in London, 1900. Frank, as Mr. Blue Beard, has just married my character, his thirteenth wife, and plans to bump her off for her money, as he did the other twelve wives. Lana and Frank pretend they are brother and sister, who plan to do the evil deed by poisoning his new bride. There was a lot of shtick where the three of us kept switching the glasses with the poison and wound up getting totally confused as a result. It was a complicated bit, but Lana nailed it every time with no problem.

After the show, a relieved Lana told me she'd had a ball.

"High Hat"

Another one of my favorites, "High Hat," was a salute to those iconic movies starring the fabulous Fred Astaire and Ginger Rogers. Our guests that week were Ken Berry and Roddy McDowall. Ken played "Jerry Travers, a millionaire devil-may-care playboy," and I played "Dale Montclaire, a sweet and simple girl with spunk." Roddy and Vicki did wonderful imitations of the famous thirties character actors Edward Everett Horton and Helen Broderick.

Our takeoff opens on an elaborate art deco scene, set in a vast hotel lobby in Venice, Italy, in the 1930s. Our dancers are twirling around to a tune reminiscent of "The Continental." Enter Roddy and Vicki as Mr. and Mrs. Travers. They check into the hotel and tell the clerk (Tim doing a zany takeoff on the comic character actor Eric Blore) to be on the lookout for Mrs. Travers's niece, Dale, and Mr. Travers's nephew, Jerry. They plan to introduce them to each other, hoping a romance will spring up. They exit and Dale enters and accidentally bumps into Jerry. He flirts with her, and she takes an instant dislike to him after she overhears Jerry asking for "Mr. Travers's room key," mistakenly thinking he's her aunt's husband! How dare he be such a cad! They join in a duet about their mutual dislike (a parody of the classic "A Fine Romance").

Ken as my devil-may-care playboy!

Singing:

DALE: *"He's foul!"*
JERRY: *"She's dumb!"*
DALE: *"He's a creep!"*
JERRY: *"She's a crumb! Well, chances are this could be a fine romance!" Etc.*

There is a mix-up with the room keys, and Dale and Jerry wind up in the same room, comically missing each other's comings and goings. Jerry sings and *tap dances* a solo claiming he's smitten with Dale, and later Dale sings a solo bemoaning the fact that she has fallen for (she believes) her aunt's husband.

The mistaken identities are cleared up when Dale and Jerry join Mr. and Mrs. Travers in the dining room. Jerry and Dale admit their love for each other, and the entire cast and dancers wind up singing and dancing once again to the parody of "The Continental."

Ken was absolutely phenomenal as his idol, Fred Astaire. He moved and sounded just like him. In fact, Fred told me once at some event that he thought Ken was a sensational performer.

Amen.

Rita Hayworth

I remember seeing the gorgeous Rita Hayworth in one of her iconic movies, *Gilda*, in 1946.

During our fourth season, we did a takeoff on *Gilda* (which we called "Golda") with Steve Lawrence doing the Glenn Ford role and Harvey Korman playing the scar-faced villain (played by George Macready in the film). Naturally, I was Golda, sporting a long red wig and a copy of the strapless black satin gown Rita wore in the famous "Put the Blame on Mame" scene. In fact, Bob Mackie's partner at the time

I am Golda in our takeoff.

Rita as Gilda in the 1946 movie.

was Elizabeth Courtney, who had made the original gown that Rita wore in the movie, so mine was an exact replica.

After our show aired, I received a telegram from Rita Hayworth herself (!) saying, "I loved it. You should have done the original."

Wow.

We got in touch with Rita and invited her to be a guest on our show, and she said yes!

Our first reading with her was Monday, January 18, 1971. We were all so excited, and couldn't wait to welcome her. She arrived, right on time, wearing a fur coat and looking beautiful at age fifty-two. We were all surprised that she came alone . . . no assistants, no secretaries, no agents or managers. She was all alone and, I might add, quite *shy*. I was also surprised at how petite she was. On the silver screen she came across a lot taller.

We were to do a sketch where Rita (as herself) was having lunch at the Brown Derby with her agent (Harvey) and Vicki and I were an obnoxious mother and daughter who kept interrupting their lunch with requests for her autograph and several photos. After that, she and I had a duet where we sang "We Belong to a Mutual Admiration Society." After our duet, I explained to the audience how I watched Rita's movies over and over when I was an usherette in a movie theater. We showed a film clip of Rita and Fred Astaire dancing in *You'll Never Get Rich*, winding up with her famous scene from *Gilda*, when she did the "Put the Blame on Mame" scene. I asked her how she'd kept that dress up, and she said, "Two good reasons!"

Since I had imitated her *Gilda* character, for the finale Rita wanted the two of us to dress up like my Charwoman character and do a song and dance together. We loved her suggestion. She enters an empty theater dressed as the Charwoman, and does an imitation of a mock striptease number that I had done many times. She looks in a mirror, and I show up as her reflection. After a brief pantomime where we match each other's movements, I join her and we finish the number together.

*Singing "We Belong to a Mutual
Admiration Society."*

I remember hearing somewhere that Fred Astaire once said that Rita Hayworth was his favorite dancing partner. She was classically trained in ballet, tap, ballroom, swing, and Spanish dancing. She was the first movie actress to partner both Astaire (*You'll Never Get Rich*, 1941) and Gene Kelly (*Cover Girl*, 1944). She had been dancing since she was three and a half! So it was a great surprise to Ernie Flatt, our choreographer, when Rita was unable to execute a simple step or two in our Charwoman dance routine. I, who had two left feet when it came to dancing, wound up working with her myself during rehearsals. She was so nervous that we decided to pretape the number so she wouldn't have to perform it in front of our live audience on the air show. Was she drinking? We didn't know, but it was evident that something was terribly wrong.

Friday came, and we were all concerned about her. She wasn't used to an audience, and I kept my fingers crossed that she wouldn't be overcome by stage fright. The word had gotten out that Rita Hayworth was our guest, and there was a huge waiting list for tickets, for both the dress rehearsal show and the air show.

The dress rehearsal began, and when I came out for the usual Q&A at the top of the show and announced that she was our guest, the audience went crazy. When she made her entrance in the Brown Derby sketch, looking gorgeous, she received a standing ovation. The same thing happened on the second show.

Rita must have felt the love pouring out to her from the studio audience, because she more than rose to the occasion. She was right at home during the sketch and our duet. The finale was played back to the audience on the TV monitors, and there was major applause for her when the number was over. Rita was beaming during the bows. We all were so very happy for her. She was so very sweet to everyone that week, and all of the angst that had been felt became a dim memory. Sadly, she succumbed to Alzheimer's disease at the age of sixty-eight.

"The Doily Sisters"

Vicki and me as the successful Doily Sisters.

One of the most popular musical movies of the forties was the Betty Grable classic *The Dolly Sisters*, starring Betty, John Payne, and June Haver. I remember seeing it with my grandmother, never dreaming that I would one day get to "be" my favorite female movie star, Betty Grable, in a send-up of the movie. We called ours

"The Doily Sisters," and we closely followed the actual plot of the real movie.

This was one particular parody that took up the *entire* show, with the exception of a brief finale where I was the Charwoman. This was one of my all-time favorites, and I wasn't alone in loving it.

After the show aired, I got a call from Jimmy and Gloria Stewart: "We absolutely *loved* it!"

PART 1 THE BUDAPEST CAFÉ. NEW YORK, 1912

Harry Handsome (Harvey) is the singing entertainer in the Budapest Café. He's upset because his opening act has left. Enter Rosie and Jenny Doily (Vicki and me), blond twins, who just got off the boat from Hungary, looking for work. They sing and dance, and Harry hires them to be the backup singers in his act. The sisters ask him, "What do you do?" He chuckles and says, "I write a song!"—and proceeds to sing (the only song he ever writes) "Hey, Mr. Moon." Dim-witted Rosie thinks he stinks, but Jenny is smitten with him and he reciprocates the feeling.

(Harvey was uncomfortable, at first, having to sing and look like the actor John Payne, who was as pretty as Betty Grable! But then, after he got into the brunet wig, with a curl in the middle of his forehead, and a cleft penciled onto his chin, he channeled John Payne, just as he did Clark Gable in our takeoff on *Gone With the Wind*.)

PART 2

Harry performs "Hey, Mr. Moon" with the sisters as his backup chorus, in vaudeville, and after their number, a talent agent, Bernie Bernie (Lyle), wants to sign them up . . . but he's looking for a "duet," not a "trio."

Dim-witted Rosie wants to know where they are going to find another person.

Jenny patiently explains that one more would be a "quartet" and Bernie Bernie wants one less—a duo. Rosie throws a tantrum, thinking her sister Jenny will leave her to go with Harry and won't take care of her like she promised their papa! Feeling guilty, Jenny decides to stay with Rosie. A hurt and angry Harry leaves, saying he at least has his song, "Mr. Moon . . ."

(Harvey was absolutely brilliant in this role and, for ages, when anything would go wrong, he would joke that "No matter what, at least I have my song—'Hey, Mr. Moon.'")

PART 3

We see a montage with the Doily Sisters and dancers touring on the road in a huge production number, "Two Natural Beauties," without makeup or fancy costumes, and then becoming more and more elaborately made up and bathed in sequins by the time they wind up starring at the Palace Theater in New York. They become the toast of the town.

PART 4

We next see poor Harry playing and singing (to a disinterested audience at a posh cocktail party in a fancy penthouse apartment) his one and only song, "Hey, Mr. Moon." The party perks up when the now famous Doily Sisters enter. Jenny spots Harry at the piano and tells him she still loves him and wants them to be together. He says he can't be with her because she's a huge star now and he's only . . .

She puts her hand over his mouth and finishes the sentence for him: "A nobody?"

He says it's over between them because he doesn't want to be known only as "Mister Doily." She tells Harry that she'll give up everything if he'll marry her and they can start all over at the bottom, as a couple of nobodies. He's thrilled and bends Jenny back for a kiss.

A uniformed soldier enters declaring that World War I has just been declared. Harry insists that these world events must take precedence and leaves to enlist, dropping Jenny on the floor.

(I have said that I survived many a sketch's physicality with, at most, a minor bruise, but when Harvey dropped me—his fervor for becoming a doughboy was perhaps a little too evident—I landed right on my tail bone and was sore for days!)

PART 5

"A Typical Trench Somewhere in France," finds WWI doughboys behind sandbags, firing their rifles at the enemy while Harry complains about all the noise because he is singing and playing "Hey, Mr. Moon" on a beat-up piano in the trench. Bernie enters with the news that Jenny and dim-witted Rosie are somewhere in France, entertaining the troops, and says wouldn't it be swell if they, somehow, showed up in this particular trench.

Voilà! The girls show up!

Harry asks them how they found him and Rosie says they couldn't hear his song for all of the noise, but they could smell it

The sisters then proceed to "cheer up" the soldiers by singing "Go Get 'Em, Doughboys!"—winding up with that promise that Uncle Sam will call on all of them again when they get home, IF they get home!

(This leaves all the soldiers weeping and wailing uncontrollably.)

Harry tells Jenny that the war has changed everything and that he will feel equal to her success because he has been chosen to lead the next charge against the enemy, and he'll be a hero! The colonel approaches Jenny, asking if the Doily Sisters will lead the charge instead, thereby boosting morale. Jenny happily agrees, and she and Rosie march over the hill to fight the enemy, leaving an emasculated Harry, while the sisters lead the charge singing a rousing song about the stinky old Kaiser!

PART 6

The war is over thanks to the heroism of the Doily Sisters! Headline: THE KAISER CAPITULATES!

It's two years later, and Jenny, Rosie, and Bernie are in a Monte Carlo casino, where Jenny is drinking heavily because Bernie has told her Harry doesn't want to have anything to do with her ever again. Rosie and Bernie get engaged, and Jenny sings a torch song about happiness being for everyone else and misery is hers, all the while winning a fortune at roulette.

A German count proposes to the distraught and drunken Jenny, and they leave to get into his car with Jenny insisting on driving. There is a crash . . .

PART 7

Harry, who is now a big Broadway star (still with only one song to his credit), has rushed to the French hospital, where he meets Bernie in Jenny's room. Jenny's bed is hidden by a screen, and Bernie warns Harry that she was pretty badly smashed up in the car wreck and that he must be strong because there is a chance he won't recognize her.

Bernie pulls the screen away to reveal: a perfectly made up and coiffed Jenny with a tiny Band-Aid on her cheek. Harry is horrified!

(In the original movie, Betty Grable's head was swathed in a bandage, but her face was fully made up . . . eyelashes, rouge, and lipstick! Hysterical! Betty called me after she saw this takeoff and said she laughed her head off . . . especially over this particular scene. She told me she argued with the studio head about having to look so perfectly made up after such a horrific car crash, and the studio argued, "Your fans want to see you beautiful at all times! Besides, this is a MUSICAL!")

The doctor enters and reveals that Jenny is going to be all right . . . she just has—he struggles for the word—amnesia.

Jenny comes to and doesn't recognize Harry, asking, "Hello, who are you?" Harry tries desperately to make her remember, to no avail.

HARRY: "Does the name 'Harry' mean anything to you?"

JENNY: "My name is Harry!"

HARRY: "No, I'm Harry!"

JENNY: (Pleased) "OH, we're *both* named Harry!"

HARRY: "No! Don't you remember the Doily Sisters on old Broadway?"

JENNY: "Nooo . . . but hum a few bars and I'll try to fake it."

HARRY: (Distraught) "It's amazing, she only remembers old jokes!"

Harry tells Jenny he's now a big star, but the whole thing doesn't mean anything without her.

He asks her to marry him for the second time, and all she can do is ask him again, "Hello, who are you?"

Crestfallen, Harry sees Rosie in the next bed, dressed like Jenny, with a small Band-Aid on her cheek.

Harry asks Bernie if she was hurt, too, and he's basically told that she's just sympathizing with her sister. Harry leaves, heartbroken. Bernie tells Rosie that it would cost the sisters every cent they have for Jenny's treatment. She doesn't care, she will do anything for her sister, until Bernie reminds her that Jenny doesn't recognize her.

ROSIE: "Oh . . . well, I'm not gonna put myself out for a total stranger. I'm no dummy."

(Vicki, as Rosie, spoke all her lines in a high, childish, whiny voice that she often used in other sketches, such as "Caged Dames," with great comedic results. Even if the line was a straight one, she would get a laugh by the way she delivered it.)

Bernie and Rosie exit. Jenny looks at herself in a hand mirror and sings the "Amnesia Song," in which she tells herself that she remembers all of the parts of the face staring back at her and parts of the body, too, but she still doesn't know who that woman in the mirror is. She ends the number with a plaintive, "Hello, who are you?"

Who are you? I wonder as I
sing the "Amnesia Song."

(The writer who got the idea for this song in this spot wrote it the night before we taped the show. I loved it. Peter Matz quickly did the orchestration, and we were able to get it done and rehearsed before the early show!)

PART 8

Five years later. Harry is being honored at an awards banquet in a New York ballroom, where he'll perform his only composition, "Hey, Mr. Moon." A confused Jenny wanders in and is hired as a waitress. Harry is introduced and laces into his song. Jenny is accidentally hit in the head by a tray and, upon hearing "Hey, Mr. Moon," begins to sing along with Harry, her memory restored! Harry jumps off the bandstand, and he and Jenny are happily reunited and engaged to be married, until . . . Rosie appears and has a crying jag, saying Bernie ran off and she has no one, laying heaps of guilt on Jenny.

Jenny asks Harry if he would do her a favor . . . "Will you marry the both of us?" Smiling, Harry responds, "Whatever!" Jenny, Rosie, and Harry and the banquet customers all sing "Hey, Mr. Moon." The three of them are carrying a suitcase that says, JUST MARRIED, MARRIED.

THE END

· · ·

WE DID ALL of the above in less than two hours for our studio audience, just like a Broadway show.

Betty Grable

B etty Grable was one of the most popular movie stars in the 1940s, when I was growing up. My grandmother and I never missed one of her movies. Those 20th Century Fox musicals starring Betty along with her various leading men, Tyrone Power, Dan Dailey, John Payne, Victor Mature, Don Ameche, etc., were always variations of the same plot, but it didn't matter, because Betty was in them. Betty Grable, the servicemen's favorite pinup girl during World War II— Betty Grable, whose beautiful legs had been insured for $1,000,000 by Lloyds of London—was going to be a guest on my show!

That week in February 1968, our other guest was Martha Raye, one of America's funniest comediennes (known for her outrageous mugging). She and Betty had known each other for years and were good friends. Martha, as usual, was over-the-top hysterical both off stage and on camera, and Betty was equally funny in a much more subtle way. This week was the first time we did our soap opera takeoff, "As the Stomach Turns."

I remember Betty was a Coca-Cola addict, drinking several Cokes a day, all that week, which resulted in unrestrained (I might say, loud) belching, which evidently was the outcome she was aiming for. Come showtime that Friday, Betty, Martha, and I were in our finale costumes waiting for the set to change, and Betty took a final swig of her Coke and came out with a doozy of a belch, causing Martha to pipe up, "Jesus Christ, Betty, why don't you just fart and save your teeth?" I lost it. Needless to say, I had a blast working with the two of them.

Betty's song-and-dance number on our show was "Hello, Dolly" in a barn setting with our dancers. Naturally, Bob Mackie dressed her in a costume that featured those gorgeous legs. She was still a terrific hoofer, and with her looking great at fifty-one, the audience ate her up.

Betty and her gams bring down the house.

Betty, Martha, our dancer, Jackie, Lyle, and Harvey in the leg contest. The winner was . . . Harvey!

Since both Betty and Martha Raye had gorgeous gams, we decided to have a "Leg Contest." We see five pairs of beautiful legs in sheer dark hose and high heels. The top halves of the owners of the legs are hidden by a curtain. I hold my hand above each pair of legs and the audience votes for the best pair by applauding. Number 5 gets the most applause. The curtain is raised and we see the contestants. Number 1 is Martha Raye. Number 2 is Betty Grable. Number 3 is one of our female dancers, Jackie Powers, and Numbers 4 and 5 turn out to be Lyle and Harvey in tuxedo jackets and black ties! Harvey, the proud winner, wielding a cigar, and Lyle exit, trying their best to saunter off stage comfortably in their high heels. The audience screamed. (So they wouldn't have to shave their legs for this bit, Bob Mackie had Harvey and Lyle wear flesh-colored tights under their sheer dark hose.)

When Joe and I moved out to California, we put a down payment on, and finally bought, a house in Beverly Hills. Guess whose house it had been in the forties? Yep! Betty and her then husband, the extraordinarily talented musician and trumpet player Harry James, had lived there with their two young daughters many years before. So we invited her to come by the house for a drink one day after rehearsals. She walked through the rooms and I saw tears in her eyes.

Five short years later, she died of lung cancer. She was quite a "dame" in the best sense of the word, and I treasure the time I got to play with her in the sandbox.

Nanny would've been thrilled.

STRESS RELIEF

I have a theory that our bodies don't know if we're *acting*, or not.

I would feel so good whenever I portrayed Eunice having one of her tantrums, or yelling as Tarzan. I would energetically squeal, wiggle, squirm, bump, and grind as Charo, or do a wild and crazy over-the-top Nora Desmond. *Phew!*

Calm. Serene. I think because, personally, I was never one to raise my voice or give in to feelings of anger or rage, so in doing these characters in these sketches, I allowed myself to really let go and vent. Even though I was *acting*, my body didn't know it and I would wind up totally relaxed. I'm sure that if I'd had a trace of high blood pressure before, it would have been significantly lower afterward.

Even now, if I'm frustrated or ticked off about something, I'll go somewhere quiet, where no one can hear me, and cut loose with a Tarzan yell, and immediately feel relief.

It works. At least for me.

THE FLIP SHOWS

After the final show of each season was taped, our cast and crew would go upstairs to the large rehearsal hall that had been turned into a restaurant, with a bar at one end and a catered buffet from Chasen's restaurant at the other. Then after everyone had finished eating and drinking, we would all return to Studio 33 and put on a show *just for us.*

When their seasons wrap, most TV shows throw a cast party, which features an "outtake reel" highlighting some of the funny goofs, etc., that occurred on their shows during the year. We did that, too, showing a few outtakes, but then went beyond the norm and proceeded to put on a *live show*!

The Annual Flip Show was fashioned to be a takeoff on the season we had just finished. I was the "producer," and the performers could be anyone connected with our show, from the cameramen to the backstage crew and even the ushers. About three weeks before the last show was taped, I would announce: "Okay, everybody, let me know if you want to perform in the Flip Show this year. Come to me with your idea and I'll put you on the bill. If someone else has come to me first with the same idea, you'll have to think of something else to parody."

The fun of it was, nobody knew what was coming . . . not even me. I just had a list of the names of the people who would be performing and a vague idea of what they planned to parody. As the emcee, I would simply announce who was on next, and then be surprised along with everybody else.

The first year, one of the "acts" was our three cameramen doing a takeoff on the number "Hey, Big Spender" that I had done with our guests Eileen Farrell and Marilyn Horne that year. The curtain parted, and there were our three big guys, in *full drag*, lip-synching to our voices and doing the same choreography! They had secretly worked with Ernie Flatt to get the moves right. In fact, everybody who was in the show would rehearse in *secret*, weeks before, and every act was a surprise.

That first year, Bob Wright, our associate producer, also got into drag. Dressed like Lana Turner, in her same flowing white gown, to which Bob Mackie had added extra material so the waistline would fit, he sailed around the floor in full makeup and a blond wig, partnering with Don Crichton and the dancers while lip-synching to Lana's recording of "Heavenly Music." At first, no one recognized him, but when we did, we were doubled over in laughter because Bob Wright was the farthest thing from being a drag queen!

Many times during the season when I did my Q&A bits, someone in the audience would want to come up on stage and give me something . . . "Can I give you this T-shirt?" I'd say, "C'mon up!" Or "Can I give you this picture I drew?" "C'mon up!" etc. I would always say, "C'mon up!" One Flip Show had one of our writers, Rudy De Luca, along with his writing partner Barry Levinson (yes, the Barry Levinson who went on to become an Oscar-winning director) doing a takeoff on me doing questions and answers, which got to be a little raucous. Rudy was me in a sad red wig and an equally sad gown. He pointed to a pre-set "plant" in the audience, "Yes, you there! What's your question?" The plant said, "Can I give you an enema?" "C'mon up!"

Not everyone got in drag. Other bits would include sending up the director's booth, satirizing various sketches and performers, etc., etc. Sometimes it could get a little blue, but it was always hilarious.

And so it went. Every year, the Flip Show became the hottest ticket in Television City.

Another hot ticket was our annual Christmas party, which would be held at the Yacht Club in Marina Del Rey. The dinner would be upstairs, and afterward we would hit the dance floor downstairs and dance to the music of a great band. Over the years the bands were led by—are you ready?—Harry James, Stan Kenton, and Count Basie, to name a few.

MORE SPECIAL MEMORIES ABOUT SOME OTHER AMAZING GUEST STARS

The Jackson 5

The Jackson 5 stole my heart.

The first time Michael, Jackie, Jermaine, Tito, and Marlon—along with their youngest brother, Randy—were on our show was March 16, 1974.

The Jacksons performed "Dancing Machine," featuring the incredibly talented sixteen-year-old Michael, and later on in the show they took part in our finale, portraying bored "students" (along with our dancers) in a classroom run by an uptight old biddy (me) attempting to teach the kids how to read music.

Pointing to a music staff written on a chalkboard, the teacher proceeds to pontificate.

TEACHER: "This is 'Mr. A,' he is sharp. This is 'Mrs. B,' she is flat. Now, if Mr. A and Mrs. B get married and move into a home, can you tell me what happens?"
JACKIE: "They give birth to the blues!"

The classroom erupts in laughter,
much to the teacher's annoyance.

TEACHER: "NO THEY DON'T! They give birth to 'Baby C'! Now to review, this is a Sharp, this is a Flat, and this is a Natural."
RANDY: (Pointing to his Afro) "No, *this* is a natural!"

My character continues trying to engage a totally disinterested bunch of kids, when out of the blue . . . *there is an earthquake!*

I mean a real earthquake.

The stage lights above us started swaying like crazy, and everybody in Studio 33 stopped breathing for a few seconds, until the jolt was over. I glanced at our audience, and no one had moved. I figured I should keep on going with the scene, and as the teacher I said, "No visiting, no visiting! The earth just moved. See what can happen when you pay attention!"

There were no more jolts and we finished the number, none the worse for wear.

The Jacksons were very shy during rehearsals, so very, very shy. But when it came time to perform, they blew the roof off the studio! They were the sweetest kids in the world, and I couldn't wait to have them back with us. They graced our show with their fantastic talents three times. I'm still sad that Michael thought he was unattractive. I thought he was beautiful.

Ray Charles

What a dear, sweet man he was. It was a thrill to watch him perform. He was on our show twice. I remember the first time I met him. He came into the music rehearsal room and was shown, by his companion, where every piece of furniture was so that he could navigate. His companion had to do this only once, and from then on as Ray walked around the room, you'd swear he could see.

Singing with Ray.

One of my favorite musical sketches was with Ray. He got a kick out of the fact that we were going to put him in a sketch as a character and not just have him do a musical number. He dove right in and learned his lines quickly.

The setting was a cocktail lounge and he was the piano player. I was a slightly inebriated customer, crying into my drink, when Ray asks if he can play something for me. I tell him I'd like to hear him sing "Happy Birthday" to Teresa.

TERESA: "Teresa's a little 'juiced.' Can I tell you something else about Teresa? Teresa's gonna get a little 'juicier' because today is Teresa's birthday, and only one person in this great big whole wide wonderful overpopulated world remembered that today is Teresa's birthday."

She tells him that person is her and then she begins to sob.

He starts to sing "Happy Birthday" and begs Teresa to join in. She does, reluctantly at first, and then, beginning to enjoy herself, she wants to hear him sing it one more time. This time Ray sweetly calls her Tessie as he sings, and she starts wailing and crying all over again. Ray asks her what's wrong, and she tells him her guy used to call her Tessie, but not anymore. Ray is endearingly sympathetic, the soul of compassion. It makes me smile just to remember.

At that point, as Teresa, I sing "Tess's Torch Song," with the lyrics describing how her best girlfriend stole her man away. Ray then says he knows exactly how she feels because the same heartache has happened to him. He invites Teresa to sit next to him and listen to his woe. He then begins to sing "Guess I'll Hang My Tears Out to Dry," with Teresa joining him. The number ends with a plaintive Teresa singing the birthday song to herself.

It was a beautiful vocal arrangement from our special material writers, along with an equally beautiful orchestral arrangement by Pete Matz. Ray told them how much he loved the whole bit.

After the show, I brought my five-year-old daughter, Jody, backstage to meet him. When she was even younger, she had fallen in love with Ray. The first time she saw him on television, she went up to the set and kissed the screen. She was absolutely mesmerized by him. One morning she was chatting with a plumber who was working in our kitchen, and I overheard her say, "I'm married to Ray Charles. He's my husband. He's blind, you know, and I have to lead him everywhere." I related this to Ray, and he laughed like crazy, and said he'd love to meet her. Jody was overwhelmed when Ray walked into my dressing room and said, "Where's my Jody?" She ran over to him and he picked her up and hugged her. She couldn't speak, but those were happy tears rolling down her cheeks.

Carol Channing

I always looked forward to having Carol on the show, because she made every straight line funny—and every funny line funnier. All she had to do was bat those great big eyes with those great big false eyelashes, smile that great big smile, deliver a line with that wonderful, one-of-a-kind raspy voice, and the audience would double over in hysterics.

Carol Channing making a straight line funny!

Everyone in show business knew that Carol never missed a show. When she starred on Broadway in *Hello, Dolly!* she performed in 2,844 shows, evenings and matinees, and never missed a curtain. She insisted that she owed her remarkable health to what she ate.

After she appeared on one of our shows, Joe and I took Carol out to Chasen's for dinner. When it was her turn to order, she asked the waiter to bring her a plate—just a plate—with nothing on it. When it arrived, she reached into a small picnic cooler she had tucked under the table and produced a huge slab of raw whale blubber, which she unceremoniously slapped onto her plate. *Splat.* This must have worked for her, because she was the picture of glowing good health.

Nevertheless, I ordered the chili.

The following season we booked Carol for another show. Early Monday morning, before the first reading with the cast and crew, Carol's husband called to say she was under the weather, but assured us that she would be right as rain by Tuesday. I was somewhat surprised (*Carol Channing . . . sick?*), but I simply said I hoped she'd feel better soon and that we'd look forward to seeing her tomorrow.

Carol was there the next morning, bright-eyed and bushy-tailed with her signature smile a mile wide. I asked her how she felt.

"Ohhh! Darlin', I'm *FINE* now, just fine!"

My curiosity got the better of me. "Great, but what happened?"

"Well, we were playing Vegas last week and I had this frozen elk flown in."

"You flew in an *elk*?"

"A *FROZEN* elk!"

"A frozen elk . . ."

"YES! And it just hit me the wrong way. Boy, did I learn a lesson!"

She took my hand and leaned in close, with those huge eyes staring at me intently. I mean we were nose to nose.

"Carol, you must listen to me and don't ever forget this."

I nodded solemnly.

"Whenever you're on the road, you must promise me to NEVER eat just *any* old frozen elk."

I swore I wouldn't. "Cross my heart, and hope to die."

Jerry Lewis

What a fascinating man. He was on our show in January 1971, which made him around forty-five years old. He didn't look it, and he certainly didn't act it.

In a sketch we called "Society Marriage," we played two nerdy rich kids who are brought together by their wealthy families hoping they will hit it off and marry. Jerry was at his manic best.

I'm Cynthia and Jerry is Dexter. He calls on Cynthia, and they're both incredibly shy and unattractive. They're also very nearsighted, and when they put on their glasses and look at each other for the first time, they both let out a scream. They sit down on the sofa and engage in a conversation about school. Cynthia confesses that she didn't have much fun because she was a very homely child.

CYNTHIA: "My father suggested plastic surgery."
DEXTER: "When are you gonna have it?"
CYNTHIA: "I had it already."
DEXTER: (Kindly) "They did a very unusual job."

The two of them warm to each other, and after an awkward kiss, they realize they're meant for each other.

Cynthia and Dexter's awkward first kiss.

Jerry's not a short person (in person), but somehow he was able to morph into a tiny, frightened, curled-up, pitiful little creature when being lectured to by his domineering father (Harvey). He could do amazing things with his body, thereby creating the type of character neurosis he wanted to get across. Also, his voice could go up several octaves when he was supposed to be scared or insecure. The audience response was overwhelming.

As the finale on my show, I was the Charwoman (who never speaks) and Jerry was a janitor in a department store after hours, and we make believe we're "fancy folks" in the store's dining room. The scene is acted out in pantomime. Jerry is a master when it comes to pantomime, and he came up with several bits of shtick during the course of the sketch. We ended up sitting on a bench and singing, "A Pocket Full of Dreams" and "Somebody." They were sung straight . . . no shtick . . . simply and sweetly sung. Jerry was wonderful, but slightly uncomfortable with the concept. I think he felt that these particular characters wouldn't switch gears like that. I did, every time I did a Charwoman finale. I would (all in pantomime) be in a setting where I was cleaning up, doing funny bits of business, and then "switch gears," sit on a bucket, and sing a (usually) sad song. Whatever his reservations, however, Jerry went with it and sang beautifully. In person and in repose, I always thought he was sexy.

One other note: He was a savant when it came to remembering numbers. During rehearsals, he would ask several of our dancers and crew members what their Social Security numbers were, and without writing down anything, he could repeat every one of them without missing a beat.

We got together again in February 2014, when he was honored by the Los Angeles Film Critics Association. I was thrilled when he asked me to present the award to him.

The Only One, but Who Needs More?

During our eleven-year run, there was only one guest who was a royal pain. I won't name him, but he wasn't a happy camper from the get-go. He complained about the material, the costuming, the music, you name it. We tried to accommodate him at every turn, to no avail. We later learned he was "on" something, which might've explained his orneriness. At any rate, it came as no surprise when he simply decided to walk the day before we were to tape the show. He was a belligerent little SOB.

I say "little" because he *was* very short, which prompted one of our writers to label him "a pony's ass."

Sid Caesar

Y*our Show of Shows*, starring Sid Caesar and featuring costars Imogene Coca, Carl Reiner, and Howie Morris, was the ultimate sketch show. I've revisited it on several occasions (lots of times on YouTube), and boy, does it hold up. When it first aired, I didn't get to watch it much for two reasons: We didn't own a television set until 1954, the year *Your Show of Shows* went off the air, and when it was on the air, I was a student at UCLA and didn't have much time to watch TV. Anyway, that changed when I went to New York in search of an acting career.

My Fair Lady was in previews and on its way to being the biggest hit on Broadway in 1956. I was a struggling wannabe, living at the Rehearsal Club, which was a haven for "young ladies interested in being in the theater." Mostly I was hoping to get an agent and land a job. I wasn't into watching much television then, either, with one exception: *Caesar's Hour*, starring Sid Caesar, Nanette Fabray, Carl Reiner, and Howie Morris, airing on Saturday nights. It was a live show, just like *Your Show of Shows*, and there were no home recording devices then, so if you missed a show you were sunk. The sketches and the performances were something to behold. The cast was beyond inventive. The writers were brilliant (Mel Brooks, Neil Simon, and Larry Gelbart, to name a few). Some of the sketches ran close to thirty minutes! I, quite simply, was hooked. Sid Caesar's stand-in was a very funny comedian, Milt Kamen. He and I were friends, and we used to meet for coffee every so often at the Stage Delicatessen. I was thrilled when he told me about his job with Sid. I went on and on about how much I loved *Caesar's Hour* and how I would never miss a show. One Saturday morning, Milt offered me the opportunity of a lifetime . . . a chance to watch a rehearsal of *Caesar's Hour* that very afternoon! Milt sneaked me into the theater, and I took a seat way up in the balcony. There, I'd be able to watch Sid and his gang *rehearse* that evening's show, and then I'd go home to the Club and watch the finished product at 8:00 that night, to see if they'd made any improvements or changes. It was heaven. I went back to the Club, eager for 8:00 to roll around, and was informed that I had won a ticket to see *My Fair Lady* (which had been donated to the Rehearsal Club by the kindly producers) that very night!

Well, it was no contest. I figured that *My Fair Lady* would run for a hundred years, but I would never get another chance to see that night's live *Caesar's Hour*. I gave my ticket to my roommate at the Club, and never regretted it, because what follows is an incredible story about what happened that night when *Caesar's Hour* aired.

As I had watched from my perch in the balcony that afternoon, one of the sketches was a parody of the play and movie *Inherit the Wind*. Sid was portraying a Clarence Darrow–type lawyer, defending Howie Morris, who was accused of murder. Carl Reiner was the pompous prosecuting attorney. The entire sketch takes place in a courtroom, complete with judge, jury, and spectators. After presenting their closing arguments, the two adversaries anxiously wait for the jury foreman to announce the verdict. The actor playing the foreman has one line to deliver, "We find the defendant GUILTY," whereupon Sid laces into a very funny tirade culminating in the jury *reversing* the verdict entirely, thereby eliciting applause from the spectators and even the prosecuting attorney! It was a monologue out of comedy heaven, and Sid was brilliant. I couldn't wait to see the final product that night.

Eight o'clock finally rolled around, and I was glued to the television set in the parlor of the Rehearsal Club. The "Inherit the Wind" sketch began and it was going swimmingly, until . . . the actor, playing the jury foreman, with the one line, said: "We find the defendant NOT GUILTY" . . . and *froze* right where he stood. He had blown his one line! The entire sketch hinged on the fact that the jury finds the defendant *guilty*, thus paving the way for Sid's "aria." I was stunned. The looks on Sid's, Carl's, and Howie's faces registered sheer horror. This was a *live* show! No retakes, thank you very much! Sid finally regained his composure and began to speak. If memory serves me correctly, he opened with something like, "Right! Sure! You say he's NOT guilty! BUT everyone in this courtroom *thinks* he IS guilty . . . and . . . and . . . and . . . I'm here to convince all of you once and for all that he's NOT guilty!" He miraculously wove his way back into the original speech and saved the sketch!!!

Pure genius.

A nice footnote to this story: The actor who played the foreman was devastated over his monumental goof and was tearing out of the stage door heading for the subway (possibly with the thought of hurling himself on the tracks) when Sid followed him, caught up to him, and said, "It's okay. You can come back next week."

I love that story.

I always admired Sid and never dreamed we'd one day be friends.

I did finally see *My Fair Lady*, never dreaming that someday Julie Andrews and I would work together and become close chums . . . but that's *another* story.

Sid's "funny business" could slay me!

I also never dreamed that I would someday have my own variety show and that Sid Caesar would be a frequent guest! So would Carl Reiner! So would Nanette Fabray!

Sid appeared with us four times, and was a delight. He constantly worked on bits of funny business ("shtick") right up to taping time.

Carl Reiner

C arl, who went on after Sid's show to create *The Dick Van Dyke Show* and write and direct several hit movies, graced us with his sketch "savvy" three times. The chemistry between Sid and Carl was so powerful and important to Sid's show, it was the main reason I wanted a talent like Harvey on my show. When Carl got in the sandbox with us to play, it was as much of a thrill for me as when Sid was a guest.

As Sid's sidekick on *Your Show of Shows*, and later on *Caesar's Hour*, Carl did it all. Versatile beyond belief, he could do hysterically funny double-talk in just about every language, matching Sid's brilliance in accents and attitudes. He was a consummate comedic actor. Sid was very smart, because when you have a partner who can lob the ball back to you, your game only gets better. That's exactly what Harvey did for me.

Carl in the sandbox with me.

Carl's wonderful wife, Estelle, was a singer. She had given up pursuing a career to raise a family. She also gets credit for delivering one of the funniest lines in movie history in *When Harry Met Sally*, directed by their son, Rob Reiner. The scene takes place in a deli where Sally proves to Harry that she can beautifully fake an orgasm and proceeds to writhe and loudly moan and finally scream "YES! YES! *YES!*" in front of all the other diners, including Estelle at the next table, who looks up at her waiter and calmly says, "I'll have what she's having."

Later on in life, she would often perform in various clubs around the Los Angeles area. I made it a point to catch her act several times. She sang with such ease and, I might add, joy. Carl would always be there to welcome the audience. Lots of times, while Estelle was singing, I would sneak a peek at Carl, who was standing in the back, and the look of love in his eyes was something to behold. They had a beautiful marriage.

I'm happy to report that Carl and I remain in touch. Not too long ago, I had dinner at his house. Among the other guests was Mel Brooks. Talk about a fun evening!

Bing Crosby

What can I say about Bing? Wow! My grandmother and I were usually the first in line whenever a Bing Crosby movie (with or without Bob Hope) was showing at our neighborhood theater. He had a cool demeanor that was very attractive to me, even as a kid, and he was a natural-born actor. I got to know him when we swapped appearances on our television shows. He was on my show twice, and I did a couple of his specials.

In one of the sketches on our show I played a starstruck waitress, and when Bing and his manager (Harvey) sit at one of her tables, she goes ape. Totally obnoxious, she badgers Bing into giving her his autograph, forcing Harvey to take a picture of her with Bing, wrapping Bing's arms around her, etc., etc., and finally ignoring Bing when she spots "a bigger star" coming into the restaurant! Enter Bob Hope!

We had been hiding Bob backstage in a dressing room during the show until it was time for his walk-on. The audience went wild, and Bing's jaw dropped. It was a complete surprise and he was really delighted.

After the sketch, Bing and Bob kidded around for the audience, trading insults, with the cameras still rolling.

BOB: "I've just been around looking for work, and I'm glad *you* found some. It's nice to see you on your feet. You look wonderful, you really do." (Caressing Bing's cheek) "You just come right from the plasterer's?" (Referring to Bing's jacket) "Very nice . . . these are coming back, y'know. Do you like my suit? I had this made for me in Glendale."

BING: "Where were *you* at the time?"

Singing with Bing. He was a real class act.

As I SAID before, I couldn't read music, so I would listen to our special material writers sing the medleys and original numbers on tape every week in order to learn the vocals. Both times he was on, we sent a tape to Bing, who also didn't read music, and he would show up for rehearsals "note perfect." He only had to hear it *once*. And some of the medleys we did were pretty complicated! What you saw on the screen was exactly what he was. Mellow, laid-back, and a real class act.

Jonathan Winters

I first met Johnny in the mid-fifties in New York when we both were starting out and had the same manager. Garry Moore had booked us on his daily morning show, long before he had his weekly variety show. Johnny was a whirlwind. His mind was always running at full speed. He was the first comedian I ever saw who really didn't have a set act. He would be given a few props on a table, such as a hat or a walking cane or a spatula or a handkerchief or whatever, and he would riff on each one, making up hysterical stories. However, we didn't actually work together until he came on my show as a guest in 1967. He was a master at improvisation, so we simply set up a situation in a sketch and let him run with it. He appeared two more times, and always amazed us with his wild musings.

Johnny was a comedy genius.

He was also a talented artist. Years ago, he invited me to see some of his work at his home, and I was thrilled when he gave me two of his paintings as a present. His humor is reflected mightily in these paintings. The first one shows a woodpecker plying his trade, destroying a wooden cross on top of a church belfry, and the title is *Evil Woodpecker*. The second one features several large birds standing up. Looking closely, you see that there are two that are belly-up, flat on their backs with their little feet poking straight up in the air. The title? *Two Dead Birds*.

Dick Van Dyke

M y first memory of working with Dick dates back to the late 1950s when we were both panelists on a show called *Panto-mime Quiz*, which was a game show based on charades, but we didn't actually perform together. Our paths crossed often over the years that followed, and we finally got to work together when we traded guest shots. He was a guest on my show, and I was a guest on his wonderful variety show, *Van Dyke and Company*.

One of my very favorite sketches that we did together was on his show. Dick played a *very* old man who is into origami, the ancient Japanese art of paper folding, and I played a *very* old woman who admires a duck he has made out of a newspaper. Actually, I was doing a character I played a lot on my show, Stella Toddler. The old man tells Stella, "It took me thirty-seven years to make this duck, and it's my most valuable possession." She takes it from him and admires his artistic endeavor, then notices that there is some "writing" on the duck. Much to the old man's horror, Stella proceeds to slowly open up the newspaper so she can read what it says, thereby destroying his pride and joy. She reads: "Stay tuned for the second half of *Van Dyke and Company*," while the old man proceeds to have a heart attack.

It was written to be just a short bit announcing a station break, nothing more. However . . . Dick's character hauled off and socked my character in the stomach! I then retaliated with a left jab to his chin. What followed was a strictly ad-libbed, *slow-motion* fistfight between these two old codgers. I repeat . . . *it was totally impromptu on our part. We had not planned it or rehearsed it!* Bob Einstein (of "Super Dave" fame) was Dick's producer and he kept the cameras rolling. Watching it, you would swear we had choreographed it and rehearsed it for days. Not so. Dick and I were miraculously on the exact same wavelength, and the ensuing fight was as funny as it was ridiculous. It was kept in the show, with sound effects added in the editing room. Dick and I had a ball. We both loved physical humor, and this was one of the most fun improvisational experiences I ever had!

In the summer of 1977, Dick and I appeared together for one month on stage in Los Angeles in the play *Same Time Next Year*. Again, we had a great time working together.

I loved working with Dick.

After my show's tenth year, Harvey was wooed away by ABC to star in his own sitcom. It was a blow, but I completely understood and we all wished him well. Going into our eleventh season, we came up with the idea of asking Dick to be my costar. I was thrilled when he accepted.

Unfortunately, a lot of the sketches that were written didn't highlight Dick's unique talents. The writers were still writing for Harvey, not Dick. After a few weeks, he was unhappy with the situation and asked to leave the show. I didn't blame him in the least, and his last show with us was around Thanksgiving.

Dick and I are still friends, and it's always a joy to see him at various functions around town. He's as nice as he is talented, but I still feel bad that we let him down when he came on board that last season.

James Stewart
....

The first time I saw him I was with Nanny at the movies. I think I was about three or four, because my feet couldn't reach the floor. I can't remember which of his movies it was, but I was transfixed. Every time he came on the screen, with his sweet crooked smile and soft drawl, he was the only person I saw.

Later that night, I couldn't get him out of my mind; I was drawn to this man in some deeply personal way. Over a cup of Ovaltine in our little San Antonio kitchen, I told Nanny that I *knew* him. She wanted to know what I meant, and I insisted that Jimmy Stewart was a friend of mine, that we just hadn't met yet, but we would. She chuckled at that, and we polished off the Ovaltine.

Well, it finally came true. The first time I did meet him was several years later, just at the start of my career. I was in my early twenties and living in Hollywood. I had been on TV a couple of times, and a famous movie director, Mervyn LeRoy, had seen me and was interested enough to invite me to lunch in the Warner Bros. commissary. He was shooting a movie on the soundstages there and even suggested that I come early enough to watch him direct a scene. I was very excited.

When the city bus stopped outside the Warner Bros. gates, I stepped off and approached the guard, who had my name on his list and pointed me to the soundstage in question. I walked into a hulking concrete building with soaring ceilings and catwalks everywhere.

Mr. LeRoy was between scenes and came over to shake my hand and tell me they had just one more short scene to do before lunch. I was shown to a chair off to the side. I watched the lights get brighter and the camera move and focus on a rolling platform that was about two feet off the floor. An actor stepped up onto it and sat behind a desk that was facing a door.

"Ready, Jimmy?" Mr. LeRoy called out.

"All set back here, Merv," said the voice I had loved for all those many years.

Mr. LeRoy called, "Action," and James Stewart walked through the door and presented a badge to the man behind the desk.

"Cut. That's a print. Lunch!" Mr. LeRoy shouted.

Over the years, I saw Jimmy Stewart in *The FBI Story* a dozen times, at least, but I never saw it without cringing at that point in the film, because what came next was one of the most embarrassing moments of my life.

Invited to meet my idol, I stepped onto the platform, gazed into his beautiful blue eyes, and watched his lips move as he spoke to me, but I couldn't hear a word because my heart was pounding like a drum. He must have worried that something was wrong, because he took my hand and looked at me searchingly. I don't know what *he* saw, but I saw his warmth, his humility, his humor, and his heart amplified a hundred times over as he towered over me. I admired many actors, I had a number of favorites, but he was different. I felt so emotional that I thought I might cry. Trying to save face, I turned to comedy—where else?—gave a silly little salute, and said, "Well, I guess it's time to tie on the old feed bag!" I whirled, stepped off the platform into a bucket of whitewash, and froze as the cold muck rushed into my submerged shoe.

There was no turning back. I decided to play it for laughs and pretend I had done this on purpose! So I proceeded to drag the bucket all the way across an acre of floor—step, drag, step, drag, step, drag. No one was laughing behind me as the whitewash squished and gurgled around my ankle and ruined shoe. I finally made it to the door and dragged the bucket out after me. The rest is vague, but I somehow made it home—and never heard from Mr. LeRoy again.

Years later, Hollywood being a small town, the actor George Kennedy and his wife introduced Joe and me to Jimmy and his beautiful wife, Gloria. Our show had premiered and Jimmy and Gloria were fans, so I invited them to a party we were giving. Gloria told me ahead of time that Jimmy was an early-to-bed, early-to-rise kind of guy and asked me if it would be all right if they left shortly after dinner. I told her I was delighted they could come at all and they should feel free to leave whenever they liked.

The other guests that night were wonderful singers and musicians: Steve Lawrence and Eydie Gormé, Paul Weston and Jo Stafford and Mel Tormé. So after dinner Paul sat at the piano in the living room and we all gathered around to sing. After the first song, Jimmy walked over and joined in. He was obviously enjoying himself immensely and he and Gloria were the last people to leave, at a little past one in the morning.

With my idol, Jimmy Stewart.

Gloria called the next day to say Jimmy had a ball and to ask me to please invite them, if we ever had a party like that one again. And I certainly did. At some point I reminded Jimmy of our first meeting and the bucket of whitewash; he was sweet enough to say he didn't remember, but I was tickled when I got a laugh out of him, nonetheless!

Fast-forward to 1978 and we are taping our final show. Tim comes over as I'm about to do my next bit and interrupts me to say, "You have a favorite performer and the guy's been here every week with his piano, but you never let him on the show." I look at Tim like he's speaking Chinese, because I haven't a clue what he's talking about. He continues, "You never let him on the show, but I think at this time, since it's our last show and everything, I'd like to give the guy a break. So do you mind?"

Suddenly the curtain rises and Jimmy is at the piano, lacing into

"Ragtime Cowboy Joe"! The audience goes wild and I shriek like a banshee.

Unable to believe my eyes! Jimmy
surprises me on our very last show.

He had never been on our show before, but he had hidden for hours in a vacant dressing room so I wouldn't see him and ruin the surprise. After he took a bow, he talked about how much he loved watching our show, and I was so overcome all I could do was stand there bawling like a baby.

In December 1983 the Kennedy Center Honors was saluting him and I was invited to be in the television segment. I sang, "You'd Be So Easy to Love," which he had performed in the 1930s musical *Born to Dance*, with Eleanor Powell.

I have a framed note on my desk at home that he sent me a few days later:

Dear Carol,

We had a fine Christmas. And the best Christmas present I got was you coming all that way to D.C. to sing to me at the Kennedy Center.

Bless your heart. All my love,
Jimmy

THE VARIETY CLUB did a show in my honor a few years later, and Jimmy surprised me by coming out on stage, pulling up a stool, holding my hand, and singing "You'd Be So Easy to Love."

It is a moment I will cherish forever.

Jimmy Stewart and I had a bond that I cannot explain. That little girl knew what she was talking about when she said he was her friend. Well, I guess some things just are what they are, and if you are lucky enough, dreams do come true.

THE NIGHT I FIRED HARVEY

Yes, I fired Harvey one night, and here's what happened:
It was during the seventh season. That Friday morning we were working on a rock-and-roll finale. There were certain times when we would have to pretape the finale because it would just take too much time to get it all set up for our live evening audience. This was one of those times. They would watch the segments on monitors, but at home it would all look seamless.

Our guests that week were Tim, who had not yet joined the cast as a regular, and Petula Clark, two of the nicest people in showbiz. We were all lip synching to our prerecorded voices, dancing in our costumes, and having fun, but something was wrong with Harvey.

Now, at times he could get into a mood. He was in an Elvis getup this particular morning and this was one of those times. He was not a happy camper, and whether it had anything to do with Elvis or not is anyone's guess. Usually I ignored his moods, because he would be back to his usual funny, lovable self before you could remember that you were annoyed with him, but not today. I could practically see the black cloud hovering over his head. He was scowling at everybody, and at one point he was actually rude to Tim and Petula.

While everyone was changing for the camera run-through, I knocked on Harvey's dressing room door. When he opened it, I asked him what was wrong, and he basically told me it was none of my business.

I told him his moods were my business when they affected our guests and our show. I said he could be short with me, but not with our guests. He told me I couldn't dictate how he should feel or act and that he'd just as soon go home and never come back after tonight's show. He walked me backwards out into the hall, and he closed the door on me.

I didn't know what to do; I was stunned. For some reason I felt that this was in my lap—it was my problem—and I didn't want to involve anyone else, not even Joe. It is not in my makeup to be confrontational, but I knew this situation called for it and I was going to have to step up. I conjured up Barbara Stanwyck and Joan Crawford, women who were strong and spoke their minds. If I acted like them, I could stand up to Harvey. Okay, showtime!

FRIDAY 12 NOON; LUNCH BREAK.

I called Harvey's agent, Tony Fantozzi, from my dressing room.

TONY: "Hey, Carol! What's up?"
ME: "Harvey's off the show after tonight."
TONY: "Whaa . . . ?"
ME: "He wants off the show, so I'm granting his wish."
TONY: "What're ya talkin' about? Does Joe know this?"
ME: "Not yet. He's in the director's booth. I'll tell him after the show, but it won't matter what anybody says or thinks. Harvey's off the show."
TONY: "What about his contract???"
ME: "If he wants off, I want him off. If there's a problem, I'll go to the union."
TONY: "Jeez . . . what did he do?"
ME: "Tony, I don't mind when he gets into one of his moods, but when he's rude to our guests, I'm not gonna put up with it! I mean, how on earth can *anybody* be mean to Petula Clark and Tim Conway??? It boggles the mind!"

TONY: "Have you told Harvey?"
ME: "After we get through the show tonight."
TONY: "Jeez . . . "

I don't think anyone had the slightest idea about the tension between Harvey and me as we did the show that night. I was a total wreck, but he was his usual professional self.

That night, after the show, still conjuring up Stanwyck and Crawford, I knock on Harvey's dressing room door.

HARVEY: "Come in."

He's sitting at his makeup table, so I sit down and look at him in the mirror.

ME: "Well, you got your wish."
HARVEY: "What are you talking about?"

He turns around to face me.

ME: "You don't have to come back anymore if you're that unhappy. I called your agent and he's aware of the situation."
HARVEY: "You called Fantozzi?"
ME: "Yep."
HARVEY: "Well . . . I have a contract . . . "
ME: "That can be taken care of. You were rude to our guests, and because of your behavior I was screwing up all over the place tonight during the show. I can't work like that, so if you want off, you're free to go."

I head for the door. He stops me.

ME: "What?"
HARVEY: "What can I do?"
ME: "Are you asking for a reprieve?"

HARVEY: "Sort of. Well, yes."
ME: (Pause) "Okay, here's what we do. This coming Monday, I want to see you *cheerful.*"

He nods.

ME: "Not only Monday, but the whole week! And you are never, ever to be nasty to one of our guests or anyone on our crew. We all have moods, but we don't bring them to work. Okay?"

He nods again.

ME: "In fact, it would tickle me pink to see you skipping around and hear you whistling in the hall!"

We shake hands.

HARVEY: "See you Monday."

In the car on the way home, I told Joe what I had done. He couldn't stop laughing. He really got a kick out of the fact that I'd had to conjure up Stanwyck and Crawford in order to confront Harvey.

The following Monday morning I was waiting for the gang and our guests to arrive for the first read-through of that week's script. I decided to run down the hall to the ladies' room before they all got there. On my way back, the elevator doors opened and there stood Harvey. For a split second neither of us knew what to do. Then he gave me a great big smile and took off, skipping, dancing, and whistling down the hall to my office. I doubled over with laughter.

Later I heard from some of the crew that Harvey had gone across the street to the local watering hole after our little discussion that night. This was a place where many in the crew went for a drink or

three after the show. They said he stood on top of the bar and gleefully told everyone what had happened.

Then he lifted his glass and toasted me!

The following week I had a plaque put on his dressing room door:

MR. HAPPY GO LUCKY

For some perverse reason, Harvey always loved telling the story of
the night he got fired.

In 2004, he was being interviewed by the Television Academy, and
he started off with a great anecdote—of course!

"I'm sure you've heard this story. Edmund Gwenn, the old movie
actor who was dying, was on his last breath, and someone came to
visit him and said, 'Teddy,' his nickname was Teddy, 'Teddy, death
must be very hard.' And Teddy said, 'Not as hard as comedy.'

"Carol was very, very smart in getting people like me and Tim
and Vicki. Because she is the kind of performer, also very theatrically
trained, that needs somebody to bounce the ball back fast. If you're
the kind of performer that is holding back, or is hesitant, that doesn't
make them look as good. But there are a lot of performers who don't
like people to be funny around them. They're threatened by them,
because often they have this insecurity thing. You will find in our
business, in theater or movies or whatever, that the biggest stars don't
necessarily have the most confidence.

"We loved each other, we had fun, we laughed. And that stuff
carries on into the work. I can't understand how people can make a
picture or a television show and not be talking to each other or having
jealousies or being competitive, or those 'diva' kinds of things. And
you know, temperament. There was no time or place for that. Carol
would not have it anywhere near.

"I was the only one that was temperamental on our show. I was
the troublemaker. One week, I think I insulted one of our guest stars
and Carol heard about it. You don't do that around Carol or on her

shows. So after the taping she came into my dressing room and she said, 'If you don't like it on this show, if you can't behave yourself, you don't have to come back.' She said, 'On Monday morning, you better come in with a smile on your face.' Now, I couldn't believe that Carol Burnett was doing this to me, 'cause I mean, it's not like her. But she's the boss and she wants it the way she wants it. And I came in on Monday morning, 'Hi, Carol!' And there was no more temperament from Mr. Korman at that point. And as a joke, she put on my dressing room door, MR. HAPPY GO LUCKY."

Harvey was asked how he'd like to be remembered: "I would like to be remembered as a good father, and a good husband . . . and somebody who cared about other people, and tried to help. I never really gave much value to my contribution to the world in terms of what I did on television or in movies. But I realize when I go out [on tour with Tim] and I meet the people and the mail I still get . . . in fact, I'm getting more mail now than I ever have, that I really have impacted people's lives, and that I have made people happier, that I have brought families together, and that I have made a difference in their lives. I think that's maybe the most important."

THE EMMYS

The year was 1974, and our show had won the Emmy for Outstanding Music-Variety Series, Writing, and Directing (Dave Powers), and Harvey won as Best Supporting Actor in Comedy-Variety, Variety, or Music. It was a big night for all of us, and after the ceremony, we all went to our favorite restaurant, Chasen's, in West Hollywood to celebrate. The place was packed with folks who had also been at the telecast, all in gowns and tuxedos.

As we were clinking champagne glasses, I looked across the room, and spotted, sitting in a booth . . . Barbara Wittlinger! She and I had gone all through Le Conte Junior High and Hollywood High together. She was a year ahead of me, so we were never in the same class. I never really knew her. Our paths crossed only when we were in the halls on our way to our classes. She was the most beautiful girl, ever. In fact, she and her two sisters, Alice and Madelyn, graced the cover of *Life* magazine one week, billed as the most beautiful teenage sisters in America. My adolescent mind figured Barbara had to be pretty stuck-up. I used to wish my stringy brown hair would shine and fall into silky waves the way hers did. I would suck in my cheeks hoping my bone structure would come close to looking like hers. I wished my two front teeth didn't stick out so much. I wished my skin was free of zits. For six years, from grades seven through twelve, she was the epitome of physical perfection, and I was . . . a *toad*.

Looking at her now—across the restaurant—sitting in a booth, she was, if possible, more gorgeous than ever, and I found myself feeling like I was that fourteen-year-old nerd all over again with stringy brown hair and buck teeth and covered in pimples.

Joe saw the look on my face and said, "What's the matter?" I gave him the whole scenario. He said, "Why don't you say hello?" Lord no. I wouldn't know what to say, "Hi, Barbara, do you remember me?" Fat chance.

I managed to get back into the swing of things with our gang, and as the evening was coming to a close, I knew that upon leaving we would be walking by Barbara's booth. Gulp. We were almost out the door when I felt a tap on my shoulder. I turned around and looked straight into that lovely face.

She said, "I don't know if you remember me, but we went to school together," and then congratulated me on our Emmy wins. She couldn't have been sweeter or more down-to-earth.

Years later our paths crossed again when she and my daughter Carrie lived on the same block in Los Angeles. They struck up quite a friendship and Barbara attended Carrie's wedding. At the reception, she and I (also) struck up quite a friendship, and she didn't make me feel like a toad at all.

HARVEY, TIM, AND Vicki were all honored with Emmy awards over the years, and I puffed up with pride every time their names were called.

ONE OF *THE* funniest moments in Emmy history was provided by . . . you guessed it: Harvey and Tim.

It was 1974, and *both* Harvey and Tim were up for Best Supporting Actor in Comedy-Variety, Variety, or Music. Before the TV ceremony, they had cooked up a plan that would depend solely on one of them winning. The envelope was opened, and the winner was announced, "Harvey Korman!" Harvey bounded up to the stage, and who was right behind him? Conway.

Harvey, holding the coveted Emmy, faced the audience and began a long and, on purpose, rambling thank-you speech during which Tim, standing directly behind the much taller Harvey, kept peeking around and lovingly staring at Harvey's prize with a sad and pitiful look on his face, showing everyone how unhappy he was that *he* didn't win. Johnny Carson, who was the host, was screaming with laughter, along with the rest of us in the audience, and undoubtedly everyone who was watching at home.

Thirty-seven years later, in 2011, the bit was repeated when Amy Poehler got the idea that when the nominees for Outstanding Lead Actress in a Comedy Series were announced, each one individually would run up on stage where all six of them would stand side by side and wait for the winner to be announced, à la Miss America. The audience was howling and gave the ladies a standing ovation while Amy, Martha Plimpton, Edie Falco, Melissa McCarthy, Laura Linney, and Tina Fey, playing it for all it was worth, waited breathlessly for the envelope to be opened . . . and the winner . . . "Melissa McCarthy!" All the ladies screamed and hugged, and Melissa was presented with a dozen roses and the Emmy, while a tiara was plopped on her head. It was a delicious moment. All awards should be presented this way.

A CONVERSATION WITH DICK CAVETT

I n 1974, I had a conversation with Dick Cavett on his ninety-minute talk show that crystallized a great deal of how I felt about comedy and show business. What follows are excerpts from the program.

DICK: "Do you have theories about comedy?"
ME: "No theories. I think you can 'theory' yourself right out of something, you know. I think . . . now I'm going to theorize . . ." (Laughter) ". . . people ask what makes you laugh. I think probably the surprise element, what you might not expect."

We then talked about doing sketches.

ME: "There are some sketches I really don't like that we have to go out and do, because I think the hardest job in the world (*I meant the show business world*) is to be a comedy writer for a variety show, because they have to come up with four or five sketches . . . different characters [every week]. It's not like a situation comedy where they know, okay, we're writing for Agnes and this is what Agnes always says and always does. But every week our writers have to sit down to a blank sheet of paper that says 'BE FUNNY' and it's a whole new sketch!

Well, you can't win them all, and consequently there are
times when we have to go out and do something none of us
are really in love with, so you just gird yourself and try to fool
yourself into thinking you love it a whole lot! When I do love
it a whole lot, I never want it to quit! It's just great fun! But
sometimes it's very difficult and I don't find my character . . .
occasionally . . . no, a lot of times, until I get into the costume.
I work, really, from the *outside in*. If I know what I'm going to
look like, sometimes it'll come to me."

Dick asked me about "playing" or acting out the movies I saw
when I was a kid. I talked about how we loved going to the "picture
show." That's how we described going to the movies.

ME: "My grandmother and I moved out from Texas to Hollywood when I was seven. To beat the prices, we'd go before
one o'clock and then I could get in for twelve cents. We'd lie
about my age. I was this tall when I was twelve, and I would
slouch so they wouldn't charge us the adult price. We'd see
as many as eight movies a week! Double features, four times
a week. I was absolutely enamored of the movies, in the late
forties. So I'd come home and I'd play Betty Grable or Joan
Crawford, Bette Davis, etc. We had this vacant lot about three
blocks from where we lived, and all of us [neighborhood kids]
would go up there and we'd play Nyoka, Queen of the Jungle,
Sheena, and . . . Tarzan."
DICK: "I played Tarzan, and years later I met Johnny Weiss-
muller, one of the greatest thrills of my life."
ME: "I played Tarzan, too." (Laughter) "My cousin Janice
always played Jane because she was shorter and looked more
like Jane, and I looked more like Tarzan." (Laughter) "And
that's where I learned to do the yell. And we'd mark off
[lines in the dirt] on the lot that was quicksand, and if you

stepped on that you were dead. I was pretty athletic as
a kid."

DICK: "Can you remember moments back then when you
first realized 'I think I can get a laugh in front of a crowd of
people?'"

ME: "Well, when we'd [the neighborhood kids] play the movies, we all laughed at each other. But in school I was very
quiet. I was interested in journalism. My mother wanted me
to be a writer. I never really kidded around that much. A lot
of people I went to Hollywood High with were very shocked
when a few years later they saw me on *The Ed Sullivan Show.*
'That's not the Carol I went to school with,' because I wasn't
'crazy' then."

DICK: (Changing the subject) "There are plenty of miserable
people in the business."

ME: "I think they'd be miserable if they were plumbers. There
are just some miserable people and some happy people. Most
of the people I know in show business are pretty terrific. Especially some of the 'biggies.' James Stewart . . . he's like he is.
Lucy's terrific."

DICK: "Yes, there are some nice people, but there are some
true swine in our business. You want to name a few of your
favorite swine?"

ME: "Porky Pig."

Dick asked me if I would like to do any of the classics, e.g., Chekhov,
etc. Serious stuff.

ME: (Laughing) "No, I don't feel the need. *Pete 'n' Tillie* was
very serious. In fact, it was a little too serious. I felt . . . I
wasn't pleased with myself in it. I was so worried that in the
first part of the film, because it's Walter Matthau and me
meeting on a blind date, that if I so much as" (Subtly making

a face) "people would think we're doing a sketch. So I so *underplayed* her that I don't know why the hell he ever asked her out for a second date, because I was so *dull*. I'd love another crack at it. I learned a lot from the director, Marty Ritt, and of course, Walter."

DICK: "Can you isolate the source of your ambition, or desire to succeed, or anything other than just liking the business? Does it have to do with any kind of insecurities?"

ME: "I was never really turned on by the idea of being a journalist, although my mother tried it. She wrote a little bit herself, and she'd say, 'No matter how old you get or what you look like, you can always write!' So I thought, well that makes sense. Then when I went to UCLA, something drew me into taking an acting course and I got up [to do a scene] and nobody knew me and I heard them *laugh*, where they were *supposed* to! And that was the biggest thrill and turn-on for me, and I went home and I said, 'I'm going to be an actress.' And my mother said, 'You're crazy, what makes you think you can be an actress?' I said, 'I know it, I feel it.' I was so gung ho about it. I wanted to go to New York and . . . I didn't know I had a loud voice until it just kind of happened, 'cause I'd always talked softly. A friend of mine at UCLA asked me if I could carry a tune. I said 'Sure!' And he put me in the chorus of a scene from *South Pacific* that the music department was putting on. I was so loud, he took me out and he and I did a scene from *Guys and Dolls*. I sang 'Adelaide's Lament.' And then I realized that it was *musical* comedy, I wanted. I wanted to be Ethel Merman and be on Broadway!"

I talked about how, after I got to New York, I made the rounds, auditioned, and had a part-time job checking hats in a ladies' tearoom. (How many ladies check their hats? That's how bright I was!) I gave myself a time limit, five years, and if I wasn't earning a living in show business, I'd give up and do something else. I would have been happy simply being in the chorus of a Broadway show. Dick asked me what happened next.

> ME: "I was almost cast in a show, and they didn't accept me because I can't read music. And then I got a job as the *lead* in *Once Upon a Mattress*! If I could've read music, maybe that's where it would've ended for me. I'm not saying don't learn to read music!"
>
> DICK: "If you'd go back to school now, what would you study?"
>
> ME: "Music. Study piano . . . DANCE! DANCE! I am the WORST! Anytime I have to do a step on our show, for the whole week, I worry about some dumb step instead of the sketches!"

Dick talked about his wife, the actress Carrie Nye, who didn't like making movies and preferred the theater because in the theater, there's a camaraderie among actors who go out together afterward and talk about the play, etc.

> DICK: "I got that feeling when I was around your TV show, when I came out [during Questions and Answers] and surprised you that time. There's a feeling around your show that it's more like a *play*, a repertory of actors who work closely together [unlike most TV shows]."
>
> ME: "Well, we don't put in all the hours that people do making film television. We're on tape, and we rehearse all week and shoot in front of an audience and go straight through, changing costumes as fast as we can without stopping, and we almost never do pick-ups, or redo anything. If it goes wrong, it goes wrong! It's more of a live feeling. And we go home! So that helps. I'm home more than I'm at work."

HARVEY LEAVES OUR SHOW

As our tenth year was coming to a close, Harvey asked Joe and me to have dinner with him. He told us he had had an offer from ABC to star in his own sitcom, and he wouldn't be coming back next year. My heart sank. An eleventh year without Harvey? I couldn't wrap my head around it. He was obviously thrilled at the prospect of having his own show, and there was no way I was going to rain on his parade.

I said, "Honey, I'm sad for our show, but I'm happy for you. Anyhow, who knows how much longer we'll last? Of course, you have to do your own thing, and now's the time." I hugged him, and he and Joe shook hands. Harvey had tears in his eyes and I'm sure he was relieved that the dinner ended on a positive note.

Joe and I drove home in silence.

FOR OUR FINAL show that tenth year, we did a ninety-minute recap of some of our favorite moments over the past decade. Tim, Harvey, Vicki, and I sat on director's chairs and reminisced while we showed a bunch of clips. At one point, I felt I had to address the fact that Harvey was going to leave us . . . and yes, I had a mega lump in my throat.

"Before we continue with the show, there are a couple of words I'd like to say right now to all of you. I'm sure most of you know this is Harvey's last show with us. He's going to have a show of his own next season on ABC and we're very, very proud of him. I have mixed emotions. I've been with the most versatile, talented actor I've ever known, and I feel kind of like a parent. You know, when your kids get married, you wish and pray for them to have every success and happiness, but you're gonna miss them like hell." I turned to Harvey and we hugged. "I love you," I said, and Harvey said, "I love you, darling."

OUR FINAL SEASON AND THE LAST SHOW

The eleventh season began. The wonderful Dick Van Dyke came on board, but as I said earlier, we didn't do his talents justice and he left the show before Thanksgiving.

Saying goodbye after eleven magical years.

Our ratings were down because *Fantasy Island*, now opposite us on Saturday night, was a huge hit. CBS moved us to Sunday nights at 10:00, where our ratings improved a lot. But even though we did some pretty good shows that season, I was getting the feeling that it might be time to quit while we were ahead. I came to the tough decision that this would be our last year. It was a hard one, but I didn't want to wait for CBS to say, "Stop doing this." Joe and I talked about it and he

agreed. We had several meetings where CBS executives tried to talk
us into a twelfth year, but we stood fast.

OUR LAST SHOW was taped on March 17, 1978, and aired March
29. It was a two-hour special where we featured highlights from the
entire run.

I was dressed as the Charwoman for the finale that took place on
the empty soundstage. Along with our dancers and singers exiting, several friends surprised me as they walked by my Charwoman character
and waved good-bye. There was my real kid sister Chris, Bernadette
Peters, Jim Nabors, Roddy McDowall, Betty White and Allen Ludden,
and then . . . Harvey! Vicki came out and we hugged . . . tightly. Tim
entered and we hugged . . . tightly. After everyone had exited through
the large studio door into the hall, I was left alone. This time I sat on
the bucket and talked to our audience as *myself*, not the Charwoman. I
hadn't shared what I was going to say to anyone, not even Joe.

I was on the brink of tears, but I managed to keep it together.

*"This is an evening of mixed emotions for me. Like graduation it's a
sad and a happy time. It can't be possible that it was 1967 when Harvey,
Vicki, Lyle, and I stepped on this stage for the first time, because it does
seem 'as if it were only yesterday.' Those clichés really have a habit of
punching you in the nose, don't they?*

*"Recently, a lot of people have been running around expressing their
own opinions as to why I decided to quit at the end of this season and
I think I should be the one to tell you, seeing as how I'm the one who
really knows.*

*"In our eleven years we have had four different time slots and we've
had our share of being up there in the ratings and down there in the ratings. Ratings do not have anything to do with my decision. If they did, I
would've called a halt to the proceedings a long time ago, because there
have been many, many times when they've been a lot lower than they've
been this season. I do think it's classier to leave before you're asked to,
and the fact that CBS picked our show up for a twelfth year, and was
quite adamant about it, is very flattering to all of us here on the show.*

However, I'm adamant, too. I'm so proud of our show, and quite sim-ply, I'm no dummy, now is the time to put it to bed and go on to other things, because change is growth. It's hard because all of us around here truly did become like a second family. We've been through marriages, divorces, deaths, and births, and I know the love that we have shared can never be measured by time.

"Our first director, Clark Jones—our first year—just wonderful. Dave Powers, who has been our director the past ten years—and he is going to other things. He's going to direct Three's Company *next year. I would like to thank our various producers, Arnie Rosen, Bill Angelos, Buz Kohan, our present producer Ed Simmons, our executive producer Joe Hamilton, whom I happen to love very much.*

"Our technical crew, our stagehands, the gang upstairs in the office. Our entire creative staff are the best anybody could have ever had. I know they know all of the love and admiration I have for each and every one of them.

"No one could feel more grateful than I do tonight for having had the opportunity to work with and learn from the brilliant talent of Harvey Korman, who has no creative limits. And we have all watched Vicki Lawrence blossom and grow from a green kid just out of Inglewood High into one of the finest young character actresses and comediennes in the industry. I'm so proud of her. Tim Conway—defies description. His brain never slows down. Those little wheels are constantly churning out original chunks of genius that amaze us all. And the fact that he is even nicer than he is talented is the best thing that you could know about him.

"On behalf of all of us, I want to thank you here tonight and all of you who have been watching us for making these years possible. You brought us together and we're all so very grateful. I love you."

I cued Pete in the band shell, and the orchestra started playing our theme. For the last time, I sang:

I'm so glad we had this time together
Just to have a laugh or sing a song

Seems we just get started and before you know it
Comes the time we have to say "so long"

There's a time you put aside for dreamin'
And a time for things you like to do
But the time I like the best is any evening
I can spend a moment here with you

When the time comes and I'm feelin' lonely
And I'm feelin' oh so blue
I just sit back and think of you only
And the happiness still comes through

That's why I'm glad we had this time together
Just to have a laugh or sing a song
Seems we just get started and before you know it
Comes the time we have to say "so long"

I pulled on my left earlobe. Now it was time for me to exit through the large studio door, which closed behind me, leaving only the mop and bucket as the last camera shot . . .

Reminiscing with Tim and Vicki.

AFTERWORD

When we finally hung it up, our show had won twenty-five Emmy awards and was listed by *Time* magazine as one of the "100 Best TV Shows of All Time." A terrific accomplishment, thanks to all the gang who contributed their talents, and *love*.

How did we get here from there? August 26, 1967, before I walked out on stage for our first taping, I got Harvey, Vicki, and Lyle together for a "Kumbaya" moment. We all hugged each other and I said, "Look, we don't know if we're going to last. CBS *had* to put us on the air, and they don't have a lot of faith in us, so I figure what we have to do is go out there and just have fun. If we have fun, the audience will. And whenever the time comes for us to leave, we can walk away knowing that we had one hell of a great time."

I didn't think it at the time, but looking back I see that we were charmed from the start. Everything miraculously fell into place with little or no angst!

As I said earlier, the head writer, Arnie Rosen, took a big chance to uproot his family and move to California. Also risking a move out from New York were Ernie Flatt, our brilliant choreographer; Harry Zimmerman, our orchestrator and conductor; and Don Crichton, our lead dancer. They all gave us a leg up at the start. Because of them, we amassed several fine comedy writers, musicians, and twelve of the best dancers in the business almost immediately!

Then along came Harvey, fresh off *The Danny Kaye Show*. The fact that Danny's show was going off the air just as we were coming on strikes me now as a minor miracle. Had Danny continued, we never would have had Harvey.

Following Carl Reiner's advice to hire a handsome announcer, we found gold in Lyle.

What are the odds of finding a talent like Vicki because of a fan letter sent by a seventeen-year-old? What made me sit up and take notice that afternoon when I was reading my mail? What was it? Something simply "spoke" to me. Whatever it was, I'm grateful I listened.

Tim. What can I say? We should've been smart enough to hire him after his very first appearance, but eventually we wised up and he came on board every week. He had had several shows of his own before, each of which wound up being canceled, causing him to have his license plates read: 13 weeks. Our show allowed him to fly, and boy did he! As I've said a million times before, the sketches he did with Harvey should go in the time capsule. Again, if Danny Kaye's show had remained on the air, and if Tim's shows hadn't been canceled, we never would have had the experience of enjoying their phenomenal chemistry.

In his interview with the Television Academy, Tim was asked about reviving *The Carol Burnett Show*:

There's no question about the fact that we could probably fire the whole thing up again in a matter of moments. You know if Carol ever said, "I think we're going to do this again," I don't think we would skip a beat.

But I'd only want to do it if we did it the way we did it, you know. Somebody had enough trust in us to know that it was going to be funny the way we were going to do it. I think nowadays we have four or five producers and six or eight assistant producers and eighty-four writers who all want to hear their lines. All the fun goes out of it. You have to have fun in order to do it the way we did.

After our show went off the air, Harvey and Tim took to the road with a show of their own, performing all over the country doing some of their favorite sketches for sold-out crowds. However, we were never parted for long. Whenever Joe and I had dinner with Harvey, Tim, and their wives, Debby and Sharkey, we'd wind up laughing so hard that I really hoped somebody in the restaurant would know how to do the Heimlich maneuver!

IN THE SUMMER of 1978, we thought it would be fun to come back and do four shows. We got in touch with Tim and Vicki and they came on board, along with comic actors Kenneth Mars and Craig Richard Nelson. Our guests in order were: Cheryl Ladd, Alan Arkin, Penny Marshall, and Sally Field. CBS couldn't do the shows at that time, so they aired on ABC.

In 1992, Harvey, Tim, Vicki, Lyle, and I got together for a twenty-fifth reunion show airing on CBS. We sat in director's chairs, fielded questions from the studio audience, and showed some of our favorite clips. In 2001, we got together again and did another special, *Show Stoppers*, which went through the roof ratings-wise. That led to another one, *Let's Bump Up the Lights*, in 2004.

Just before Christmas of 2007, Harvey got very sick. He had several operations, and pulled through every one of them. He was a fighter, but he lost the battle in May 2008. His wife, Debby, and his family were at his side.

I will remember and love "Mr. Happy Go Lucky" forever.

THE ARTIST ENTRANCE

I n 1998, Studio 33 in Television City, where we had taped all eleven years of my show, had been renamed "The Bob Barker Studio," in honor of the long-running host of *The Price Is Right*, who had also taped his show there.

*The plaque on the wall in the entrance
moved me to tears.*

Early in 2015, a suggestion was made by CBS to put up a plaque at the foot of the stage in Studio 33. The plaque would read THE CAROL BURNETT STAGE. I was thrilled with the whole idea. However, it wasn't well received by Bob, so it was shelved out of respect for his wishes.

What happened, as a result, was that CBS decided to rename the Artist Entrance. *For me, it was an even better suggestion!*

On September 28, 2015, at Television City in Hollywood, I was pretty much close to tears when CBS president and CEO Leslie Moonves unveiled a plaque and also a large photograph of me, with the cartoon version of the Charwoman, on the walls in the entryway. Outside, the entrance doors read: CAROL BURNETT ARTIST ENTRANCE.

At the dedication: What an honor!

Asked to say a few words, I talked about all the wonderful times when I had walked through those doors on the way to rehearse and tape our show . . . about how much I loved Harvey, Vicki, Lyle, and Tim . . . about how much the crew meant to me . . . and about how absolutely overwhelmed I was with this honor.

Wow.

And, in closing, I just want to add . . .

WRAPPING IT ALL UP

Fifty years have passed since we "pushed the button" to do the show. Sure, I'd like to be younger, but then I could never do today what we did back then. Sadly, variety shows like ours have gone the way of the dodo bird. A variety show today can never duplicate what we did. Why? Money. The cost of clearing the songs and music alone would sink the *Titanic*. Sixty to seventy costumes a week? No way. A twenty-eight-piece orchestra? Twelve dancers? A rep company of five? Six to eight sketches a show? Major guest stars? Block the entire show and rehearse with the orchestra in one day? The following day tape the whole shebang in two hours? Dream on.

We all get older, if we're lucky. So, if I had to choose, I'm happy I was there at that *time* . . . to have a laugh or sing a song.

OUR SHOW HAD gone into syndication while we were in our last season. The syndicated show, *Carol Burnett and Friends*, was cut down to a half hour, showing only the sketches and none of the musical features. Recently, because several of the entire one-hour shows have been released on DVD and also as a result of us being on YouTube, we've garnered a whole new generation of viewers.

Every so often I go around the country and do a Q&A evening. I'm thrilled that the audiences' ages can range from nine to ninety. Not too long ago, I was performing in a theater in my hometown, San Antonio, and a little boy in the second row raised his hand and I called on him.

ME: "Hi there! What's your name?"
LITTLE BOY: "Andrew."
ME: "How old are you, Andrew?"
ANDREW: "Nine."
ME: "And you know who I am?"
ANDREW: (Pause) "Surprisingly, yes."

How lucky am I?

APPENDIX 1:
SHOWS AND GUESTS

SEASON 1

1. #001. First taped show. Airdate: January 1, 1968. Regulars: Harvey, Vicki, and Lyle. Guests: Lynn Redgrave and Mike Douglas.

2. #002. Airdate: November 20, 1967. Regulars: No Vicki (no "Carol and Sis" sketch). Guests: Martha Raye and Juliet Prowse.

3. #003. Debut. First air show. Airdate: September 11, 1967. Regulars. Guest: Jim Nabors.

4. #004. Airdate: September 18, 1967. Regulars. Guests: Sid Caesar and Liza Minnelli.

5. #005. Airdate: September 25, 1967. Regulars. Guests: Jonathan Winters and Eddie Albert.

6. #006. Airdate: October 2, 1967. Regulars. Guests: Lucille Ball, Tim Conway, and Gloria Loring.

7. #007. Airdate: October 9, 1967. Regulars: Harvey and Lyle (no Vicki because there was no "Carol and Sis" sketch that week and we hadn't started using her elsewhere yet). Guests: Imogene Coca and Lainie Kazan.

8. #008. Airdate: October 16, 1967. Regulars. Guests: Phyllis Diller, Gwen Verdon, and Bobbie Gentry.

9. #009. Airdate: October 23, 1967. Regulars. Guests: The Smothers Brothers, Diahann Carroll, and Richard Kiley.

10. #010. Airdate: February 5, 1968. Regulars. Guests: Jack Palance and Liza Minnelli.

11. #011. Airdate: November 6, 1967. Regulars: No Vicki. Guests: Sonny and Cher, and Nanette Fabray.

12. #012. Airdate: November 13, 1967. Regulars. Guests: Richard Chamberlain, Gloria Loring, and Kay Medford.

13. #013. Airdate: November 27, 1967. Regulars: No Vicki. Guests: Don Adams and Lesley Ann Warren.

14. #014. Airdate: December 4, 1967 (Christmas theme).

Regulars. Guests: Jonathan Winters and Barbara Eden.

15. #015. Airdate: December 11, 1967. Regulars. Guests: Mickey Rooney and John Davidson.

16. #016. Airdate: March 18, 1968. Regulars. Guests: Tim Conway and Jack Jones.

17. #017. Airdate: December 25, 1967. Regulars: No Vicki. Guests: Sid Caesar and Ella Fitzgerald.

18. #018. Airdate: January 8, 1968. Regulars. Guests: Lana Turner and Frank Gorshin.

19. # 019. Airdate: January 15, 1968. Regulars: No Vicki. Guests: Trini Lopez and Ken Berry.

20. #020. Airdate: January 22, 1968. Regulars. Guests: Shirley Jones and George Chakiris.

21. #021. Airdate: January 29, 1968. Regulars. Guests: Jonathan Winters and Dionne Warwick.

22. #022 Airdate: February 12, 1968. Regulars. Guests: Betty Grable and Martha Raye. (First "As the Stomach Turns" sketch.)

23. #023. Airdate: February 19, 1968. Regulars. Guests: Art Carney and Nanette Fabray.

24. #024. Airdate: February 26, 1968. Regulars. Guests: Garry Moore, Durward Kirby, and John Gary.

25. #025. Airdate: March 4, 1968. Regulars. Guests: Imogene Coca and Mel Tormé.

26. #026. Airdate: April 29, 1968. Regulars. Guests: Tim Conway and Shani Wallis.

27. #027. Airdate: March 25, 1968. Regulars. Guests: Soupy Sales and Gloria Loring.

28. #028. VTR date: March 2, 1968. Airdate: April 29, 1968. Regulars. Guests: Sid Caesar and Barbara McNair.

29. #029. Airdate: April 15, 1968. Regulars. Guests: Peter Lawford and Minnie Pearl.

30. #030. Airdate: May 13, 1968. Family show. No guests. Final show of the first season.

SEASON 2

1. #101. First taped show of the second season. Airdate: December 9, 1968. Regulars. Guests: Imogene Coca and Vic Damone.

2. #102. Airdate: October 10, 1968. Regulars. Guests: Nanette Fabray and Trini Lopez.

3. #103. Airdate: September 23, 1968. Regulars. Guests: Jim Nabors and Alice Ghostley.

4. #104. Airdate: September 30, 1968. Regulars. Guest: Carol Channing.

5. #105. Airdate: October 14, 1968. Regulars. Guests: George Gobel and Bobbie Gentry.

6. #106. Airdate: October 21, 1968. Regulars: No Vicki. Guests: Tim Conway and Edie Adams.

7. #107. Airdate: November 11, 1968. Regulars: No Vicki. Guests: Don Rickles, Mel Tormé, and Nanette Fabray.

8. #108. Airdate: November 4, 1968. Regulars. Guests: Lucille

Ball, Eddie Albert, and Nancy Wilson.

9. #109. Airdate: November 18, 1968. Regulars. Guests: Sid Caesar and Ella Fitzgerald.

10. #110. Airdate: November 25, 1968. Regulars. Guests: Garry Moore and Durward Kirby.

11. #111. Airdate: December 2, 1968. Regulars. Guests: Michele Lee and Flip Wilson.

12. #112. Airdate: January 6, 1969. Regulars. Guest: Tim Conway.

13. #113. Airdate: December 16, 1968. Regulars. Guests: Marilyn Horne and Eileen Farrell.

14. #114. Airdate: December 30, 1968. Regulars. Guests: Mickey Rooney and Nancy Wilson.

15. #115. Airdate: January 20, 1969. Regulars: No Vicki. Family show. No guests.

16. #116. Airdate: January 27, 1969. Regulars. Guests: Mel Tormé and Martha Raye.

17. #117. Airdate: February 3, 1969. Regulars. Guests: Chita Rivera and Vince Edwards.

18. #118. Airdate: February 17, 1969. Regulars. Guests: Ken Berry and Shirley Jones.

19. #119. Airdate: February 24, 1969. Regulars. Guests: Soupy Sales and Barbara McNair.

20. #120. Airdate: March 3, 1969. Regulars. Guests: Tim Conway and Ethel Merman.

21. #121. Airdate: March 10, 1969. Regulars. Guests: Ross Martin and John Davidson.

22. #122. Airdate: March 17, 1969.

Regulars. Guests: Martha Raye and Mike Douglas.

23. #123. Airdate: March 24, 1969. Regulars. Guests: Barrie Chase and Larry Hovis.

24. #124. Airdate: March 31, 1969. Regulars. Guests: Vikki Carr and Ronnie Schell.

25. #125. Airdate: April 7, 1969. Regulars. Guests: Robert Goulet and Imogene Coca.

26. #126. Airdate: April 28, 1969. Family show. No guests.

SEASON 3

1. #301. First taped show of third season. Airdate: October 10, 1969. Regulars. Guests: Tim Conway and Ken Berry.

2. #302. Airdate: November 3, 1969. Regulars. Guests: Pat Boone and Gwen Verdon.

3. #303. First air show of third season. Airdate: September 22, 1969. Regulars. Guest: Jim Nabors.

4. #304. Airdate: January 12, 1970. Regulars. Guests: Nanette Fabray and Nancy Wilson.

5. #305. Airdate: September 29, 1969. Regulars. Guests: Bernadette Peters, Nancy Wilson, and the Burgundy Street Singers.

6. #306. Airdate: October 6, 1969. Regulars. Guests: Steve Lawrence and Edward Villella.

7. #307. Airdate: October 13, 1969. Regulars. Guests: Scoey Mitchell and Bobbie Gentry.

8. #308. Airdate: November 10,

1969. Regulars. Guests: Bing Crosby, Ella Fitzgerald, and Rowan and Martin.

9. #309. Airdate: November 17, 1969. Regulars. Guest: Andy Griffith.

10. #310. Airdate: November 24, 1969. Regulars. Guests: George Carlin and Lucille Ball.

11. #311. Airdate: March 9, 1970. Regulars. Guests: Nanette Fabray and Trini Lopez.

12. #312. Airdate: December 8, 1969. Regulars. Guests: Martha Raye and Tim Conway.

13. #313. Airdate: December 15, 1969. Regulars. Guests: Garry Moore and Durward Kirby.

14. #314. Airdate: December 29, 1969. Regulars. Guests: Donald O'Connor and Nancy Wilson.

15. #315. Airdate: January 5, 1970. Regulars. Guests: Audrey Meadows and Kaye Stevens.

16. #316. Airdate: January 19, 1970. Regulars. Guests: Flip Wilson and Vikki Carr.

17. #317. Airdate: January 26, 1970. Regulars. Guests: Mel Tormé and Soupy Sales.

18. #318. Airdate: February 2, 1970. Regulars. Guests: Joan Rivers and Barbara Feldon.

19. #319. Airdate: February 16, 1970. Regulars. Family show. No guests.

20. #320. Airdate: February 23, 1970. Regulars. Guests: Jack Jones and Pat Carroll.

21. #321. Airdate: March 2, 1970.

Regulars. Guests: Tim Conway and Jane Connell.

22. #322. Airdate: March 16, 1970. Regulars. Guests: Nancy Wilson and Ronnie Schell.

23. #323. Airdate: March 23, 1970. Regulars. Guests: Mel Tormé and Martha Raye.

24. #324. Airdate: March 39, 1970. Regulars. Guests: Tim Conway and Peggy Lee.

25. #325. Airdate: April 13, 1970. Regulars. Guests: Nanette Fabray and Michele Lee.

26. #326. Airdate: May 4, 1970. Regulars. Family show. No guests.

SEASON 4

1. #401. Airdate: November 9, 1970. Regulars. Guest: Juliet Prowse.

2. #402. Airdate: September 14, 1970. Regulars. Guest: Jim Nabors.

3. #403. Airdate: September 21, 1970. Regulars. Guests: Cass Elliot and Pat Paulsen.

4. #404. Airdate: October 12, 1970. Regulars. Guests: Nanette Fabray and Ken Berry.

5. #405. Airdate: January 1, 1971. Regulars. Guests: Pat Carroll and Art Carney.

6. #406. Airdate: September 28, 1970. Regulars. Guests: Nanette Fabray and Steve Lawrence.

7. #407. Airdate: October 5, 1970. Regulars. Guests: Eydie Gormé and Joan Rivers.

8. #408. Airdate: November 2,

1970. Regulars. Guests: Ricardo Montalban and Cass Elliot.

9. #409. Airdate: October 19, 1970. Regulars. Guests: Lucille Ball and Mel Tormé.

10. #410. Airdate: October 26, 1970. Regulars. Guests: Bernadette Peters and Donald O'Connor.

11. #411. Airdate: December 7, 1970. Regulars. Guests: Don Rickles and Mel Tormé.

12. #412. Airdate: November 16, 1970. Regulars. Guests: Martha Raye and Ross Martin.

13. #413. Airdate: November 23, 1970. Regulars. Guests: Dyan Cannon and Paul Lynde.

14. #414. Airdate: November 30, 1970. Regulars. Guests: Debbie Reynolds and John Davidson.

15. #415. Airdate: December 14, 1970. Regulars. Guests: Steve Lawrence, Durward Kirby, and Julie Budd.

16. #416. Airdate: December 28, 1970. Regulars. Guests: Pat Carroll, Robert Goulet, and Rich Little.

17. #417. Airdate: January 11, 1971. Regulars. Guests: Jerry Lewis and Leslie Uggams.

18. #418. Airdate: January 18, 1971. Regulars. Guests: Mel Tormé and Michele Lee.

19. #419. Airdate: January 25, 1971. Regulars. Guests: Martha Raye, Edward Villella, and Violette Verdy.

20. #420. Airdate: February 1, 1971. Regulars. Guests: Rita Hayworth and Jim Bailey.

21. #421. Airdate: February 15, 1971. Regulars. Guests: Ken Berry and Totie Fields.

22. #422. Airdate: February 22, 1971. Regulars. Guests: Chita Rivera and Bob Newhart.

23. #423. Airdate: March 1, 1971. Regulars. Pat Carroll, Tim Conway, and Karen Wyman.

24. #424. Airdate: March 8, 1971. Regulars: No Vicki. Guests: Mike Douglas and Bernadette Peters.

25. #425. Airdate: March 22, 1971. Regulars. Guests: Eileen Farrell, Marilyn Horne, and David Frost. (Taped in New York.)

26. #426. Airdate: March 29, 1971. Regulars. Guests: Paul Lynde and Nanette Fabray.

SEASON 5

1. #501. Airdate: December 8, 1971. Regulars. Guests: Andy Griffith and Barbara McNair.

2. #502. Airdate: March 22, 1972. Regulars. Guests: Karen Black and Paul Lynde.

3. #503. Airdate: November 10, 1971. Regulars. Guests: Bernadette Peters and Cass Elliot.

4. #504. Airdate: September 15, 1971. Regulars. Guest: Jim Nabors.

5. #505. Airdate: September 22, 1971. Regulars. Guests: Tim Conway and the Carpenters.

6. #506. Airdate: October 6,

1971. Regulars. Guests: Steve Lawrence and Carol Channing.

7. #507. Airdate: October 13, 1971. Regulars. Guests: Ken Berry and Cass Elliot.

8. #508. Airdate: October 20, 1971. Regulars. Guests: Peggy Lee and Dom DeLuise.

9. #509. Airdate: October 27, 1971. Regulars. Guests: Tim Conway and Diahann Carroll.

10. #510. Airdate: November 3, 1971. Regulars. Guests: Bing Crosby and Paul Lynde.

11. #511. Airdate: November 17, 1971. Regulars. Guests: Mel Tormé and Nanette Fabray.

12. #512. Airdate: November 24, 1971. Regulars. Guests: Eydie Gormé, Shecky Greene, Improv Group.

13. #513. Airdate: December 1, 1971. Regulars. Guests: Tim Conway and Cass Elliot.

14. #514. Airdate: December 15, 1971. Regulars. Guests: Dionne Warwick and Ken Berry.

15. #515. Airdate: December 29, 1971. Regulars. Guests: Steve Lawrence and Dick Martin.

16. #516. Airdate: January 5, 1972. Regulars. Guests: Paul Lynde and Peggy Lee.

17. #517. Airdate: January 19, 1972. Regulars. Guests: Ken Berry, Nanette Fabray, and the Carpenters.

18. #518. Airdate: January 26, 1972. Regulars. Guests: Tim Conway and Ray Charles.

19. #519. Airdate: February 2, 1972. Regulars. Guests: Eydie Gormé and Vincent Price.

20. #520. Airdate: February 16, 1972. Regulars. Guests: Kaye Ballard and Steve Lawrence.

21. #521. Airdate: February 23, 1972. Regulars. Guests: Nanette Fabray and Burt Reynolds.

22. #522. Airdate: March 1, 1972. Regulars. Guests: Tim Conway and Eydie Gormé.

23. #523. Airdate: March 8, 1972. Regulars. Guests: Jack Klugman and Tony Randall.

24. #524. Airdate: March 29, 1972. Regulars. Family show. No guests.

SEASON 6

1. #601. Airdate: October 4, 1972. Regulars. Guests: Steve Lawrence and Paul Sand.

2. #602. Airdate: October 18, 1972. Regulars. Guests: Joel Grey and Cass Elliot.

3. #603. VTR date: August 4, 1972. Regulars. Airdate: November 29, 1972. Guests: Carl Reiner and Melba Moore.

4. #604. VTR date: August 11, 1972. Airdate: February 14, 1973. Regulars. Guests: Anthony Newley and Bernadette Peters.

5. #605. Airdate: September 27, 1972. Regulars. Guests: Andy Griffith and Helen Reddy.

6. #606. Airdate: September 20, 1972. Regulars. Guests: Carol Channing and Marty Feldman.

7. #607. Airdate: September 27,

1972. Regulars. Guest: Jim Nabors.

8. #608. Airdate: October 11, 1972. Regulars. Guests: Eydie Gormé and Jack Gilford.

9. #609. Airdate: November 15, 1972. Regulars. Guests: John Davidson and Ruth Buzzi.

10. #610. Airdate: November 1, 1972. Regulars. Guests: Peggy Lee, Jerry Stiller, and Anne Meara.

11. #611. Airdate: October 25, 1972. Regulars. Guests: Tim Conway and Pearl Bailey.

12. #612. Airdate: November 8, 1972. Regulars. Guests: Steve Lawrence and Lily Tomlin.

13. #613. Airdate: November 22, 1972. Regulars. Guests: Ray Charles and Vincent Price.

14. #614. Airdate: December 23, 1972. Regulars. Guests: Steve Lawrence and Tim Conway.

15. #615. Airdate: January 6, 1973. Regulars. Guests: Tim Conway and Jack Cassidy.

16. #616. Airdate: January 20, 1973. Regulars. Guests: Ruth Buzzi and Jack Gilford.

17. #617. Airdate: January 27, 1973. Regulars. Guests: Tim Conway, Kaye Ballard, and Burt Reynolds (Q&A).

18. #618. Airdate: February 3, 1973. Regulars. Family show. No guests.

19. #619. Airdate: February 10, 1973. Regulars. Guests: John Byner and Petula Clark.

20. #620. Airdate: February 17,

1973. Regulars. Guests: Valerie Harper and Tim Conway.

21. #621. Airdate: February 24, 1973. Regulars. Guests: Ken Berry and Eydie Gormé.

22. #622. Airdate: March 10, 1973. Regulars. Guests: David Hartman and Paula Kelly.

23. #623. Airdate: March 17, 1973. Regulars. Guests: William Conrad and Peggy Lee.

24. #624. Airdate: March 24, 1973. Regulars. Family show. No guests.

SEASON 7

1. #701. Airdate: September 22, 1973. Regulars. Guests: Tim Conway and Charo.

2. #702. Airdate: October 6 and December 29, 1973. Regulars. Guests: Helen Reddy and John Byner.

3. #703. Airdate: September 15, 1973. Regulars. Guest: Jim Nabors.

4. #704. Airdate: November 10, 1973. Regulars. Guests: Tim Conway and Petula Clark.

5. #705. Airdate: September 29, 1973. Regulars. Guest: Gloria Swanson.

6. #706. Airdate: October 13, 1973. Regulars. Guests: Eydie Gormé and Paul Sand.

7. #707. Airdate: October 20, 1973. Regulars. Guests: Ken Berry, Jack Weston, and Tim Conway.

8. #708. Airdate: October 27, 1973. Regulars. Guest: John Byner.

9. #709. Airdate: November 3,

10. #710. Airdate: December 8, 1973. Regulars. Guests: Tim Conway, Edward Villella, and Lucette Aldous.

11. #711. Airdate: December 1, 1973. Regulars. Family show. No guests.

12. #712. Airdate: December 1, 1973. Regulars. Guests: Ruth Buzzi and Richard Crenna.

13. #713. Airdate: December 22, 1973. Regulars. Guests: Anthony Newley and Dick Martin.

14. #714. Airdate: January 5, 1974. Regulars. Guests: Steve Lawrence and Tim Conway.

15. #715. Airdate: January 12, 1974. Regulars. Guests: Eydie Gormé and Paul Sand.

16. #716. Airdate: January 19, 1974. Regulars. Guest: Carl Reiner.

17. #717. Airdate: February 2, 1974. Regulars. Guests: Steve Lawrence and Tim Conway.

18. #718. Airdate: February 9, 1974. Regulars. Guests: Joel Grey and Vincent Price.

19. #719. Airdate: February 16, 1974. Regulars. Guests: Bernadette Peters and Tim Conway.

20. #720. Airdate: February 23, 1974. Regulars. Guests: Tim Conway and Eydie Gormé.

21. #721. Airdate: March 9, 1974. Regulars. Guest: Steve Lawrence.

22. #722. Airdate: March 16, 1974. Regulars. Guests: Roddy McDowall and the Jackson 5.

This was the premiere of "The Family."

23. #723. Airdate: March 23, 1974. Regulars. Guests: John Byner and Francine Beers.

24. #724. Airdate: April 6, 1974. Regulars. Family show. No guests.

SEASON 8
LYLE IS NO LONGER A REGULAR.

1. #801. Airdate: November 16, 1974. Regulars: No Harvey. Guests: John Byner and Kenneth Mars.

2. #802. Airdate: October 5, 1974. Regulars. Guests: Jack Weston and Michele Lee. (This was during the CBS strike.)

3. #803. Airdate: September 14, 1974. Regulars. Guest: Jim Nabors. (This was during the CBS strike.)

4. #804. Airdate: September 28, 1974. Regulars. Guests: James Coco and the Pointer Sisters. (This was during the CBS strike.)

5. #805. Airdate: September 21, 1974. Regulars. Guest: Steve Lawrence. (This was during the CBS strike. This is the last show during the strike. Thankfully the strike ended.)

6. #806. Airdate: October 12, 1974. Regulars. Guests: Telly Savalas and the Smothers Brothers.

7. #807. Airdate: October 26, 1974. Regulars. Guests: Eydie Gormé and Rich Little.

8. #808. Airdate: November 2, 1974. Regulars. Guests: Alan King and Lena Zavaroni.

9. #809. Airdate: November 9, 1974. Regulars. Guests: Helen Reddy and John Byner.

10. #810. Airdate: November 23, 1974. Regulars. Guests: Maggie Smith and Tim Conway.

11. #811. Airdate: December 7, 1974. Regulars. Guests: Steve Lawrence, Tim Conway, and Steven Warner.

12. #812. Airdate: December 14, 1974. Regulars. Guests: Ken Berry and Carl Reiner.

13. #813. Airdate: December 21, 1974. Regulars. Guest: Alan Alda.

14. #814. Airdate: January 4, 1975. Regulars. Guests: Joan Rivers and Vincent Price.

15. #815. Airdate: January 11, 1975. Regulars. Guest: Tim Conway.

16. #816. Airdate: January 25, 1975. Regulars. Guests: William Conrad and the Jackson 5.

17. #817. Airdate: February 15, 1975. Regulars. Guests: Rock Hudson and Nancy Walker.

18. #818. Airdate: February 8, 1975. Regulars. Guests: Tim Conway and the Pointer Sisters.

19. #819. Airdate: February 22, 1975. Regulars. Guest: Tim Conway.

20. #820. Airdate: March 8, 1975. Regulars. Guests: Wayne Rogers and Buddy Ebsen.

21. #821. Airdate: March 15, 1975. Regulars. Guests: Roddy McDowall and Bernadette Peters.

22. #822. Airdate: March 22, 1975. Regulars: No Vicki. Guests: Steve Lawrence and Sally Struthers.

23. #823. Airdate: March 29, 1975. Regulars: No Vicki. Guests: Jean Stapleton and Phil Silvers.

24. #824. Airdate: April 5, 1975. Regulars. Guest: Tim Conway.

SEASON 9
TIM IS A NOW A REGULAR.

1. #901. September 20, 1975. Regulars. Guest: Sammy Davis, Jr.

2. #902. Airdate: November 1, 1975. Regulars. Guest: Roddy McDowall.

3. #903. Airdate: October 4, 1975. Regulars. Guest: Shirley MacLaine.

4. #904. Airdate: November 8, 1975. Regulars. Guest: Helen Reddy.

5. #905. Airdate: September 27, 1975. Regulars. Guest: Cher.

6. #906. Airdate: September 13, 1975. Regulars. Guest: Jim Nabors.

7. #907. Airdate: October 11, 1975. Regulars. Guest: Bernadette Peters.

8. #908. Airdate: October 25, 1975. Regulars. Guests: The Pointer Sisters.

9. #909. Airdate: November 15, 1975. Regulars. Guest: Maggie Smith.

10. #910. Airdate: October 18, 1975. Regulars. Guest: Maggie Smith.
11. #911. Airdate: November 27, 1975. Regulars. Guest: Betty White.
12. #912. Airdate: December 6, 1975. Regulars. Guest: Eydie Gormé.
13. #913. Airdate: December 20, 1975. Regulars. Guest: Steve Lawrence.
14. #914. Airdate: November 29, 1975. Regulars. Guests: The Pointer Sisters.
15. #915. Airdate: December 13, 1975. Regulars. Guest: Jessica Walter.
16. #916. Airdate: January 3, 1976. Regulars. Guest: Rita Moreno.
17. #917. Airdate: January 10, 1976. Regulars. Guest: Steve Lawrence.
18. #918. Airdate: January 24, 1976. Regulars. Guests: The Jackson 5 and Emmett Kelly.
19. #919. Airdate: January 31, 1976. Regulars. Guests: The Pointer Sisters.
20. #920. Airdate: February 7, 1976. Regulars. Family show. No guests.
21. #921. Airdate: February 14, 1976. Regulars. Guest: Joanne Woodward.
22. #922. Airdate: February 21, 1976. Regulars. Guests: Dick Van Dyke and Tony Randall.
23. #923. Airdate: March 6, 1976. Regulars. Guest: Jack Klugman.
24. #924. Airdate: March 13, 1976.

Regulars. Family show. No guests.

SEASON 10

1. #0001. Airdate: October 16, 1976. Regulars. Guest: Madeline Kahn.
2. #0002. Airdate: November 13, 1976. Regulars. Guest: Dinah Shore.
3. #0003. Airdate: October 2, 1976. Regulars. Guest: Sammy Davis, Jr.
4. #0004. Airdate: September 25, 1976. Regulars. Guest: Jim Nabors.
5. #0005. Airdate: October 23, 1976. Regulars. Guest: Steve Lawrence.
6. #0006. Airdate: October 9, 1976. Regulars. Family show. No guests.
7. #0007. Airdate: October 30, 1976. Regulars. Guest: Roddy McDowall.
8. #0008. Airdate: November 6, 1976. Regulars. Guest: Kay Cole.
9. #0009. Airdate: November 20, 1976. Regulars. Guest: Ken Berry.
10. #0010. Airdate: November 27, 1976. Regulars. Guests: The Pointer Sisters.
11. #0011. Airdate: December 4, 1976. Regulars. Guest: Alan King.
12. #0012. Airdate: December 11, 1976. Regulars. Guest: Betty White.
13. #0013. Airdate: December 25, 1976. Regulars. Family show. No guests. (No Q&A on this show.)

14. #0014. Airdate: December 18, 1976. Regulars. Guest: Dick Van Dyke.

15. #0015. Airdate: February 5, 1977. Regulars. Guest: Helen Reddy.

16. #0016. Airdate: January 15, 1977. Regulars. Guest: Glen Campbell.

17. #0017. Airdate: January 22, 1977. Regulars. Family show. No guests.

18. #0018. Airdate: January 29, 1977. Regulars. Guests: Steve Lawrence and Rock Hudson.

19. #0019. Airdate: March 5, 1977. Regulars. Guest: Hal Linden.

20. #0020. Airdate: February 12, 1977. Regulars. Guest: Eydie Gormé. (No Q&A.)

21. #0021. Airdate: February 26, 1977. Regulars. Guest: Ben Vereen.

22. #0022. Airdate: March 26, 1977. Regulars. Guest: Ken Berry.

23. #0023. Airdate: March 19, 1977. Regulars. Guest: Neil Sedaka.

24. #0024. Airdate: April 2, 1977. Regulars. Family show. No guests. (90-Minute special; Harvey's last show.)

SEASON 11
Harvey gone. Dick Van Dyke is a Regular.

1. #0101. Airdate: October 15, 1977. Regulars. Guest: Nancy Dussault.

2. #0102. Airdate: October 15, 1977. Regulars. Family show. No guests.

3. #0103. Airdate: October 1, 1977. Regulars. Guest: Steve Lawrence.

4. #0104. Airdate: September 24, 1977. Regulars. Guest: Jim Nabors.

5. #0105. Airdate: October 8, 1977. Regulars. Family show. No guests.

6. #0106. Airdate: October 29, 1977. Regulars. Guest: Ken Berry.

7. #0107. Airdate: October 22, 1977. Regulars. Family show. No guests.

8. #0108. Airdate: November 5, 1977. Regulars. Family show. No guests.

9. #0109. Airdate: November 19, 1977. Regulars. Guest: Ben Vereen.

10. #0110. Airdate: November 26, 1977. Regulars. Family show. No guests.

11. #0111. Airdate: December 3, 1977. Regulars. Guest: Bernadette Peters.

12. #0112. Airdate: December 11, 1977. Regulars: Dick Van Dyke was not on the show from show #0112 on. Guest: Rock Hudson.

13. #0113. Airdate: December 18, 1977. Regulars. Guests: Helen Reddy and Ken Berry.

14. #0114. Airdate: January 1, 1978. Regulars. Guest: Steve Lawrence.

15. #0115. Airdate: January 8, 1978. Regulars. Guests: Roddy McDowall and Ken Berry.

16. #0116. Airdate: January 22, 1978. Regulars. Guest: Eydie Gormé.

17. #0117. Airdate: January 29, 1978. Regulars. Guests: Steve Lawrence and the Captain (Daryl) and Tennille (Toni).

18. #0118. Airdate: February 5, 1978. Regulars. Guests: Natalie Cole and Ken Berry.

19. #0119. Airdate: February 19, 1978. Regulars. Guest: Ken Berry.

20. #0120. Airdate: February 26, 1978. Regulars. Guest: Steve Lawrence.

21. #0121. Airdate: March 5, 1978. Regulars. Guests: Steve Martin and Betty White.

22. #0122. Airdate: March 12, 1978. Regulars. Guests: James Garner, George Carlin, and Ken Berry.

23. #0123. Airdate: March 19, 1978. Regulars. Guests: Steve Lawrence and Bernadette Peters.

24. #0124. Airdate: March 29, 1978. Regulars. Family show. No guests. (Last show.)

APPENDIX 2:
WRITERS BY SEASON

SEASON 1: 1967–1968
Director: Clark Jones
Writing Supervisor: Arnie Rosen
Writers:
Bill Angelos
Barry E. Blitzer
Ray Brenner
Stan Burns
Don Hinkley
Buz Kohan
Mike Marmer
Gail Parent
Kenny Solms
Saul Turteltaub
Special Music Material Writer:
Artie Malvin

SEASON 2: 1968–1969
Director: Dave Powers
Writing Supervisor: Arnie Rosen
Writers:
Bill Angelos
Stan Burns
Hal Goldman
Al Gordon
Don Hinkley
Buz Kohan
Mike Marmer
Gail Parent

Kenny Solms
Special Music Material Writer:
Artie Malvin

SEASON 3: 1969–1970
Director: Dave Powers
Writing Supervisor: Arnie Rosen
Writers:
Bill Angelos
Stan Burns
Hal Goodman
Don Hinkley
Larry Klein
Buz Kohan
Mike Marmer
Gail Parent
Bob Schiller
Kenny Solms
Bob Weiskopf
Special Music Material Writer:
Artie Malvin

SEASON 4: 1970–1971
Director: Dave Powers
Writing Supervisor: Arthur Julian
Writers:
Roger Beatty
Stan Burns
Stan Hart

Don Hinkley
Coleman Jacoby
Arthur Julian
Heywood "Woody" Kling
Mike Marmer
Jack Mendelsohn
Gene Moss
Gail Parent
Arnie Rosen
Larry Siegel
Kenny Solms
Jim Thurman
Saul Turteltaub
Paul Wayne
Special Music Material Writers:
Dick DeBenedictis
Artie Malvin
David Rogers

SEASON 5: 1971–1972
Director: Dave Powers
Writing Supervisor: Arnie Rosen
Writers:
Art Baer
Roger Beatty
Stan Burns
Stan Hart
Don Hinkley
Ben Joelson
Heywood "Woody" Kling
Mike Marmer
Arnie Rosen
Larry Siegel
Special Music Material Writers:
Artie Malvin
Ken and Mitzie Welch

SEASON 6: 1972–1973
Director: Dave Powers
Head Writers:
Stan Hart

Larry Siegel
Writers:
Bill Angelos
Roger Beatty
Robert Hilliard
Heywood "Woody" Kling
Arnie Kogen
Buz Kohan
Gail Parent
Tom Patchett
Jay Tarses
Special Music Material Writers:
Artie Malvin
Ken and Mitzie Welch

SEASON 7: 1973–1974
Director: Dave Powers
Writing Supervisor: Ed Simmons
Writers:
Roger Beatty
Gary Belkin
Dick Clair
Rudy De Luca
Barry Harman
Arnie Kogen
Barry Levinson
Jenna McMahon
Gene Perret
Bill Richmond
Special Music Material Writers:
Artie Malvin
Ken and Mitzie Welch

SEASON 8: 1974–1975
Director: Dave Powers
Writing Supervisor: Ed Simmons
Writers:
Roger Beatty
Gary Belkin
Dick Clair
Rudy De Luca

Barry Harman
Arnie Kogen
Barry Levinson
Jenna McMahon
Gene Perret
Bill Richmond
Special Music Material Writers:
Artie Malvin
Ken and Mitzie Welch

SEASON 9: 1975–1976
Director: Dave Powers
Writing Supervisor: Ed Simmons
Writers:
Roger Beatty
Gary Belkin
Dick Clair
Rudy De Luca
Ray Jessel
Bo Kaprall
Arnie Kogen
Barry Levinson
Jenna McMahon
Gene Perret
Pat Proft
Bill Richmond
Special Music Material Writers:
Artie Malvin
Ken and Mitzie Welch

SEASON 10: 1976–1977
Director: Dave Powers
Writing Supervisor: Ed Simmons
Writers:
Roger Beatty
Dick Clair
Tim Conway
Elias Davis
Rick Hawkins
Jenna McMahon
Gene Perret
David Pollock

Bill Richmond
Liz Sage
Adele Styler
Burt Styler
Special Music Material Writers:
Bobby Gorman
Artie Malvin
Ken and Mitzie Welch

SEASON 11: 1977–1978
Director: Dave Powers
Writing Supervisor: Ed Simmons
Writers:
Roger Beatty
Gary Belkin
Dick Clair
Tim Conway
Elias Davis
Rudy De Luca
Rick Hawkins
Robert Illes
Ray Jessel
Bo Kaprall
Arnie Kogen
Barry Levinson
Jenna McMahon
Gene Perret
David Pollock
Pat Proft
Bill Richmond
Liz Sage
Larry Siegel
Franelle Silver
James R. Stein
Adele Styler
Burt Styler
Special Music Material Writers:
Stan Freeman
Bobby Gorman
Artie Malvin
Ken and Mitzie Welch

ACKNOWLEDGMENTS

My everlasting thanks to my editor, Shaye Areheart, whose suggestions and guidance made this whole experience a joy from start to finish. This process took a lot longer than I expected, and Shaye helped me so much, every step of the way, with her optimism and savvy. "Grateful" isn't a big-enough word.

I also want to thank my literary agent, Phyllis Wender, for her constant encouragement, love, and smarts. This is our third book together, and I hope there will be more.

My thanks to Crown's senior editor, Mary Reynics, for her sharp insight and kind support while expecting her first baby.

Thanks also go to Crown's editorial director, Trish Boczkowski, who seamlessly took over after Mary had her beautiful baby boy and guided this book to its finish.

And thanks to my daughter, Jody Hamilton, for putting together the lists and airdates of all 276 shows, plus the list of our writers for each of the eleven seasons.

ABOUT THE AUTHOR

CAROL BURNETT has been an actor on Broadway, on television, and in the movies, and she was the star of the long-running *The Carol Burnett Show,* which won twenty-five Emmy Awards. She has been awarded the Presidential Medal of Freedom, the Mark Twain Prize for American Humor, and the Kennedy Center Honors, among other singular achievements of a woman comedian who is nothing less than a pioneer and a role model for today's stars.

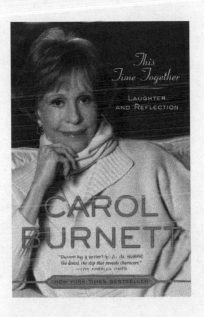